SMART 1,001 Travel Tips

D0047612

Fodor's

Fodor's Travel Publications
New York, Toronto, London, Sydney, Auckland

1001 Smart Travel Tips

Editor: Melisse Gelula
Editorial Contributors: Andy Collins, David Downing
Design: Guido Caroti
Cover Photo: Digital Vision/Getty Images

Copyright

First Edition
ISBN 978–1–4000–1939–7
ISSN 1541–289X

Important Tip

Although all prices, opening times, and other details in this book
are based on information supplied to us at press time, changes
occur all the time in the travel world, and Fodor's cannot accept responsibility for facts that become outdated or for inadvertent errors
or omissions. So **always confirm information when it matters,** especially if you're making a detour to visit a specific place.

Special Sales

Fodor's Travel Publications are available at special discounts for
bulk purchases for sales promotions or premiums. Special editions,
including personalized covers, excerpts of existing guides, and cor-
porate imprints, can be created in large quantities for special needs.
For more information, contact your local bookseller or write to
Special Markets, Fodor's Travel Publications, 1745 Broadway,
New York, NY 10019. Inquiries from Canada should be directed
to your local Canadian bookseller or sent to Random House of
Canada, Ltd., Marketing Department, 2775 Matheson Boulevard
East, Mississauga, Ontario L4W 4P7. Inquiries from the United
Kingdom should be sent to Fodor's Travel Publications, 20
Vauxhall Bridge Road, London SW1V 2SA, England.

PRINTED IN THE UNITED STATES OF AMERICA
10 9 8 7 6 5 4 3 2 1

At DHL, meeting the needs of our customers is at the heart of everything we do. For example, take our unique approach to international shipping.

We understand the complexities that many businesses face when dealing with multiple vendors across the globe, varying currencies and a myriad of international regulations.

To give our customers the hassle-free international shipping experience they desire, we keep it simple. We provide real door-to-door delivery, with an all-inclusive price, on a single invoice, in only one currency.

We also have more experience shipping to more international destinations than any other company. In fact, we were at the forefront of reliable overseas shipping. And that spirit continues today, as we cover more than 225 countries and territories around the globe, providing unparalleled customer service.

And just as DHL knows international shipping, Fodor's knows international travel. I hope you'll turn to this book for ideas on how to make travel easier and more enjoyable. And I hope you'll turn to DHL the next time you're looking for a stress-free shipping experience.

Enjoy.

Hans Hickler
CEO
DHL Express, United States

Contents

Getting the Trip You Want

Fodor's 1,001 Smart Travel Tips covers every aspect of every conceivable kind of trip: deciding where and when to go, packing the right gear for wherever you're headed, choosing the right way to get there—whether it be car, plane, boat, train, or bus—figuring out what to do once you arrive, eating well and finding a great place to stay, and keeping safe and healthy the entire time. Here you'll get the scoop on how best to prepare for trips to dozens of countries all over the world, and where to turn to when you encounter obstacles.

We've tried to consider some ideas, and potential pitfalls, that you might not think of: what always to have in your trunk in the event that your car breaks down, which activities to choose—and which to avoid—when planning a trip for the entire family, how to get compensation when your travel arrangements are blundered by somebody other than yourself. Even a minor setback, perhaps being overcharged by an unscrupulous taxi driver or experiencing an especially acute case of jet lag, can ruin a trip. Knowing how to avoid unpleasant surprises is one key to a happy vacation—and knowing how to remedy a negative situation that simply cannot be avoided is still another.

Some travel advice has made sense for years, if not for generations: pack lightly, read the fine print, avoid motion sickness by focusing on the horizon, and never carry all your money in one place. But other strategies for planning the perfect trip emerge as the world constantly changes around us. On a positive note, technological improvements have made it possible for travelers with even a modicum of computer know-how to plan virtually every aspect of their trip from the comfort of their living room—and without necessarily having to use a travel agent (although, as you'll learn in this book, a skillful and experienced agent can be any traveler's best friend). If you can navigate the best travel sites out there, you can nearly always save money and time better spent enjoying other aspects of your vacation.

A newer and perhaps more significant development has been the recent focus on travel safety and security, a necessary response to our increasing vulnerability to terrorist attacks and other threats related to political strife. Not only do we use more caution about where we go, but increased security at airports, train stations, hotels, government buildings, monuments, and even museums requires that we exercise forethought and patience in our travels.

Many of this book's tips reflect the uncertain times we are living in, but you'll notice that not one single suggestion recommends that you simply stay home, or that you avoid going any place that you truly wish to see. In fact, travel has always required taking certain risks. For many of us, giving up travel is simply not an option. So the best thing you can do is plan as carefully as possible, try to anticipate what you'll encounter wherever you're going, and go with confidence.

There may not be a single recommendation in this book that applies to every single traveler—we all travel with different priorities and sensibilities, our own ideas about what constitutes a bargain or a rip-off, or what we find deathly dull or intensely entertaining. Whether you're seeking romance with your significant other, a hassle-free business trip by yourself, or a family vacation that your kids will remember for the rest of their lives, we have included a wealth of ideas and suggestions. But read on with an open mind and a discerning eye, and consider when a tip truly applies to you, and when you're better off following your own instinct.

Above everything else, let the guidance in this book or any magazine article, guide, travel brochure, or Web page help you to plan your trip and allow your adventures to take shape as you want them to. But avoid the temptation to overplan or rely too heavily on any one suggestion or idea. Much of the joy that comes with travel occurs when we take the unexpected road or go with our intuition. A great travel tip can make a nice vacation even sweeter and can also salvage a trip that might have begun to feel doomed. But the best travel tips will end up being the ones you learn through your own experiences, by exploring with an open mind and trying new things.

Who Says?

The tips in this book have been contributed by the editors and several authors of dozens of Fodor's guidebooks, and they represent everything from tried-and-true strategies to quirky tidbits culled from a wide variety of resources—items that have been passed on to us by sage locals, lessons some of us have learned the hard way (and hope will spare you similar disappointments), pleasant discoveries we've made during our globe-trotting adventures, and even letters and e-mails we've received from readers gracious enough to share them. In fact, for some of us, parting with these pearls of travel wisdom hasn't been easy. Sometimes you just want to keep a great tip all to yourself.

Your guides through this maze of travel wisdom are pros, your editors.

▶ **Andrew Collins,** a former Fodor's editor, has contributed to more than 100 Fodor's travel guides in the past 10 years. He also conceived of, authored, and regularly updates *Fodor's Gay Guide to the USA*, for which he received the 1996 Lowell Thomas Travel Journalism bronze award from the Society of American Travel Writers in the category of "best guidebook." His articles have appeared in magazines, such as *Travel + Leisure*, and he writes a biweekly travel column, "Out of Town," which appears on Web sites and in gay/lesbian newspapers throughout North America. When he's not traveling, which isn't often, he lives in Santa Fe, New Mexico.

▶ **Melisse Gelula** has covered Aruba to Zimbabwe as an editor for Fodor's and has also contributed to many guides, covering hotels, shopping, spas, and, well, El Salvador as a writer. She has traveled significantly—particularly to Central America, her favorite region—and regularly dispenses her advice as a Fodor's media spokesperson. Since joining Fodor's in 1998, she has appeared on the Travel Channel and television news programs nationwide. *USA Today*, CNN.com, and *Redbook* have also interviewed her for travel tips and advice. As an editor, Melisse has created a half dozen new travel guides to such destinations as Nantucket, Seattle, and Central America. Currently a resident of Brooklyn, New York, she has also lived in Toronto, Chicago, and San Francisco.

▶ **David Downing,** a former Fodor's editor whose travel features have appeared both on Fodors.com and on New York Times on the Web, has learned the ins and outs of smart traveling, oftentimes the hard way. He shares his insider's tips in the "Fodor's Fix It" boxes that appear throughout the book. His work also appears in Fodor's guides to Florida, Mexico, and New York, where he currently lives.

Please Write

We hope that by sharing some of our favorite tips, you'll feel inspired to do the same, and to write or e-mail us with some of your best recommendations and savvy tips. Contact the *Fodor's 1,001 Smart Travel Tips* editor at editors@fodors.com or c/o Fodor's at 1745 Broadway, New York, NY 10019.

Planning

Although it might sound silly, getting the trip you want takes work. Determining where and when to go, scouting out the best deal, and doing a bit of guidebook and on-line research takes effort and time—and that's before you've even left for the airport. Though as any successful traveler (or Boy Scout) will tell you, what you put into planning and preparing at the beginning pays off later in Vacationland when you can relax knowing you've taken care of all the potential pitfalls. For tips on what to do now so that your trip is effortless later, read on.

WHEN TO GO

▶ **Be flexible when possible.** All aspects of travel are based on supply and demand, so be aware of your destination's peak season. If it's from December through April and you're coming at the end of April, you might save hundreds of dollars if you change your travel dates by a week or two. (Many properties will charge you the peak-season rate for your entire stay even if you straddle the change between peak and off-peak seasons, so be sure to ask when the rates go down.)

▶ **Pay attention to exchange rates.** Sometimes a whole country will go "on sale," when its economy is going through a soft spot. New Zealand, for instance, has been yielding about $1.85 for every American dollar. Mexico, Australia, and Canada also have good exchange rates for Americans, so be sure to factor this in when choosing when and where to go.

▶ **Go when you get a good deal.** Last-minute e-saver tickets and other money-saving travel deals often reward those with a drop-and-run lifestyle while punishing the rest of us hardworking souls who need to plan to take time off. If you can arrange to take a weekend excursion, even if you can't really do all, say, of Paris in three days, you may just have an experience and a deal you'll remember and brag about indefinitely. Heck, that's what "personal days" are for.

▶ **Avoid holidays if you can.** Don't even try to travel when everyone else is on the road. Be a contrarian instead, and do what the hordes don't do. At Thanksgiving, for instance, get your traveling done on Tuesday—or wait for Thanksgiving Day. Christmas

Eve is actually a great time to travel—all the normal people are already holed up with their loved ones.

▶ **Don't forget about spring break.** Whether you want to join it or avoid it, be advised that spring break takes place between the end of February and mid-April. This means a lot of vacationing college students, beach parties, sports events, and entertainment aimed at young ones.

▶ **Watch the weather.** Hurricane season in the Caribbean is from about June 1 through November 30, with greatest risk for a storm from August through October.

▶ **Consider local holidays.** Tourists crowd the major art cities of Europe at Easter, when Italians flock to resorts and to the country. From March through May, busloads of eager schoolchildren on excursions take cities of artistic and historical interest by storm.

▶ **Heed popular midsummer European travel times.** You don't want to be, say, on an Italian beach in August if you can help it—unless it's a private beach—or you'll not have a scrap of sand on which to lay your towel, and resorts charge more then as well. (Italian beach vacations are best taken in June and September.) On the other hand, from mid-July through August you'll find Paris somewhat abandoned (albeit hot and stuffy) when the locals flee the city on beach trips of their own.

▶ **Know international holidays.** Many businesses, restaurants, and shops may be closed for holidays which are not observed in the United States. Your guidebook can tell you when religious holidays, like the feast days of patron saints, for example, are observed locally, and when services are likely to be closed. Some religious holidays, like the Day of the Dead in Oaxaca, Mexico, or the week before Easter in Antigua, Guatemala, might be an excellent time to visit, when the cities come alive with colorful and elaborate festivities.

▶ **Consider playing courier.** If you really can get up and go at a moment's notice and travel light, sign up with a courier agency, such as the Air Courier Association and the International Association of Air Travel Couriers—you're likely to end up paying less than half the lowest fare. The return time varies from a few days to as much as six months, and the frequent-flier miles are yours to keep. You might even get a deal on a companion ticket, especially if you're willing to take different outbound flights.

▶ **Use your miles for a last-minute trip.** Some airlines will charge a $75 fee to use your miles at the last minute. But you'll still pay far less than full fare if seats are still available. Seats are more likely to be open to business destinations since frequent-flier miles are used more often for leisure travel. The best days to use frequent-flier miles are Tuesday and Wednesday, when there are fewer vacation travelers.

▶ **Assess whether you want to vacation during the most popular time.** In Central America, for example, dry season runs from mid-December through April. From mid-December until early February in particular, you have the combined advantages of good weather and lush vegetation. Of course, hotels are more likely to be full during this time of year, making advance planning all but essential.

▶ **Consider visiting during the rainy or off-season.** This is a good way to avoid crowds and high prices. In countries with a rainy season, beaches might be wet in the afternoon but sunny and dry in the morning. But check into what transportation is like, as flights can be delayed during hurricane season and roads can be washed out. Local climates might also be unbearably cold or hot, thereby turning your vacation into an episode of *Survivor*.

▶ **Watch out for shifting shoulders.** The definitions of in- and off-season used to be a lot clearer, pre-air-conditioning and before local tourism boards got the bright idea of expanding their markets. Room-rate charts will give you a good idea of peak booking periods. If you do opt for off-season, keep in mind that certain attractions and modes of transportation may well be closed.

▶ **Keep tabs on new properties.** Often hotels will start up with a "soft opening"—like a test run—to make sure all systems are go. If you're willing to put up with patchy service—and, sometimes, a bit of lingering construction—you can not only get a good deal but be among the first to visit what could be a hit.

▶ **Always book flights for early in the day.** That way, if your flight is delayed or you miss a connection, you stand a much better chance of getting on another flight and not being stranded overnight.

A Little Bit of Business, A Little Bit of Vacation

▶ **Turn your business trip into a vacation.** Having your airfare covered by your employer means you have more money left in your pocket to bring your significant other(s) along or simply stay for a while and explore. If you're being sent to Toronto, Berlin, or Hong Kong, you may as well see more than the convention center or hotel. Negotiate with your employer for a flexible departure and return date on your next trip, or offer to take that business trip others in your office are reluctant to and know your airfare and biggest expense is covered.

▶ **Know what your destination city is known for.** Make it your business to know the great seasonal sights of Toronto, say, or Miami before you go. If a meeting is canceled or you have free time, you'll know exactly how to use it. (How many cities do businesspeople visit without ever getting the sense of having been there?)

▶ **Plan a layover.** Having to rush to make connections can ruin a perfectly good excuse to visit another city on your way to or from your intended destination. Airfare is often cheaper if you are flexible about connection cities and times, so put a positive spin on that overnight layover in Helsinki or Cape Town and take a taxi tour and great meal in a new city you might not otherwise have seen. Who knows, that unintended layover stop may become a destination the next time you plan a vacation.

WEB RESOURCES

▶ **Set up a customized travel page.** Expedia.com and Travelocity.com, for example, allow you to select your preferred travel destinations, departure city, price, and more by signing up. Then every time you log on, you'll get a pared-down selection of travel options that pertain specifically to your preferences. You can also store personal information, like your credit card number and regular traveling companion's information—which make booking a quick procedure—and have the system keep track of your miles.

▶ **Have the best deals find you.** If you sign up for "Fare Tracker" on Expedia.com or Travelocity.com, you'll get an e-mail the moment a fare meeting your price requirement is available to cities you specify. If you register with SmarterLiving.com, it will notify you weekly of the discounted flights departing from the gateways closest to you.

▶ **Go directly to the source.** Many airlines e-mail a list of weekly specials (typically on Wednesday for the next or following weekend); all you have to do is sign up—it's free. Also, by consulting their sites, you'll be eligible for special deals not available elsewhere, and perhaps entitled to bonus frequent-flier miles.

▶ **Read all the rules for "reverse auction" sites.** When entering a "name your own price" bid with a service such as Priceline.com or Cheapfares.com, make sure you know exactly what you're committing to, because later changes aren't allowed—even for an extra fee, and regardless of whether you made a mistake.

▶ **Leave leeway when bidding in on-line auctions.** The bidding period for travel products offered at sites like eBay.com, Bid4vacations.com, and Skyauction.com generally lasts several days, and you need to keep checking back to make sure you haven't been outbid. Also, you may need to pay the seller by check or credit card, which adds to the delay.

▶ **Research before you bid.** To get a ballpark figure, you'll need to research the regular prices, calculate the related taxes, and set yourself a bidding limit of 10%–15% below the total. Although your chances of besting the 14-day advance-purchase price are good, you don't want to start the bidding too low, because you may only get a couple of chances to come up with an acceptable price.

BREAKING THE "TRAVELSPEAK" CODE

After many hours of looking at brochures and consulting with their travel agent, Greg and Marcia were looking forward to their island honeymoon. They were impressed with the idyllic photos they'd seen and were looking forward to spending a romantic week in their waterfront love nest. But when the happy couple arrived at the posh resort, they were surprised to learn that the room they reserved was not on the beach but on an adjacent man-made inlet that reeked of stagnant tidewater. Overgrown marsh grass obstructed what little view they had: They'd come expecting Fantasy Island and wound up on Love Canal. Despite the couple's complaints, the management contended that the room was exactly what the couple had reserved. Besides, it was high season and the hotel was completely booked so nothing could be done. Greg and Marcia were incensed because they believed they had been taken, but the hotel maintained it had fulfilled its promise of a waterfront room. Who is to blame?

▶ FODOR'S FIX

Here we have the sad result of ambiguity created by slick PR firms and misleading brochure language that some call "travelspeak": It's the same style of writing that refers to a closet-size hotel room as "intimate." In destinations where the beach is the attraction, many businesses do their best to disguise the fact that some (or all) of the rooms at their properties are not directly on the beach. In cases such as this, always be on the lookout for ambiguous terms like "waterfront," "water view," and "ocean view." Although those words might seem clear, the reality is that just because a room has as view of the water does not mean the room—or any part of the hotel—is necessarily waterfront. And just because your room is waterfront, does not mean it is oceanfront. Be sure to ask exactly what body of water you are fronting, or you might end up with a commanding view of a duck pond in the far inland reaches of an oceanfront resort. In other words, never trust the description you see in a promotional brochure or Web site, because one hotel's "oceanfront" is another's "ocean view."

The Bottom Line: No doubt about it, Greg and Marcia got taken by an unscrupulous—or lamentably ignorant—travel agent. Still, before you commit to a hotel in any destination, do some research and check the lay of the land if location is important to you. Also, always talk with a representative directly at the hotel—not with a reservations agent at an 800 number—and ask pointed questions about your room's location. And be sure to get the name of the agent: it'll lend your case credibility if your room isn't what—or where—you expected.

▶ **Don't wait until the last minute.** Despite all the publicity touting "last-minute" fare bargains, the closer you book to departure, the greater odds that a glitch—or a simple shortage of tickets—will thwart your plans. To make the Web work for you, leave plenty of time for shopping around (don't expect a single site to meet all your needs) and then compare options.

▶ **Be careful how you click.** It's all too easy to throw your plans off by a day or even a month with one slip of the finger. Before you proceed to the "Buy It Now" level (every site phrases the stage slightly differently), double-check every single detail—including the airport code! Certain acronyms are so misleading they could put you on the wrong side of the globe.

▶ **Always print your confirmation and carry it.** In the case of an e-ticket, that may be all the documentation you get. To play it extra safe, call the reservations line of the airline in question a few days beforehand to reconfirm your booking, make sure you have the itinerary you requested, and double-check details such as seating or special meal requests. Even if you have to spend some time on hold, you're likely to get better service than if you wait until check-in time.

BUDGETING

▶ **Plan your budget before you book.** Calculate exactly how much the trip will cost. Be comprehensive: cover every category, including long-distance and local transportation, lodging, meals, beverages, entertainment, gratuities, events, and activities. Also factor in any shopping you may want to do (whether local specialties and deals or sundry necessities), and include those costs in your estimate. And after you've done this add at least another $100 to approximate your true budget.

▶ **Use a current guidebook to help estimate costs.** A good travel guide should tell you the price of a local taxi ride, a beer or a cappuccino, a concert ticket, a museum entrance fee, a three-day bus pass, and so on. You can also call the local tourist office, visit a local magazine Web site (such as *Bermuda Magazine* for a trip there), or e-mail the various businesses to inquire about specific details.

▶ **Check and double-check details.** The last thing you want to do is arrive at a hotel and find that what you thought was a double-room rate is in fact per person, or what is usually Modified American Plan rate (including breakfast and dinner) reverts to European Plan (no meals) during the slow season. Also, room occupancy taxes can be substantial in certain locations; check the rate before you book.

▶ **Call the hotel's local toll-free number.** You'll often get a better price than from the central reservation line.

▶ **Check the cost of incidentals at the hotel you've chosen.** Seemingly petty details such as surcharges on local phone calls, local taxes, and parking can really add up. Some hotels tack on hidden gratuities, too.

▶ **Define what is meant by "all-inclusive."** The term can be nebulous, often in the resort's favor. For instance, the wine that comes free with dinner could cost you as an afternoon aperitif, or the much-vaunted water sports could incur an extra charge. Determine beforehand exactly what's included.

▶ **Stay at a condo, cottage, or an efficiency.** Having a kitchen at your disposal will significantly cut down on the cost of meals—especially if you've got children in tow or are staying for a week or so.

▶ **If traveling in a group, negotiate a deal.** You should be able to work out a volume discount on transportation and lodging. For 20 or so rooms, contact the group sales department of the hotel, resort, or cruise line. Depending upon the season, properties might be flexible with the minimum number of rooms required and extend discounts beyond their published policies. Smaller parties may benefit from making a quick phone call inquiry.

▶ **When budgeting for a group, accommodate individual differences.** Hold a group meeting to settle on an agreeable budget, but be flexible. If some people in your group like to maintain a higher level of comfort than others can afford, don't just compromise: why should everyone suffer in the middle? The high rollers could go first class and book a suite while budget travelers travel in coach and bed down in a motel. Both will have a better time.

▶ **Start by scouring newspaper travel sections.** Read beyond your local press. Papers from your destination usually have more and deeper discounts, in the editorial, advertising, and classified-ad sections. You can obtain newspapers via a news service or through the mail; easier still, many of the major papers now have Web sites you can access free of charge.

▶ **Watch out for the term "from" when it comes to pricing.** That baseline figure, although an effective come-on, might apply to an undesirable property. The minimally acceptable, mid-level options could be quite a hike up.

▶ **Consider working with a travel agent.** It's a matter of personal predilection (some of us are die-hard individualists); however, a good travel agent could easily steer you to money-saving alternatives—package trips, especially—that would more than compensate for the consultation fee that is now the norm. Shop around: If an agent simply hands you a packet of travel brochures, keep looking.

▶ **Get all promised services down in writing.** If you do find an agent who seems to be on your wavelength, you still need written confirmation of the arrangements you've agreed to, in case anything should go wrong with the travel company or any of the service providers. If it does, a good travel agent will act as your advocate to resolve any complaints—either upon your return or, better yet, while there's still time to ameliorate the situation.

▶ **Read the fine print.** The typical "Terms and Conditions" appended to most travel brochures may not make the most riveting reading, but you're better off forewarned when it comes to such potential headaches as deposit and payment due dates (with attendant forfeits), cancellation penalties, order processing and change fees, gratuity policies (an automatic 15% add-on can be a very big deal), complaint and refund procedures, and trip-protection insurance options.

▶ **Buy insurance policies from an insurance company.** If you buy from the service provider (airline, cruise line, or tour operator), there's always the chance that they could go out of business and leave you holding the bag. You should be okay, though, if you book with a member of the National Tour Association or the U.S. Tour Operators Association, or a company that participates in the American Society of Travel Agents' Tour Operator Program, all of which have programs to cover costs or mediate in case of default.

▶ **Check your health and home-owner's policies.** It's costly—and pointless—to be doubly insured. Before buying any travel insurance, check to see what contingencies may already be covered by your existing plans.

▶ **Be prepared to negotiate.** If the task makes you squeamish or you're just not very good at it, consider delegating this task to a friend or family member who can finesse it. It really pays to haggle for a price below the published rates (known in the biz as "rack rates"). Ask about special promotional rates (which might be even lower than any group rate quoted). Having researched the norm, start by offering a rate well below what you're willing to pay, then dicker upward.

▶ **Play on your strengths.** Are you traveling off-season, when the property might otherwise have to absorb the costs of some empty rooms? Also, explore every angle: Would they consider a discount if you pay by check rather than credit card? Might they match lower rates offered by nearby competitors? Or perhaps they'll throw in a bonus, such as an extra night's stay or a sports-activity package? A little polite wheedling could save you big bucks.

▶ **Keep tabs on fare and rate changes.** Even as you're making your air reservations, ask what your options are should the fare later drop: you might be able to receive credit for the value of the price reduction. Even if you have to pay a handling charge of $100 or more per person for re-ticketing, the savings could be worthwhile. As for hotels, request that, if the room rate drops radically, the difference be credited toward in-house meals, activities, or other extras.

▶ **Give some thought to your at-home expenses.** As you work up an estimate for your vacation, keep an eye on the bottom line at home. What's your monthly discretionary income? Do you have any major nontravel expenses looming (e.g., taxes, home improvement, auto repairs, medical bills, tuition)? Are you already carrying high credit card debt? Taking such concerns into account, you might want to curtail any overlavish plans—it's no fun coming home to a financial crisis.

▶ **Look into packages.** You don't necessarily have the flexibility that you have when you put all the pieces together yourself, but if you're truly going for price/quality then a package can be very affordable and easy to plan. (Don't forget that your planning time is worth money as well.)

▶ **Use an alternative airport.** You can often save money if you are willing to drive to another airport near your departure city. The low-fare airlines tend to use them and the passenger loads are smaller, and therefore priced to go!

▶ **Try a consolidator.** These travel-booking services have contracts with airlines that allow them to sell tickets up to 50% off published fares because they buy in bulk.

▶ **Consider what organizations you belong to.** Are you a member of the American Dental Association or the American Bar Association? Even if you do nothing more than carry your membership card and pay yearly dues, you can take advantage of low rates that many organizations and unions negotiate with hotels and car-rental companies. These can sometimes be the best deals around.

"WHERE SHOULD WE GO?"

▶ **Determine your druthers.** Once you've determined who's going, and how much they're willing to spend, the trick is settling on the ideal itinerary. Choices, choices! Just for starters: Domestic or international? By land, air, or water? City or country? Beach or mountains? Weekend or extended sojourn? Single destination or constantly on the move? And what matters most to you: adventurous activities outdoors, cultural opportunities, or luxury accommodations and gourmet food? Of course, there's no reason you shouldnt try to have it all.

▶ **Ask everyone you know for suggestions.** Soon enough, patterns will emerge among your friends, families, and coworkers who have made great choices or disappointing ones.

▶ **Go to the bookstore and look at the travel guides.** One of the most frequent questions travel editors are asked is, Where should I go? There are so many fantastic places, and so many variables, it's a tough question to answer. Only you know best what and where will make you happy. Plop yourself down in the travel section of your local bookstore, and promise yourself you'll pick up lots of books that simply catch your eye.

▶ **Match your destination to your fantasy.** Which of the following pops out? Rome and Florence. Caribbean beaches. Canadian ski resorts. Disney in Orlando. Camping in Colorado. A Napa Valley inn. Bird-watching in Central America. Cruising the Mediterranean. A chichi safari tour in Kenya. This list represents broad types of travel, and your answer might reveal just what kind of travel mood you're in.

▶ **Go with your gut.** Many future travelers have an idea about what kind of a place they'd like to visit, even if it's mostly built on fantasy. If you've always wanted to go to Italy, for example, but know nothing about it, do a little research to see if it matches up with your fantasy. It's likely it will. And paying less for a trip elsewhere just might not satisfy.

▶ **Let the ideas fly freely.** In the brainstorming phase, the point is not so much to come up with concrete plans as to make sure that everyone feels heard—and feels comfortable revealing pipe-dream fantasies, even those that are admittedly outlandish. You can always winnow down the flurry of wishes later.

▶ **Decide if you're willing to consider "gray areas."** If you're the adventurous sort, you might find some real bargains in areas with iffy reputations, or others recovering from a bad rep. Before you commit, though, and also before you go through with the trip, check current State Department warnings at http://travel.state.gov/travelwarnings.html.

▶ **Draw on a variety of resources.** The Web, guidebooks, media (magazines, newspapers, TV), travel agents, friends and acquaintances—all are helpful in honing in on some specific destinations. Check one source against another: That dreamy photo you clipped from a glossy magazine or a friend's rhapsodic recommendation might not give the whole story, and Web sites, like brochures, can be guilty of glossing over potential downsides, such as dingy rooms or a major highway cutting right past a presumably peaceful retreat. The more sources you check, the more rounded the picture.

▶ **Narrow your choices down to a short list.** This is the fun part, when pie-in-the-sky plans start to come down to earth. Budgeting concerns may impose certain restrictions, but you're getting close to a viable plan.

▶ **Remember that you still have options.** When the time has come to pick "the one," continue to comparison shop and pay attention to subtle differences. For instance, not all Caribbean islands are alike (some, like Saint Martin/Sint Maarten, even have distinctive, disparate sides). Similarly, there's a world of difference between a cruise on a small yacht and one on a ship the size of a small metropolis.

▶ **Look up recent "Best Of" issues.** Most newspapers publish "best of" editions at the end of the year, so if you're traveling soon after the winter holidays, this can be a great resource for the best-of-the-best selections for new restaurants, shops, or nightlife spots. Monthly city-focused magazines, like those in Los Angeles, New York, or Chicago, have annual editions that spotlight the best places in town as well, which give great insider information on fresh hotspots as well as perennial favorites. Both newspaper and magazine articles of this sort can generally be accessed on-line.

▶ **Consider an organized tour.** They're a great way to see a new place. Companies run from the refined Abercrombie & Kent variety to ones that appeal to go-getters who'd prefer to ride a bike across Cambodia. Niche travel is up, so whatever your pleasure, there's sure to be a tour to match.

Different Types of Travelers

▶ **Sketch out travel profiles.** Any group is likely to encompass several types, and in fact, even individuals can be blends. But a preliminary "typecasting" is a good way to start thinking about what kind of place will please whom:

Go-getters like to fill every moment, from dawn to midnight, with productive and/or pleasurable activities: big cities, resorts with sports facilities, and theme parks will meet their need for constant stimulation.

Culture vultures are only happy when expanding their aesthetic horizons: they're best matched with big cities, foreign destinations, and places boasting unique festivals and events.

Relaxation-seekers are intent on mellowing out at all costs: they might cope with plenty of stress in real life, but to them the ideal vacation means a chance to slow down—at a beach, perhaps, or deep in the peaceful countryside, or at a spa or on a cruise ship.

Sports and adventure enthusiasts want to play hard: for those who experience life at its fullest only when they're striving to meet new challenges (ace that tennis serve, tackle that mountain or Class III rapids), the answer is a beach, ski, or golf resort, the wilderness to be found within national parks, or an organized adventure tour.

▶ **Match-make creatively.** With a little ingenuity, a zany destination can meet mixed needs. Cities have it all, or almost all: nonstop action for the go-getters, culture to spare, sophisticated spas. Outdoorsy types may not be in their optimal element, but they can usually find some kind of sporting activity (consider New York's urban adult playground, Chelsea Piers), and if not, there's always the hotel gym. Beach vacations can be weak on the cultural front: if that's a must, pick an exotic locale, or one steeped in history.

▶ **Consider your special requirements.** Social butterflies are likely to thrive in any setting, barring utter isolation; privacy seekers, on the other hand, will be miserable if it's nowhere to be found. Older travelers or those with chronic health problems may need to ensure that there are good medical facilities nearby.

▶ **Decide who is responsible for which travel duty.** One of you might book flights and rental cars and the other might handle hotel arrangements; one of you may be more comfortable practicing his/her Portuguese or French for asking for information from the locals, and the other may be better equipped to deal with maps/itineraries/public-transport issues or to handle the driving.

▶ **Discuss your travel fantasy with your prospective fellow travelers before booking.** Spell out how you'd like to spend your time before you make your plans, or you might find your traveling companions don't share your feelings about nonstop sightseeing and shopping.

▶ **Devise a plan before your trip.** You don't want to waste time in your exotic destination trying to figure out where you want to go and who's interested in going there. Think about how difficult simple consensus is at home, such as choosing a video to rent or what to make for dinner. Avoid bickering later, and plan now.

▶ **Regularly refer to the wish list of sights.** Plan things day by day, and keep the itinerary (and your minds) flexible—with lots of room for breaks. All this makes it easier to avoid the three feelings that lead to fights: resentment, disappointment, and fatigue.

FAMILY VACATIONS

▶ **Don't expect a vacation to resolve familial disputes.** Are there tensions among family members that might spoil other people's enjoyment of the trip? If Aunt Gertrude and Aunt Marcy can't put aside their differences at Thanksgiving dinner, the one time of the year they meet, it's probably unwise to see if they can work things out on vacation.

▶ **Don't ignore the hesitancy of family members.** Maybe Uncle George isn't feeling like he can say no, but he'll go along with your plan for the 12-day hike through the Australian Outback not to upset you. You may find yourself left holding Uncle George's unclaimed airline ticket or hotel bill at the last minute— or his hand, so to speak, as he laboriously whines his way through your trekking vacation.

▶ **Consider physical challenges.** Multigenerational trips are hard on everyone. When kids can't keep up they feel left out, and it's not right to leave older family members behind on some of the best bonding activities. Honestly evaluate who can do what and consider activities that resolve the problem of physical limitations, adding in lots of opportunities to rest, so everyone enjoys the trip.

▶ **Put one person in charge.** That's true even if your vacation involves dozens of family members. Many resorts insist on dealing with one individual who is responsible for all payments. This person needs experience either planning large business meetings or social gatherings. Whoever planned the last wedding will view this as a piece of cake!

▶ **Involve children in planning.** Make the trip interesting for children by showing them maps and brochures and renting movies or reading books about your destination. Such information puts the destination in a context the child can relate to. Although you might be going for the vineyards and culture, they might be more enthusiastic about a destination because it was a movie location or because a great sports figure or team is based there. Whatever the reason for their enthusiasm, their involvement now will go a long way to a successful trip later, when everyone wants to be there.

▶ **Consider using a family-friendly travel agent.** They can recommend destinations, hotel, and car-rental companies with a track record for catering to families. Between your agent and their contacts, you'll have less planning to do when they remember you'll need a car seat with your rental car and a hotel with child-care programs and in-room cribs.

▶ **Take your kids with you on business.** The Travel Industry Association of America reported in 2000 that more than 32 million business trips in the United States included children. For this reason, sophisticated city hotels such as the Ritz-Carlton and the Four Seasons now offer elaborate activities for their youngest guests and daily children's programs. The Four Seasons Boston has outfitted rooms for tykes with potty seats and outlet covers and offers fun features such as restaurant menus via View-Masters. Although urban hotels generally don't have kids' clubs, they will help you secure child care in a pinch.

▶ **Consider the type of hotel you'll need and whether you'll share a room.** A stay with wee ones at a B&B is probably not a great idea—the furniture and objects may be fragile antiques and the rooms tend to be less soundproof and less likely to include two beds. Many families prefer generic all-suite hotels, where the furnishings are sturdy, two double or queen beds are standard, and a kitchen is at your disposal. Rather than heading straight for a roadside chain motel or an all-inclusive, consider a furnished rental property or stay open to other good deals in circulation. For example, medium-price hotels, particularly those in business districts, often offer lower weekend rates to attract families.

▶ **If you have extra to spend, get adjoining rooms.** Especially if your kids are old enough or you're traveling with other family members, you'll all enjoy yourselves better with a little space. Rooms on the same floor allow some visitation rights without feeling that you are with each other every minute of every day.

▶ **Take the whole family into account.** Families with young children need to determine whether resorts are truly family-friendly or just paying lip service. Although good-parenting techniques are just as important on the road as they are at home, you don't want to feel as if you have to apologize for your children when they're just acting their age.

▶ **Consider your tolerance for togetherness.** Does the vacation represent a long-awaited chance to hang out? Or are you yearning for a little alone time? Parents who already spend a great deal of time with their children—and vice versa—might appreciate the organized children's activities to be found at a family-oriented resort.

▶ **Make sure there's something for everyone.** Toddlers might prefer a placid, nonthreatening pond; pre-teens might want to be brandishing boogie boards and looking to get pounded by the waves. Teenagers, of course, want the opportunity to take off and hang out with their peers. So the same setting may not suffice year after year. As you shop around, try to find at least one element to delight each member of the family—including yourself.

PLANNING HEALTHFUL TRIPS

We all start out with the romantic notion that travel refreshes. The reality, though, is that often, even in the best of circumstances, it's physically draining. We head out starry-eyed and return home suffering from travel's Bermuda Triangle: fatigue, stress, and weight gain. Planning ahead can minimize the damage.

For further information on vaccinations, travel insurance, and tips for travel to extreme destinations, see the Health and Safety chapter.

▶ **Assess the status of your health.** Make a list of any conditions that might affect your plans—anything from serious conditions like asthma and high blood pressure to more minor complaints like tennis elbow or foot calluses. Create a packing list of any special needs: such as medications, ice packs, and so on, and consider creative ways to cope with your health needs when away from home, like having your prescriptions called into a pharmacy in your destination.

▶ **Pack plenty of your prescribed medicines.** Pack more than you anticipate needing, just in case you get stranded. And pack them in their original containers in your carry-on bags, not your checked luggage, which could go astray. If you'll need to refill a prescription while you're away, have your doctor use the generic name on your slip and have him clarify the dosage, as product names and dosages can vary.

▶ **Get your shots early.** Some countries require immunizations of international travelers; for others, especially remote destinations in southerly climes, you might want to take some extra precautions. The Centers for Disease Control (cdc.gov) lists what shots are required or recommended by country; they can also inform you about common diseases and how best to protect yourself. Some shots may be required as much as six weeks before you go or require several shots spaced over several weeks, so get going on this right away.

▶ **Go over your insurance.** Check with your insurance company on what the provisions are for emergency care outside your coverage area. What kind of documentation should you bring? Whom should you contact if you fall ill? If heading overseas, you might want to purchase additional coverage through a separate travel insurance company if it's not already included. Be sure to keep your emergency information with you at all times.

▶ **Choose a healthful seat.** Not all seats are created equal. Aisle seats are generally the most healthful, since you can more easily get up and stretch. On the other hand, windows are coziest for would-be nappers. (If you're not happy with your seat assignment, call a day or two in advance to inquire about cancellations; you might be able to move.)

▶ **Travel early.** Early flights are most likely to be on time—but are also likely to be fuller than mid-morning to early afternoon flights—thereby often allowing you to have a day comprised of events unrelated to getting to and from your destination.

▶ **Find out about in-flight meal options.** Airline meals are increasingly a thing of the past, but when they are offered, the choices can be wide (e.g., diabetic, gluten-free, bland, soft, low-calorie, low-carbohydrate, low-sodium, low-cholesterol/fat, sulfite-free). Whichever you choose, get the specifics when booking your flight; don't assume the meal will be suitable. On some airlines, for instance, the vegetarian option is the tastiest of all; on others, it can be a bad joke. Just as in a restaurant, you have a right to know what you'll be served.

▶ **Write down your current fitness plan.** You'll find it easier to follow your exercise regime if you put it in writing. Write down all your daily fitness goals, and narrow them down to the top five. As an example: (1) Walk whenever possible; (2) Eat smaller portions; (3) Use the hotel fitness facilities or tennis court; (4) Stretch for five minutes morning and night; (5) Do at least 20 minutes of aerobic exercise. Pack that list to help you stay on track. But don't go on a guilt trip if you miss a few: the point of the list is to keep you healthy and relieve stress, not add to it.

▶ **Find a pool or a gym.** Consult a travel guide or your hotel for local gyms, and ask about bicycle rental for getting around. Can't do without a daily swim? Swimmers Guide Online at Lornet.com/sgol lists 10,000 pools worldwide.

▶ **Think outside the box.** Can't find any of the activities you know and love? Try a new one. Call the local chamber of commerce (locatable on Chamberofcommerce.com) in your destination city and ask what's out there: a dance studio, perhaps, or bowling alley, skating rink, or rock-climbing wall. Maybe it's time you took up in-line skating or boogie-boarding.

▶ **Map out coping strategies in advance.** Don't want to be munching airline peanuts all day? Bring your own snacks. Your hotel lacks an exercise room? Call ahead to find out if there are pleasant walking/running routes nearby. As long as you look around for smart ways to adapt, you can find a way to adhere to your fitness goals.

▶ **Try to eat normally.** If your usual morning meal is a bagel and juice, a solid week of breakfast buffets could get you in trouble. Though it's true that, while traveling, you have less control over what you eat and when, do your best to approximate your normal routines—while allowing for opportunities to sample local cuisines.

▶ **If you're a vegetarian, call ahead.** All too often, at regular restaurants the "vegetarian" options are limited. Call the restaurant before you go, to see if they can come up with something a little more interesting (at the better restaurants in bigger cities, vegetarian entrées are common). Or pick an all-vegetarian dining spot through a Web site such as Vegdining.com.

▶ **Get the hotel lowdown.** It's not enough to know there's an in-house gym: How big is it? (Some are virtual closets.) What are the hours? What kind of equipment is available? (Ask the brand name if you prefer a particular type.) What kinds of classes are offered, and are there extra fees? Does the pool have lap lanes, or is it a family free-for-all? Are there laundry facilities for your gym clothes? If the hotel's facilities are inadequate to your needs, ask if they have any deals with other clubs nearby.

▶ **Get a custom fit.** Planning to exercise in your room? Make sure you'll have enough floor space. To soothe the ensuing sore muscles, you might want a tub, or better yet, a Jacuzzi. If you find you get depressed without loads of natural light, or want access to fresh air at night, ask. And whatever you're promised, get a written confirmation with your room number and bring it with you. Many hotels overbook, then play fast and loose with room assignments. If you find you've been baited-and-switched, complain politely but persistently until a supervisor makes it right.

▶ **Create your own meal plan.** Get the hotel to fax you its menus and, if possible, those of restaurants nearby. Check out guidebooks and consult the local chamber of commerce to find the kinds of places you prefer. Then reserve well in advance (all the research in the world won't do you any good if the restaurants are all booked up). Also, you don't have to eat out for every meal—that can get tedious as well as expensive. If there's an in-room fridge or minibar, ask about good groceries and delis in the neighborhood: you can stockpile some healthful nibbles.

▶ **Don't throw your home rules to the winds.** Travelers often joke that, on the road, "Calories don't count"—if only! It's a challenge, when traveling, to stay firmly in control of your own health and well-being. If you identify your fitness goals before you start your trip and then stick to them, the outcome won't be left to chance. The trick to not sabotaging your goals is to ask yourself the question: Is this what I'd do at home?

▶ **Have fun.** Staying healthy should be fun—otherwise, why bother? If you're making yourself miserable by trying too hard to stick to the straight and narrow, lighten up a bit. Don't get too fixated on your routine: You don't have to put in a half hour on the cross-trainer—try something new, like a kayaking trek. You don't need to dread every restaurant visit: sharing a dessert from time to time can be salubrious. Keep your mind open to the possibilities—that's why you're traveling, after all.

KNOW YOUR PASSPORT

▶ **Get a passport.** Not only does it verify both your identity and nationality—good enough reasons to have one—but you need a passport now more than ever. U.S. citizens must have a passport when traveling by air between the United States and several destinations for which other forms of identification (e.g., a driver's license and a birth certificate) were once sufficient. These destinations include Mexico, Canada, Bermuda, and all countries in Central America and the Caribbean (except Puerto Rico and the U.S. Virgin Islands). Soon you'll need a passport when traveling between the United States and such destinations by land and sea, too.

▶ **Take the right steps.** You must apply in person if you're getting a passport for the first time; if your previous passport was lost, stolen, or damaged; or if your previous passport has expired and was issued more than 15 years ago or when you were under 16. All children under 18 must appear in person to apply for or renew a passport. Both parents must accompany any child under 14 (or send a notarized statement with their permission) and provide proof of their relationship to the child. There are 13 regional passport offices, as well as

7,000 passport acceptance facilities in post offices, public libraries, and other governmental offices. If you're renewing a passport, you can do so by mail. See the state department's Web site (http://travel.state.gov/passports) for details.

▶ **Know your fees and forms.** Forms are available at passport acceptance facilities and online (http://travel.state.gov/passports). The cost to apply for a new passport is $97 for adults, $82 for children under 16; renewals are $67.

▶ **Time it right.** U.S. passports are valid for 10 years. Allow six weeks for processing, both for first-time passports and renewals. For an expediting fee of $60 you can reduce this time to about two weeks. If your trip is less than two weeks away, you can get a passport even more rapidly by going to a passport office with the necessary documentation. Private expediters like Passport Express (www.passportexpress.com) and American Passport Express (www.americanpassport.com) can get things done in as little as 48 hours, but charge hefty fees for their services.

▶ **Don't let a name change foil your trip.** If you've changed your name, you must have your current, valid passport amended. To do so, mail your passport with your Court Order, Adoption Decree, or Marriage Certificate showing your name change, and a completed passport application form DSP-19 to the passport agency nearest you.

▶ **Know the guidelines of the country you're visiting.** Some countries require your passport to be valid for at least six months after the date you arrive. Some countries also require a visa in addition to a passport. And still other countries require that you have blank pages (for a visa stamp) at the very front and/or very back of your passport. Knowing the rules will allow you time to renew your passport early, get the necessary visa, or have extra pages added to your valid passport.

▶ **Pack a copy of your passport.** Before your trip, make two copies of your passport's data page (one for someone at home and another for you to carry separately). Or scan the page and e-mail it to someone at home and/or yourself.

2

Packing

Although we often want to get away from our daily life and cares when we travel, we also feel oddly compelled to bring along everything from our everyday world when we do. It's not enough that we're going on vacation, as outfit after outfit is layered in the suitcase like an enormous wedding cake; it's as if we want our things to have the experience, too. It's hard to remember after each glorious trip, that we really would have been happier if our bags had been lighter and our responsibilities to our stuff less pronounced. Below are some ideas on how to lighten your load, navigate the tendency to overstuff bags, and meet the ever-tightening airline industry luggage limits without feeling like you're missing anything more than the delivery of your hometown paper.

DEVELOP A PACKING PLAN

▶ **Have a plan, and stick to it.** Packing is like most enterprises in life: The better the plan going in, the more successful the venture will be. Map out the stages, and you'll never be stuck in the bind of having to pack fast—and sloppy.

▶ **Draw up a rough itinerary.** How will you be spending your days—in a series of daylong meetings, perhaps, or lolling, sarong-wrapped, on the beach? Will you be staying put or moving nightly? Seeing the same people for the duration or meeting new ones daily? Knowing what you'll be doing is the first step toward planning what you'll be wearing.

▶ **Consider the destination.** Look into local customs as you plan. In some resort areas, an anything-goes dress code applies; others might expect fancy dress for dinner. If you're going abroad, local mores may vary: in the Middle East, for example, women are expected to dress modestly (long skirts, no pants). Before you start assembling your wardrobe, check with the country's tourist office or consult a good guidebook.

▶ **Anticipate the weather.** If you're traveling fairly soon, check the *New York Times,* CNN International, or the Weather Channel; call 900/WEATHER; or check the Web to get forecasts. If your trip is a few weeks (or months) off, consult guidebooks and local tourism boards so you'll know what conditions to expect.

▶ **Make a comprehensive list.** A mental list is never quite as effective as a written one. Think about everything you'll need to take, from travel kits (see below) to incidentals and electrical items, and write everything down. Check your itinerary and note possible outfits next to each activity or meeting, including shoes and accessories. In this way you'll become aware of your clothing needs and begin to form a tentative travel wardrobe.

▶ **Make a separate clothing list.** This list should include only the clothing you've chosen. Study it carefully, noting how many times you've listed a specific item and consider the colors of the clothes. If shorts are listed seven times for the week, for instance, you can probably make do with two or three pairs. Those lime-green Manolo Blahnik pumps, listed only once? Better leave them home in favor of more versatile shoes.

▶ **Mix and match, then edit.** Figure out how many outfits you can make with each article of clothing. Black pants, for instance, can be dressed up or down. Most women find that separates work better than dresses, although you may need a few dresses for certain occasions. Considering all the variables calmly, you can begin to edit your wardrobe.

▶ **Focus on a couple of colors.** If you coordinate your wardrobe around two or three complimentary colors (e.g., black, gray, and red or brown, green, and beige), you'll have greater latitude in your outfit choices because everything goes with everything else, and you'll get more mileage out of fewer accessories.

▶ **Choose a travel outfit.** Drawing on the items you've selected, select an outfit to travel in. You might want to opt for the heaviest clothes on your list; wearing those means you'll have less to pack. If traveling casually, wear neat-looking, loose-fitting clothing that breathes, and do a bit of layering: cabin temperatures often vary. If you're heading south, leave your heavy winter coat in the car trunk or back at home.

▶ **Be ready to jump in.** If you're a man traveling directly from the airport to a business meeting, you may want to wear a dress shirt, suit jacket, and comfortable pants, bringing your suit pants and a tie in a carry-on so that you can change just before or after landing. Women could practice a similar maneuver, switching at journey's end from comfortable clothes into something more formal.

▶ **Get your clothes travel-ready.** Go over the clothes you've selected and see which ones need washing, dry-cleaning, and mending—and get it done. If traveling with children, have them try on their vacation clothes in advance—they may have outgrown some since the last trip.

▶ **Go shopping.** If there's one key element that would tie your wardrobe together—for instance, a dressy blouse that would turn your suit skirt into a dinner outfit—go out and get it (don't wait for serendipity). If your children have outgrown key clothing items, budget the time to get them reoutfitted.

▶ **Scope out your hotel.** Inquire about laundry services, hair dryers, irons, ironing boards, cribs, high chairs, toiletries, and other amenities. Knowing that you can maintain your wardrobe on-site and dispense with some of these accoutrements could make your suitcase a bit lighter.

WHAT NOT TO PACK

▶ **Never pack valuables.** The big no-nos are cash, jewelry, medicines, keys, passports, tour vouchers, business papers, and irreplaceable or fragile items, cameras, eyeglasses, or the big round of Gouda you just bought in the Amsterdam airport.

▶ **Don't bring anything you'd hate to lose.** Depending upon your trip, it might be best to wear a few simple articles of clothing and basic jewelry that works with everything.

▶ **Don't wear jewelry that looks expensive.** Remember the old adage: Less is more. Wearing a lot of jewelry while traveling, even costume jewelry, can be risky and draw the attention of thieves, who may not be able to tell the difference between a gold-colored chain and one that's 24K. Besides, the more you take along, the greater the risk of leaving something behind. Similarly, a plastic watch is the way to go if you wear one at all—in many places, you can keep perfectly on top of the time by checking clock towers and clocks in other public places. If you do take good jewelry, make a point of never removing it, even when sleeping; once it's off, it's too easy to forget.

▶ **Give your jeans a break.** They're less dressy than men's trousers or khakis, they weigh a lot, and they take forever to dry. If these things matter to you, try going it without them.

▶ **Don't pack miniskirts.** There are so many places where these won't serve you well: developing countries, religious countries, cold countries. The list goes on. If you must bring yours for a trip to a nightclub, make sure your vacation destination can handle it.

► **Inquire about local fashion taboos.** Each city has its customs and quirks. In New York City, you will stand out in a windbreaker and fanny pack, since locals tend to leave home confidently attired like they're film stars acting in a city street scene. In Paris, women are far less likely to wear open-toed shoes, especially in any kind of business setting. In Italy, the jeans, sneakers, and baseball hat combo doesn't go over too well. If not standing out is important to you, know before you go.

► **Bring no appliances.** There is almost never a good reason to bring an iron, clothes steamer, or blow dryer, as most hotels provide them, even if they're not in-room. Forget electric razors or toothbrushes—the manual versions are easier on the road.

► **Don't bring bars of soap.** Almost every hotel provides soap, plus it's messy. If you don't like hotel soap, consider a bottle or tube of shower gel that can double as a clothes cleanser or even as shampoo. And to keep liquids you do take from leaking, cut a small piece of plastic wrap, unscrew the cap and place the plastic over the top of the opening then screw the top back on. This provides a seal in case the top becomes a little loose in transit.

► **Leave risky items at home.** Security restrictions being what they are, you shouldn't bring anything pointy, unusual, risky, or weaponlike. If you're in any doubt about what's a no-no, call your airline and find out in advance how best to transport it or visit the Transportation Security Administration Web site, www.tsa.gov for the latest list of prohibited items.

PERSONAL BAGGAGE

▶ **Bring one bag to carry on and one to check.**
Because of security concerns, restrictions on carry-on seem to be getting tighter every day. Most carriers now permit one carry-on plus one "personal item" (e.g., laptop or purse). Here's a checklist of what you might want: one change of clothing, plus a bathing suit; laptop, cell phone, camera, iPod or MP3 player; valuables, toiletries (per TSA guidelines), eyeglasses, and prescription meds (in original packages); in-flight reading, including guidebooks; and your personal and travel documents. Everything else should go in a checked bag. For more info check the TSA Web site (www.tsa.gov.)

▶ **Consider borrowing luggage instead of buying.**
Most travelers just need two bags: one that meets the approved carry-on dimensions (45 linear inches) and a large, sturdy model with wheels that can hold enough items for a two-week trip. Luggage is the type of thing that people are typically happy to lend. If you can, borrow something. Don't lay money out for luggage that you could otherwise spend on the trip.

▶ **Compare the interiors of several bags when shopping.** Consider whether the space allocation makes sense to you. Would you prefer to have two compartments or one big one? Also, spend some time experimenting in the store to see which size works best. Garment bags come in several different lengths, the longest up to 56 inches. This may not be an issue for men who are packing only suits, but for a woman, a short bag means that the hems of longer dresses and coats must be folded back. A taller person should have no trouble carrying a 45-inch bag; someone of average height may feel more comfortable with one that measures 40 inches.

▶ **Don't just use any old suitcase.** Consider your particular trip. Do two small bags make more sense than one big one? It may, if you're flying on tiny airplanes. Find out if you'll have to claim your luggage and recheck it or whether you'll be required to make a 500-yard dash to make a connecting flight and need wheels.

▶ **Decide now: Are you going to check it or carry it?** As long as it's under the luggage weight requirement, you might as well bring a medium or big bag with wheels and check it. On the other hand, a carry-on bag packed only with the essentials can lighten the burden of worrying about your belongings while on vacation, especially if it's a brief one. Light bags mean fewer worries—and less time spent at luggage claim.

▶ **Abide by the luggage weight requirement.** Know the specific luggage limits for your particular airline (there's no Federal requirement) and the class of your ticket. An economy ticket on a Virgin Atlantic or US Airways transatlantic flight gets you 70 pounds worth of luggage (two checked, one carry-on max). You get more if you're flying business or first class and less if you're flying domestically.

▶ **Anticipate having to check carry-ons.** Carry-on bags can be no larger than 45 linear inches (the total length, width, and height). Not much will help your case if yours are simply too big or if you and your luggage have been selected because your flight is full and the overhead compartments are stuffed. In these instances, a flight or counter attendant may ask you to check your bag. You will probably feel more comfortable cooperating if you've put a sturdy luggage tag on your bag and segregated all carry-on no-nos—including jewelry, medications, and paperwork—in one section of the bag so that they can be easily removed.

▶ **ID all luggage.** Label it both inside and out, with your name and telephone number or your business card. Add a copy of your itinerary in an outside pocket, so that the airline can track you down if need be. Skip your home address: If thieves get a look at it, they might head off on a little business trip of their own. If the airline requires an address, use your company's. If you work at home, include a firm name to make it look like a business address. And make sure a phone number or some other kind of contact information is taped or attached to very important items, such as cell phones, laptop computers, pocketbooks, and small carry-on bags. Also ID easily-lost items—coats, sweater, hat, gloves, cell phone, PDA. You'll be more likely to get it back if the finder knows where to return it.

▶ **Individualize your luggage.** Inevitably, someone's going to have your exact bag. To prevent them from innocently taking off with it, add a distinguishing mark—a bright ribbon, an identifiable sticker or kitschy luggage tag, a pause-inspiring strip of duct tape. This distinction will help not only on the baggage carousel, but anywhere luggage accumulates, such as a crowded hotel lobby.

▶ **Pack a collapsible duffel or large tote bag.** Will you buy out the store? Be prepared. Store an empty bag inside your medium-size checked bag rather than bringing a huge suitcase to accommodate future purchases—you can use it as a day pack in the meantime. To travel even lighter, ship gifts and souvenirs home.

Make room in your checked luggage for some bubble wrap, tape, and scissors.

THINK RESOURCEFULLY

▶ **Bring critical items from home.** Don't assume you can get anything you need at any time anywhere in the world. If there are certain things you can't live without—for business or personal reasons—bring them from home.

▶ **Bring resealable plastic bags in different sizes.** Plastic bags are indispensable and can be used for anything from packing shoes and wet swimsuits to trash in the car and exploding shampoo and sunscreen bottles.

▶ **For carrying delicate clothing items, try tissue paper.** Lay the item face down and place tissue paper on top. Fold it up with the tissue paper inside. Use additional layers of paper as you fold the garment so it is completely wrapped in paper. You might want to use a lingerie bag or large freezer bag with a zipper for it, too.

▶ **Sleep soundly by providing your own white noise.** Raucous Parisian partying keeping you up at night in your hotel? Pack a small radio and turn the dial to one of the channels that beams only "static"—white noise that sounds like an air-conditioner. Play this at sufficient volume and the noisy world outside your window will disappear.

▶ **Bring a travel alarm clock. But remove the batteries!** How would you feel if your suitcase was the one beeping from within the plane's cargo hold—and surrounded by airport police? In fact, never leave the batteries in anything you pack.

▶ **Consider going nonelectric.** Your appliances should work fine anywhere in the United States, Canada, Mexico, Japan, Korea, Jamaica, Bermuda, and the Bahamas; anywhere else, you'll need an adapter (other countries have four different pin configurations) and a converter. Unless having your own device is absolutely essential (e.g., a laptop), you'll have fewer headaches using hotel equipment.

▶ **Keep a toiletries travel kit.** Frequent travelers would do well to double up on toiletries and keep one set at home, the other permanently packed inside their luggage. Even if virtually every hotel now provides the basics, you never know what key items may be missing (or not to your liking). As long as you have your own essentials, you're set. Use a sealed, plastic-lined pouch or case—in a bright color, ideally, so that you won't accidentally leave it behind in the hotel bathroom.

▶ **Check carry-on restrictions.** Research restrictions with the TSA. Rules vary abroad, so check them with your airline if you're traveling overseas on a foreign carrier. Consider packing all but essentials (travel documents, prescription meds, wallet) in checked luggage. This leads to a "pack only what you can afford to lose" approach that might help you streamline.

▶ **Follow the 3-1-1 Rule.** The TSA allows you to carry on personal-care products in 3-ounce containers. All the containers must be in a clear 1-quart resealable bag. Each person is allowed one such resealable bag.

▶ **Be smart about packing toiletries in checked luggage.** Buy inexpensive, reuseable, travel-size containers and fill them with your own products, which often come in enormous containers that take up a lot of room in your suitcase. (Never fill containers to the top: changes in air pressure during a flight could cause the contents to expand and leak.) To play it extra safe, put toiletry bottles in a resealable plastic bag within your kit. And put the kit itself in a sealed plastic bag. If, after all this, you still end up with sunscreen on your Bruno Maglis, the travel gods simply have it in for you.

▶ **Pare every ounce of extra weight.** The small stuff adds up. Packing pros know, for instance, to remove facial tissues from their bulky boxes and slip them into resealable plastic bags. Ditto for baby wipes—useful for waterless hand washing and, some contend, stain removal.

▶ **Determine your feelings about doing laundry.** For some, the idea of doing laundry en route is anathema. Others are willing to do a little hand washing in exchange for a lighter load. Either way, it can't hurt to pack a small bottle of detergent or Woolite (the travel packets are great) to cope with unanticipated spills.

▶ **Double up.** Look for ways to make your daily routine more travel-friendly. Why pack hand, body, and face creams when one all-purpose moisturizer will do? Why pack clothes cleaner when your shampoo will do? Or forget shampoo, and go with a Dr. Bronner's soap that's everything in one.

▶ **Pack an all-in-one tool.** A Swiss Army knife or the equivalent provides a scissors, toothpick, nail file, bottle opener, screwdriver, and small knife in mere inches of space. But remember: Pack it in your checked bag, not your carry-on, or it'll be confiscated at the security gate.

▶ **Include a basic sewing kit.** Pick one up at a drugstore or grocery store (the better hotels provide little kits). Or make your own, with a credit-card-size piece of cardboard: pierce it with a couple of needles and pins, wind on various colored threads, then attach a safety pin with a couple of buttons.

▶ **Provide children with a carry-on fun pack.** Whether in the air or on an extended car trip, a portable toy stash can be indispensable. Keep it off-limits until the trip itself (lest the novelty wear off), and include such items as new audiotapes for the Walkman, books, a clipboard and colored pencils (because crayons melt and markers leak), handheld games, puzzles, and one-piece toys without small parts that could get lost. Let your child add a tried-and-true toy, too.

▶ **Wear a watch with a 24-hour clock dial.** Unless you've got a military background, or have spent a lot of time in countries that tell time this way, trying to read the opening hours of a restaurant or a movie's show times may require constant math (you subtract 12). It isn't hard but it sure can be frustrating.

GETTING IT INTO THE BAG

▶ **Don't bring everything you own.** You are likely to be the one responsible for lugging your bags to the airport, across a busy terminal, off the luggage carousel, into a taxi, and up to your hotel room. And back. Note that shopping on a trip is also likely. Travel light.

▶ **Divvy the load.** If you're traveling with a spouse or companion, figure out where you don't need to double up. She's got the shampoo? You'll get the toothpaste.

▶ **Cross-pack.** A pair of people flying together could also pack some of each person's essentials in the other's suitcase. That way, if one bag doesn't make it to the destination, both will still be covered.

▶ **Customize your "night before" routine.** Since packing can be stressful, set aside enough time and set the desired mood (whether New Agey and calming, or pumped-up Rolling Stones). If you're a perfectionist, set up an ironing board next to your suitcase: ironed clothes lie flatter and arrive neater.

▶ **Try different folding techniques.** Each school has its passionate advocates. You might do best to match the method to your luggage. Rolling items works well with duffels and soft-sided bags, and will meet the needs of a casual traveler. "Interlocking" (wrapping slacks, say, around a bulky sweater) and the "dress-maker's dummy" approach (layering your garments progressively over one another) are other good ways to minimize wrinkles.

▶ **Fold clothes together.** Take two or more garments, for example trousers, and lay half of one pair on top of the other. Fold the one on the bottom over the pair on the top. Then take the other and fold it on the top. This gives each pair some cushion where they're folded it so it's less likely to crease or wrinkle in the folds.

▶ **Organize for efficiency.** Small items have a way of disappearing, especially in the undifferentiated space of a duffel or pack. Plastic bags, or the mesh bags made for laundry and delicates, help in sorting and keeping categories cohesive. Pack extras for dirty clothes.

▶ **Utilize every inch.** Shoes should never be empty: they're ideal for stuffing with underwear, socks, or a travel umbrella. Nor should they travel in pairs: one by one (and wrapped, of course), they're easily wedged into unused crannies.

▶ **Refine and record your list.** Some travelers recommend halving the packing list at the last minute, but if you've prepared well, you'll probably only need to do

CELL PHONES: AN AMERICAN ABROAD

Dan realized after a brief hotel stay here at home that he could save a bundle by using his cell phone for local calls instead of paying the exorbitant fee—sometimes as high as $2—the hotel charged for local calls. Although his company picked up the tab, he thought his boss would appreciate the cost-saving measure. His conscientiousness paid off, and when he was promoted to handle European accounts, he planned on doing the same thing in Europe. But on his first trip to London he learned the hard way that his American cell phone didn't work there—in fact, it didn't work anywhere in Europe. He was forced to use the hotel phone and wound up paying more for his phone calls than he did for the room. What happened? What should Dan have done to make his cell phone European compatible?

▶ FODOR'S FIX

Just like plugs, adaptors, and electrical currents, cell phone technology is different on the other side of the pond. The problem stems from the fact that cell phones gained popularity in Europe long before they caught on in the United States, and the result has been something of a compatibility mess. The major American providers use different technologies—AT&T Wireless uses something called TDMA, Verizon Wireless uses CDMA, and VoiceStream uses GSM, for example—while all European providers use only GSM. What makes it worse, though, is that this one technology they share in common, GSM, broadcasts on 1900 Mhz in the United States and on 900 Mhz and 1,800 Mhz in Europe. In other words, technologically speaking, it's Babel out there.

The Bottom Line: If Dan didn't lose his job after his boss got a look at his hotel phone bill from his first European trip, he might want to consider switching to what's called a "tri-band" or "global" phone—one that can communicate on any one of the three GSM bandwidths currently used in the United States and Europe. These phones are more expensive and harder to find—for now, anyway—due to a lack of demand for them in both markets. Of course, even if you have a tri-band phone you'll still be assessed roaming charges, so be sure to get the details from your provider before deciding to take your phone along. Alternatively, consider renting a European phone once you get there.

some light editing. Place a copy of your revised list in your personal documents kit (see below)—as a checklist for when you're repacking to head home, for reference on the next trip, and also as a record in case your luggage is lost or stolen. To play it double safe, add a photograph of your luggage to your personal documents kit (see below).

ESSENTIALS

▶ Assemble a personal documents kit. This is a pouch or envelope of the stuff that, if you lost everything else, you'd still be basically okay. Include a photocopy of the first page of your passport (also give a copy to a friend at home for safekeeping), a few traveler's checks, copies of prescriptions for medications and eyeglasses, a list of your credit card numbers (along with phone numbers to call for assistance), and key phone numbers such as family, neighbors, doctors, work associates (you could photocopy or print out your address book). Keep it with your suitcase until you're ready to travel.

▶ **Always hand-carry your documents.** Put your personal documents kit in your carry-on as backup, adding maps and guidebooks as necessary. When it's time to go, carry on your person your passport, airline tickets, hotel confirmations or other necessary receipts, and more traveler's checks.

▶ **Start out with a little local currency.** Before a foreign trip, convert about $50 to $100 into local currency—enough to cover a cab ride from the airport, and incidentals or a late-night meal. Have enough small bills to cover tips (dollar bills will do in the Caribbean). Carry the rest of what you'll need in traveler's checks, if you're going someplace where they're accepted, or make other arrangements, like visiting an airport ATM machine.

▶ **Carry your wallet in your left front pocket.** Thieves usually go for the right-hand one. Scatter the rest of your money, leaving some in the in-room safe, some in a wallet, some with your travel partner, and even some between the insole and bottom of your shoe. You'll be in better shape if some is stolen. Money should be accessed only as needed, though. If possible, use local ATMs.

▶ **As a daypack, use what locals carry.** If you don't want to be taken for a rich American, consider using something for a daypack that's familiar to your vacation setting and less of a magnet for thieves. Your fancy

American backpack will stand out among, say, the handwoven bags and canvas totes of Central America.

▶ **Don't forget sunscreen, sunglasses, and a hat.** You might also want to pack some Pepto-Bismol and Imodium tablets and a bottle of water. Rich food or food in new places can really do a number on your stomach.

▶ **Pack an extra pair of contact lenses.** Disposable varieties are handy for traveling, and are less expensive than eyeglasses. If contacts aren't for you, make sure you have a spare set of glasses or an eyeglass repair kit.

▶ **Have addresses and phone numbers for where you'll be staying.** These will be crucial during trips to the lost luggage counter or if your ground transportation is unreliable and you have to get to your hotel yourself.

▶ **Send your jars of baby food ahead.** Rather than schlep it with them, an ingenious couple vacationing with their new baby in the Caribbean decided to ship a package to their hotel a week ahead of their arrival. (Local provisions were miles and miles away, and sold at hefty price.) They discussed their intentions with the hotel and were able to confirm the package's arrival before leaving the United States. You could do the same and save yourself a whole lot of extra luggage.

WHAT TO WEAR

▶ **Wear your bulkiest clothes on the plane.** It's either that or carrying them. Which would you prefer?

▶ **On a city vacation, dress as if for business.** Nothing marks a yahoo like workout pants and a sloppy tee. If you want to be treated respectfully, dress respectably. (You can wear shorts if you prefer in season, but make them pressed linen.) Don't insult locals by wandering around dressed as if you were hanging out in your backyard.

▶ **Pack only multipurpose items.** Try to have everything you pack serve at least a couple of different purposes. Don't take an item you'll wear only once unless you absolutely can't live without it. And forget about having your suitcase give you the variety of your closet at home—one of the wonderful things about taking a trip is that you get away from all that.

▶ **Pack black trousers.** They are the perfect multifunctional item; they can be dressed up or down, depending on what you put on top and on your feet.

▶ **Go with two pairs of shoes.** It might be hard to imagine that two pairs of shoes can cover all occasions, but they can. Bring a dressy pair that looks great with a skirt or pants, and a casual (but not beat-up) pair that you can walk across Rome in. Unless you plan to run, you won't need running shoes.

▶ **Slip into a skinny pair of flip-flops or sandals.** They're a must for a beach vacation and around any hotel room.

▶ **Consider the multiple uses of a jacket.** A navy or olive-green blazer looks great over jeans as well as with business slacks. A windbreaker makes for a waterproof shell. A long, fancy coat dresses up casual outfits.

▶ **Look for lightweight and wrinkleproof fabrics.** As you evaluate your options and narrow your choices, go for items that are light in weight, wrinkle resistant, compact, and washable. If you notice the resilience of a particular item over the course of a workday, pack it! If you've considered a microfiber skirt, buy it now.

▶ **Pack for social or religious customs.** In the fashion capital of Milan, women visiting the famous cathedral are expected to cover their heads and bare shoulders with a scarf. Consult the Destinations chapter of this book or a guidebook on the place you're visiting, or check with a local tourism board to find out about local mores.

▶ **Layer, even if you think you won't need to.** Forget what you've read about sunny California: San Francisco in summer is subject to finger-numbing fogs, and even Los Angeles has its chilly days. Also, malls, museums, cinemas, and airline cabins are often air-conditioned to a wintry degree. The best bet is a lightweight, waterproof jacket, stuffable into your carry-on. A shawl-size scarf—virtually weightless and warm—is a woman's best friend, and can act as a beach cover-up or a wrap.

▶ **Pack the kitchen sink when you cruise.** Luckily, since you'll only need to unpack once, you can pack everything you need for activities on board and ashore. Most cruise lines issue a list of suggested clothing. You may want to pack the required formal wear in a garment bag and the rest in a suitcase or duffel. Also, be sure to bring a daypack for excursions (to carry your camera, sunscreen, water, an extra sweater, etc.).

PACKING FOR KIDS

▶ **Co-pack.** Most kids—like more than a few adults—feel compelled to have their "own bag." Still, try to pack in communal bags as much as possible, especially on a road trip.

► **Abide by the motto: Last in, first out.** Pack swimsuits, pajamas, fresh underwear, and other important items last so they're on top. Keep handy whatever they will need to settle down fast at the end of a long journey.

► **Use mesh or large resealable plastic bags.** The big bags can hold a complete outfit—pants, shorts, tops, underwear, and socks—for each day. With everything together, you'll spare yourself endless rummaging for missing essentials. Bags are easy to pull out of the suitcase and a great way to separate dirty clothes from clean ones.

► **Make sure everyone gets a carry-on.** Busy children are happy children. Have your child help fill a manageable carry-on bag with items to play with during your trip. A book-on-tape may be a new and exciting experience, preferable to school work. And tossing in a few familiar snacks won't hurt either. Don't forget extra batteries.

► **Bring a baby backpack.** Some hotels have strollers—or can get one for you—but backpacks are less cumbersome for strolling around town. With your baby safely ensconced, your hands are free to haul out tickets, lug bags, or quickly maneuver streets.

PACKING YOUR PET

► **Bring your pets-approved information.** Have the information handy that your airline or hotel mailed or faxed to you, so you have proof that someone has endorsed your pet's transportation or stay.

► **Have your pet wear two tags when traveling.** One should list your permanent address and telephone number and another a way to contact you on the road. A trick is to staple a card or matchbook from your lodging to your pet's collar.

▶ **Consider attaching a bell to your pet's collar.** This is a great backup safety measure if, say, your pet gets loose in the woods on a camping trip.

▶ **Bring a good leash.** Pets may be fine on a junky, chewed-up leash for their local walks. But for new places and modes of transportation a new, sturdy one is worth the investment.

▶ **Make sure your pet carrier is airline-approved.** If it's vetoed at the airport, it could foul up your travel plans big time and you might incur a financial penalty if you need to change your ticket. Some airlines sell carriers, but they can be more expensive than at a pet store and your particular airport may not have the right size on hand. An approved model is well ventilated and large enough for your pet to stand up, turn around, and lay down; it must also contain two plastic food and water dishes.

▶ **Acquire a Sherpa bag for a small pet.** These soft-sided carriers, some with a "sun roof," resemble gym bags or totes and are airline-approved for carry-on. Some pets find them more comfortable than crates and are more willing to climb into them voluntarily. You can buy a model with a removable "travel tray," which is lined, washable, and absorbent. Or one with wheels.

▶ **Pack a current photo.** Taking every imaginable precaution doesn't guarantee your pet won't get lost on your trip. As a safety measure, be sure to have some current photos and a detailed description of your pet's markings in case you need to put up signs.

▶ **Don't forget to assess how the temperature may affect your pet during transport.** Rumors circulate about the chilly temperature of a plane's cargo hold and the cabin, as people know, can be hot. Try to anticipate what your pet might need.

▶ **Put down bedding in the carrier or car.** Depending on your animal's preferences, pack a bed, blanket, or carpet sample.

▶ **Bring health and vaccination records and extra ID tags.** You and your pet are out of your normal surroundings, so it's good to take extra precautions in the event anything goes awry.

▶ **Just say no to drugs.** Never give your pet any drugs, especially tranquilizers, without your veterinarian's approval; most do not recommend tranquilizers because they can have adverse side effects at high altitudes. On the other hand, if your pet often gets car sickness, a holistic remedy might help. Many people have had success with Rescue Remedy, which is a mixture of flower essences. This option should be discussed with your vet.

▶ **Buy a clip-on minifan.** These can come in handy in the hotel room or the car.

▶ **Pack the right toys and comfort objects.** Sterilized hollow white bones or Kong toys can be stuffed with meat, cheese, kibble, or peanut butter (good for dogs and cats). Pet stores sell ingenious cat toys, though the easiest and cheapest one is a piece of crumpled paper or a square of cardboard tied to a string. If your pet has a personal attachment, say, to a dish scrubber or a stuffed toy, be sure to pack that, too.

Food and Water

▶ **Consider going disposable en route.** Paper plates and a collapsible water bowl are light to carry and easy to dispose of. You can bring plastic bowls for your destination.

▶ **Don't forget a can opener and a spoon.** You'll need them if you use canned food.

▶ **Instead of canned food, bring dry soup mix.** If you usually add a bit of moist food to the dry food but prefer not to take heavy cans with you, take a few packets of mild dry soup mix. Sprinkle a bit over the kibble and mix with warm water to make a tasty gravy. If you have a finicky eater, you might want to try this at home first.

▶ **Pack the familiar kibbles.** If you routinely use a local brand that may be difficult to find while traveling, pack enough for the whole trip. (A sudden change in your animal's food could cause an upset stomach.)

▶ **Bring a spray bottle to avoid dehydration.** On the road you may find it convenient to use a spray bottle to squirt water in your pet's mouth—unless, of course, your pet will think upon sight of it that it's being asked to get down from the kitchen counter or stop spraying the plants.

▶ **Bring a container or two of water.** If your pet has a sensitive stomach and may be affected by drinking new water, you might want to bring enough along and stick to bottled water when in your destination.

▶ **Plan for "accidents" en route.** Sure, your perfect pet knows the litter box or would rather hold it for hours than go in the house, but new environments can set off even the most well-trained cat or dog. Unless you've traveled together extensively, don't assume your pet will be fine. Accidents are normal given the stress of travel on animals. It's best if you bring along a few clean-up supplies, rather than find yourself without them and in need. Baby wipes and plastic bags can come in handy for all kinds of circumstances.

▶ **Bring a few essential hygiene or first-aid items.** Bring more than a few if you're going camping. Some essentials may include: prescription medicines, a first-aid kit, a slip-on muzzle, tweezers (for removing burs and ticks), baby wipes, paper towels, a spray bottle of cleaner, room deodorizer, grooming tools, and, for cats, a litter box, litter, a plastic bag (to slip over the box), and two large rubber bands (to hold the bag in place). Sweater-size plastic storage boxes and disposable plastic casserole-size bake-and-serve containers work well as substitute litter boxes—and come with their own snap-on lids.

PACKING YOUR CAR

The On the Road chapter gives more tips on packing for a road trip.

▶ **Buy maps or a road atlas.** Flag the relevant pages with Post-it notes, and consider highlighting your route or important towns. If you're not the navigator, share your plans with the person who is before you get in the car. It's no fun to be made responsible for getting you there and having to interpret the map at the last minute.

▶ **Bring extra keys!** Make sure at least one of the passengers carries an extra set of car keys. (Never leave them locked up in the car!) Better still, leave a third set with someone who can easily Fed Ex them to you should you be locked out.

▶ **Put essentials within reach.** Every passenger should have an extra shirt or a jacket for a pillow and for darting in and out of the car, as well as his or her own book or Walkman. Except for a trash bag and roll of paper towels, everything else should be stashed in the trunk.

▶ **Pack "on the way" items separately.** The most important thing about packing a car is to pack what you'll need on the way to your destination separate from what you'll need once you get there. This way, you won't have to unload the whole trunk each time you stop en route.

▶ **Pack from back to front.** Place "there" bags, packed with clothes and supplies you'll need when you arrive at your destination, at the back of the trunk or under other bags. "Getting-there" suitcases—clothes for the trip, enough to get you from home to your destination—should be accessible and loaded last.

▶ **Clean out your trunk.** Before putting anything into the trunk, take out seasonal items that don't apply. Get rid of everything you won't need on your trip.

▶ **Check the air in the spare tire.** If you have a trunk light, make sure that it works. See that the lock is properly lubricated.

▶ **Don't bury the emergency kit.** Leave it out until after you load all of your bags and then find a corner where it will be easily accessible if needed.

▶ **Consider a roof rack.** If you have skis or other special sports gear that takes up lots of space, think about a roof rack. Things like boogie boards and beach chairs are hard to fit under the seats.

▶ **Plan for spills and quick changes.** Put helpful extras inside the car. Bring paper towels for clean-ups. Have a couple of large T-shirts handy in case someone spills coffee or dribbles ice cream. A quick change and you're on your way without having to unpack the trunk.

▶ **Give the kids plastic containers.** Let each child have his or her own square plastic container that can double as a lap desk. Fill it with games, books, music, journals—whatever might entertain them on the road.

▶ **Pack a small cooler.** A small cooler filled with treats for children and adults will reduce costs and help make car travel fun.

▶ **Pack a few emergency items.** Not everyone needs a flare and a fire blanket. A cell phone with a car charger, extra wiper fluid, a spare tire and jack, jumper cables, and your AAA membership card should do it.

WORK AWAY FROM THE OFFICE

▶ **Create a portable office.** Bring letter-size envelopes to hold receipts, as well as for correspondence; add some 10x13 manila envelopes for sending material home, so you don't have to lug it around. Take stamps if you're traveling in the United States. Add a Ziploc bag of useful small stuff: e.g., business cards, calculator, tape, paper clips, Post-its, miniature stapler.

▶ **Plan your outfits.** Knowing what you need before you pack means you'll carry less and worry less when getting ready for meetings.

▶ **Evaluate whether an overnight bag will suffice.** There are many occasions when one carry-on bag does the trick. Is this one of them? Don't overpack, if it is. Many of your clothes will never see the light of day, and you'll regret having towed them around.

▶ **Always bring one casual garment.** Choose an outfit (a pair of khakis or a casual skirt) that can mix with dressier work pieces and shoes. You'll feel more comfortable in your hotel room, exploring the city, or on your return flight.

▶ **Pack for the circumstances.** Clearly, what you'll be doing dictates what you'll need. On a multipurpose trip—for instance, business mixed with a bit of beach-combing—you'll have to be all the more strategic to conserve space.

▶ **For business, err on the conservative side.** Different countries' definitions of "business casual" vary widely: an open-collar shirt that goes over in Singapore marks you as a rube in London. Check with colleagues or the destination's tourism bureau to learn more about the local business norms.

▶ **Try to blend in.** A splashy tie could make a strong impression—in the worst way. If you'll be moving from place to place, meeting new people, you can get by with a versatile, minimalist wardrobe with minor variations. When keeping the same company, opt for an unobtrusive style, and people will be less likely to notice if your wardrobe tends to repeat itself.

▶ **Buy good luggage.** Professional travel calls for professional-looking luggage. It's an incontrovertible fact that image counts. You'll score negative points if spotted with a raggedy backpack. Consider investing in a good garment bag and wheeled Pullman, ideally in a matching set.

▶ **Make room for recreation.** Business travelers need all the destressing they can get, so take your running gear, gym clothes, or bathing suit, on the chance you'll get to squeeze in a workout. Add any accessories you might need, such as an iPod with exercise program downloads, bands for resistance exercise, plastic bottles to fill with water and use as hand weights, or a jump rope.

▶ **Coddle your feet!** If you're heading to a meeting or trade show where you'll be standing for hours on end, bring comfortable, broken-in shoes—flats or low heels for women. Choose these as well for days involving lots of walking. The era of the sneaker-sporting female exec may be long gone, but comfort still counts.

PACKING FOR THE COMPUTER AGE

▶ **Have your laptop extremely handy.** Most people who routinely travel with their computers are security-savvy. You'll save yourself some misery by following their lead; have your laptop packed so that you can easily take it out and put it away, with no other items in the same compartment, locks open, and so on. Have it fully charged so you can turn it off at security checkpoints if requested.

▶ **Always carry your Ethernet connector.** This is a must as more and more hotels offer high-speed Internet connections.

▶ **Carry a 12- to 20-ft telephone line.** Phones are not always convenient to hotel desk surfaces, and are often closer to the nightstand. You'll need the extra length if you're using a dial-up connection.

▶ **Consider buying a telephone adapter for phone plugs outside the United States.** You haven't schlepped your laptop this far to not be able to dial up, and phone plugs do differ. Radio Shack or other such store will be able to help you select the right one for your destination. For the United Kingdom, visit www.multitel.co.uk for information.

▶ **Get your ISP's local phone number before your trip.** This is particularly important when going abroad, and staying in a hotel. You don't want to accrue astronomical long-distance bills for your time spent on-line.

▶ **Leave your computer at home and use an Internet café.** Ask your hotel staff or visit www.netcafeguide. com before your trip to locate Internet cafés in cities you're visiting.

▶ **Make sure your computer has a firewall.** If you take your computer to a place that has a wireless network, such as Starbucks, others may be able to "eavesdrop."

▶ **Disguise your expensive photo equipment.** Traveling through a congested, sometimes mugger-prone city (like Naples and Barcelona)? Get a shopping bag with handles from a local department store or boutique, then "camouflage" your camera within the bag. The bag will also help you blend into the crowd and you'll be less marked as a "tourist."

▶ **Before you rent a cell phone, read the fine print.** Although renting a cell can make life easier—www.internationalcellular.com is one such rental outlet—if the phone is stolen, you often need to file a police report, or they won't refund your deposit, which can be hefty.

3

On the Road

Road trips appeal to our sense of wonder and imagination, our yearning to know what lies just around the bend, and what happens if we choose one fork in the road over another. Where trains, planes, and buses are captained by others, automobiles go pretty much where we want them to go. Other forms of travel limit our luggage allowances, force us to follow somebody else's schedule, and cramp our style; car trips allow us the ultimate freedom and flexibility.

Perhaps the biggest decision you'll need to mke before planning a road trip is whether you intend to use your drive as a relatively quick means to get to where you're ultimately headed, or whether you want to make the very automobile journey its own linear and evolving destination. The wide, speedy superhighways are great for getting where you want to go with maximum efficiency. But, according to die-hard road-trippers, you understand the places you're visiting—their contours and climates, the local architecture and social histories, the longtime inhabitants and their long-practiced customs—only by sticking to narrow, two-lane roads through country villages and bustling cities.

There are so many other reasons to travel by automobile. A long car ride provides the easy pace and close quarters conducive to good conversation—a road trip is the perfect way for passengers to connect, or reconnect, not only with the land as they pass over it, but with each other.

As you are saving time or money driving versus flying or even taking a train, you are also freeing yourself from the trappings of home and the constraints of other transportation modes. Best of all, simply hopping into your car and gliding down a twisting road—windows down—feels totally empowering. There really is no better way to see the world around you.

KEEPING TRAVEL COSTS DOWN

▶ **Borrow books-on-tape from the library.** Books-on-tape are a wonderfully diverting way to pass the time during a long road trip, but audiobooks often cost two or three times more than printed versions. If you're planning a trip that's shorter than two weeks, it's worth checking out some audiotapes at your local library. Even if you won't be home in time to return the books in person, it can still be worth borrowing audiobooks from the library and shipping them back to your library once you're finished. The chain restaurant Cracker Barrel, which has many roadside franchises, has a program where you rent a book-on-tape for a small fee and then return it to any other Cracker Barrel location.

▶ **Pick up the latest hotel coupons.** Roomsaver.com prints hotel-coupon books on every region in the United States, and they reprint them seasonally. These are available free at many highway rest stops and fast-food restaurants and in some visitor information centers, but you can also log onto the Web site and print out the coupons from the convenience of home. Keep in mind, however, that although these coupons often provide the lowest hotel rates around (even better than what you'll find on Expedia.com or Priceline.com), they're good only for walk-ins and are subject to availability. They aren't honored for guaranteed reservations. You can hedge your bets by calling a hotel ahead a day or even a few hours ahead of time and asking if they're likely to have availability that night, and confirming that they'll be accepting coupons.

▶ **Park at a commuter bus or train station instead of driving into big cities.** Especially in the northeastern United States, driving in cities like Boston, New York, and Washington can be intimidating, and parking can cost $20, $30, or even $40 per day in some areas. If you're using a car to get from city to city, save yourself hassles and money by parking just outside the city limits. Instead of driving into Manhattan, for instance, you could park at the secure and covered garage at the Metro North train station in Stamford, Connecticut for just $8 per day, paying about $8 to $10 for the one-hour train ride into the city.

▶ **Conserve gasoline.** The way you drive greatly affects your car's gas mileage. Making sudden stops and starts, driving with the air-conditioning or with all the windows down, using underinflated tires, and idling unnecessarily—such as while you eat at a fast-food restaurant or talk on your cell phone—waste gas and pollute the environment.

▶ **Fill the tank of your rental car at least a few miles from the airport.** Gas stations nearest airports and car-rental agencies charge the highest rates. You can save several dollars on a full tank of gas by filling up well away from the airport. But make sure you're not so far away that you'll have less than a full tank of gas when you return your vehicle.

▶ **Stock up on road food at warehouse shopping clubs.** By far the most expensive place to buy snacks and toiletries when traveling are the convenience stores attached to roadside gas stations. At the very least, try to buy groceries at discount department or grocery stores before you leave. Members of warehouse superstores, like Costco and Sam's Club, can save a huge amount stocking up on bulk foods and even toiletries at these places. Best bets include bottled water, crackers, cookies, chips, trail mix, sports bars, nuts, and breath mints, as well as aspirin and pain relievers, antacid tablets, laundry detergent, and film.

▶ **Bring a list of warehouse shopping club locations.** In addition to low-cost snacks, warehouse shopping clubs usually have the cheapest gas prices around, and many are just off major interstates or along other well-traveled routes.

▶ **Look for clusters of gas stations when refueling.** If you're driving down the interstate looking for a place to refill your gas tank, avoid the exits that have just one or two stations. You'll save money at exits with three or more stations, as competition helps drive down prices.

▶ **Find out which states have the cheapest gas before you go.** Gas prices are greatly influenced by state gas taxes. So if alternate routes are an option, it's not a bad idea to find out where gas prices are lowest as you plan your route. On the Web, you can get a sense of this at www.gasbuddy.com, www.fueleconomy.gov, or www.gaspricewatch.com (which relies on reports from consumers). Sometimes the differences are great.

▶ **If you drive an unusual car, bring a list of repair shops.** Mechanics who specialize in Saabs, Volvos, Audis, Mercedes, Jaguars, and similar luxury cars are rare outside major urban and suburban areas—in some states you actually can't find a dealer of these kinds of vehicles. Plan your route with this in mind, keep a list of repair shops around the country in your glove compartment (most car dealers can supply you with a free directory), and avoid using a truly exotic car for long periods in remote areas.

▶ **Join the American Automobile Association (AAA).** If you need emergency road repair, your AAA membership (www.aaa.com) includes many fees related to towing and roadside assistance. Memorize the number for long trips: 800/AAA–HELP (800/222–4357).

SMART ROAD-TRIP PACKING

▶ **Bring along a set of spare car keys.** Make sure your traveling companion has a set or, if you're going solo, pack an extra set in your luggage in case yours are stolen or misplaced. Maybe stash a copy of the door key in your wallet, in the event you lock yourself out. As an added backup, it's not a bad idea to leave an additional set with a friend or relative back home who can send them via overnight mail.

▶ **In cold weather, pack appropriate supplies.** It's invaluable to have warm gloves, deicer spray, an ice scraper, a small snow shovel, antifreeze, and a bag of rock salt or sand when traveling in areas where snow and volatile winter weather is likely. Keeping a bag of sand in the trunk is useful for traction if your car gets stuck in snow or ice, and the added weight in the back of your car will help to negotiate slick roads and snow-covered hills.

▶ **Keep spare change in an out-of-view container.** Having a bag or cup of change can be useful for tolls, parking meters, and other small expenses, but be sure to keep it in a discreet place, maybe the glove compartment, the ashtray, or under a seat. Thieves have been known to break into cars just to steal a few nickels and dimes.

▶ **Keep a spare toiletry kit in your car.** Anybody who travels regularly by car knows how frustrating it is to run out of toothpaste, razor blades, or pain relievers on the road. Hotel gift shops and even many convenience shops charge exorbitant prices and aren't always around when you need them. Keep a bag in the trunk of your car containing spares of your most important toiletries, and replenish your supplies when it's convenient, ideally between trips.

▶ **If traveling with a camera, keep it cool and dry.** Many parts of the cabin of your car are susceptible to intense heat, and your trunk can easily become damp. Store film and smaller camera equipment in a tight, waterproof bag and keep it away from direct sunlight. And cover your camera and lens. Wrapping equipment in a towel is a good way to keep it clean and also camouflaged so that potential thieves aren't tempted.

▶ **Keep folding chairs in your trunk.** You can guarantee yourself a comfortable front-row seat wherever you are by packing collapsible nylon chairs (they resemble director's chairs) in your trunk. Even if you fly somewhere and rent a car, consider buying a couple of cheap folding or beach chairs for your rental car— they're very inexpensive at most discount department stores. And at the end of your trip you can give the chairs to fellow travelers.

▶ **Use plastic drawers to organize your trunk.** You can buy cheap, stackable plastic drawers at most department stores. Put a few of these in your trunk, filling one with books and maps, another with office or work supplies, another with toiletries, and maybe one more with music tapes or CDs (if you don't mind risking the high trunk temperatures), and you'll have an efficient system for even the longest trip from home. Use bungee cords to keep the drawers from opening or sliding.

▶ **Photocopy important documents.** Before you leave, make copies of your driver's license, passport, insurance papers, credit cards, and car documents and store one set at home or with a friend or relative, and other set in your luggage. Even better: scan these documents into your computer and take them along with you as a file on your laptop, or leave the file with a friend at home with a computer.

▶ **Carry your car-insurance card in your wallet.** It's okay to keep a copy in your glove compartment, although some drivers prefer not to for the simple reason that if the car is stolen, the illegitimate driver will have a much tougher time talking his or her way out of a traffic stop without an insurance card. But definitely keep one in your wallet at all times, so you'll always have it handy should yours provide coverage for cars you rent or borrow.

▶ **Bring your passport for international road trips, even to Canada.** With the increased security measures, even drivers crossing between the United States and Canada or the United States and Mexico will be asked to supply a valid passport, whereas a driver's license typically sufficed in the past.

▶ **Separate your "getting there" and "there" clothes.** If you're planning the kind of trip that involves a stay at some place bracketed by a long drive there and back, keep the clothing you plan to use once you arrive in one piece of luggage, and store this in the least accessible part of your trunk. Fill lighter and smaller duffel bags or luggage with the clothing you'll be using during your drive there and back, and keep these in an easier-to-reach place.

▶ **Travel with baby wipes or water-free soap.** How many times have you used the lavatory at a roadside gas station only to learn that it's out of soap? Or have you eaten a messy meal in your car with no place to wash up? Baby wipes are great for cleaning up your hands, and they're also perfect if you're traveling with children or babies who need a quick cleanup. Liquid hand sanitizer such as Purell requires no water, kills germs, and dries without a towel—it's ideal for cleaning up in a car. And given the dreary state of many rest rooms, it's not a bad idea to keep a supply of toilet paper or even disposable toilet-seat covers in your car, too.

▶ **Affix a compass to your dashboard.** Portable compasses designed just for use in automobiles have become increasingly sophisticated in recent years.

▶ **Get directions on-line.** Yahoo and Mapquest are two of the biggies that allow you to access map locations if you have the address or point-to-point driving directions. They can't take all factors like construction into account, though, so compare the routes to a map. And check local directions, off the highway, with someone at your destination; the on-line services occasionally contain erroneous information as well. If you have an AAA membership, your local office will plan a route for you and provide all the relevant maps with several weeks' notice.

▶ **Buy road-tripping software.** Especially if you're traveling with your laptop, software such as Microsoft Streets & Trips and Delorme Street Atlas USA can be indispensable for planning road trips, as these programs allow you to pinpoint the location of almost any address in the United States (and often Canada, depending on the software), and to determine the fastest or shortest route between two points, complete with detailed directions. Many of these programs also show hotels, restaurants, and other services and points of interest along the way.

▶ **Never leave luggage or valuables visible.** Even if thieves aren't interested in the exact contents left on your backseat, a car with luggage or bags is a much more likely target. Even loose change, music tapes or CDs, and snack food should be stowed in the glove compartment or the trunk.

▶ **Store a set of bungee cords in your trunk.** These elastic cords, which can be wrapped around boxes and luggag, are ideal for keeping the contents of your trunk from sliding around. And they're also perfect for securing any items you might need to transport on the roof of your car or in an open pickup truck.

▶ **Leave big suitcases at home on long road trips.** There are few things less pleasant than having to haul a giant suitcase around when traveling. If you're driving long distances and staying in several places for just a night or two, pack only a carry-on-size suitcase with two or three nights' worth of clothing. Keep the bulk of your clean clothing in a laundry basket in the trunk of your car, and repack your carry-on suitcase every few days as needed, storing your dirty laundry in a separate bag.

▶ **Watch for dampness in the trunk.** Car trunks are highly prone to dampness—wetness from one big storm can remain in your trunk for long periods and ruin food, clothing, luggage, and other goods that you store there during long car trips. It's a good idea either to line the bottom of your trunk with a waterproof tarp or, better yet, with some kind of slightly elevated platform, which allows air to circulate between the base of your trunk and the goods stored in it.

▶ **Travel with a soft, collapsible cooler.** Collapsible coolers are ideal for car trips, and because they fold up compactly and can fit inside your suitcase, they're also worth taking with you when you fly somewhere and rent a car. These lightweight coolers are great for stowing leftovers, keeping drinks cool on hot days, and protecting fruit and other perishable snacks.

▶ **Keep an electricity power inverter in your car.** These adapters, which plug into your cigarette lighter and cost from about $40 to $60, depending on wattage, can power virtually any appliance that runs on electricity—alarm clocks, cell-phone chargers, hair dryers, electric razors, mini-refrigerators, TVs, hot pots, and so on. Port-A-Wattz is one of the most reliable brands on the market. You can also buy an adapter that allows you to plug two items into your cigarette lighter, or use a dual-plug attachment to power multiple appliances. Just remember that you can run power appliances only when your engine is running, and that you need to be careful not to overload the adapter.

▶ **Consider getting satellite radio for long road trips.** Two satellite radio servers, XM Radio and Sirius, began offering service in 2001, with a subscription costing about $10 to $13, plus anywhere from about $160 to $249 for the actual satellite radio receiver (which adapts to any existing car stereo). This device enables you to tune into roughly 100 music and news channels, with few or no commercials—and the reception is good nationwide, no matter how remote your location.

▶ **If you've got a cell phone, buy a hands-free adapter.** Hundreds of U.S. cities and regions have banned driving while talking on a cell phone, and it's looking likely that this practice will be banned virtually everywhere before too long. However, using a phone with a hands-free adapter, which allows you to keep both hands on the steering wheel while you talk, is legal, and these adapters are generally small and inexpensive—they can fit easily into your glove compartment.

RENTING A CAR

▶ **Obtain an international driving permit.** Abroad, your driver's license may not be recognized. Consult the AAA Web site (www.aaany.com/travel/travel_services/IDPform2.asp?) for the requirements of each country. If needed, international driving permits (IDPs) are available from the American and Canadian automobile associations and, in the United Kingdom, from the Automobile Association and Royal Automobile Club. These international permits, valid only in conjunction with your regular driver's license, are universally recognized; having one may save you a problem with local authorities. In the case of an accident, local police could confiscate your paperwork, and it's far better to surrender this temporary permit than your actual driver's license.

▶ **Consider renting an RV instead of a car.** RV travel has become increasingly popular in recent years, and certain circumstances make this form of getting around more enjoyable—and potentially more economical—than traveling by car. RVs especially make sense if you're planning to visit parks and/or areas with campgrounds and you're traveling with a family or group of friends.

▶ **Check for deals on wheels.** When renting a car, find out if any of your frequent-flier mileage programs or credit cards entitle you to a discount.

▶ **Use a travel agent who will shop around.** Some travel agents work regularly with just one or two car-rental agencies or won't shop around for the best deal unless you ask. It pays to find an agency that will search for bargains.

▶ **If you're under 25, be prepared to pay a surcharge.** Most rental-car agencies impose a surcharge of $5 to $25 on drivers under age 25, and some will not rent to drivers under 25; in most instances, drivers under 21 will not be permitted to rent a car at all. There are certain exceptions: some rental companies waive the age restriction and possibly even the fee for employees of companies with which they have special corporate agreements.

▶ **Ask about drop-off charges or one-way service fees.** Most agencies charge a hefty fee for returning a car to a different location from where you picked it up, but there are some exceptions.

▶ **In Europe, consider renting from a wholesaler.** These are companies that do not own fleets but rent in bulk from those that do and often offer better rates than traditional car-rental operations. Prices are best during off-peak periods. Rentals booked through wholesalers often must be paid for before you leave home. Top European car-rental wholesalers include Auto Europe, Europe by Car, Destination Europe Resources, and Kemwel.

▶ **Abroad, rent from U.S.–based company.** In the event of a problem, you'll have an easier time reaching an employee who speaks English.

▶ **Remember the extra costs in Europe or abroad.** Gasoline costs three to four times more in Europe than in the United States, collision insurance (your own U.S. car insurer most likely will not cover you abroad) can be very costly, and renting a car as a walk-in—without a reservation—can be expensive.

▶ **Look before you leave.** Before you drive away in a rental car, always check for damage, and take the time to point out anything you notice to an agency staffer—otherwise you could be charged for damage.

▶ **Choose the right car for your style of driving.** Avoid tiny economy cars if you're driving in mountainous, high-altitude areas. Make sure the car you rent can accommodate not only you and your passengers but everybody's luggage. Will you need air-conditioning where you're traveling? A ski rack? In some countries you're more likely to find cars with manual rather than automatic transmissions.

▶ **Learn about your car before you leave the lot.** Some good things to check: Locate the gas tank—make sure the gas cap is on and can be opened. Check the trunk for spare and jack. Test the ignition—make sure you know how to remove the key. And test the horn, headlights, blinkers, and windshield wipers.

▶ **Jot down details about your rental car.** Want to be able to remember which unfamiliar car is yours? Always carry with you a slip of paper on which you've noted the model, make, color, and license plate number of your rental car.

▶ **Know the local traffic laws.** It may seem obvious, but it's important to familiarize yourself with the local rules of the road, which often vary considerably from country to country (especially with regard to right-of-way and right turns on red). Even within the same nation, laws often vary from state to state or city to city.

▶ **Know where you're allowed to go—and not.** In Hawaii, rental-car companies routinely forbid drivers from taking their car onto certain dangerous but popular roads. Because of the high car-theft rate, many European agencies don't want their cars taken into Eastern Europe. You'll need a special sticker in order to drive on the autobahns of Switzerland and Austria. Make sure your agency knows where you plan to use the car.

▶ **Rent a cell phone from your car-rental agency.** Some agencies rent cell phones, which can be handy and even cost-effective in countries where your own cell phone doesn't work.

▶ **Call local car-rental offices to compare rates.** The price you're offered for a rental car on a national chain's Web site, or through its toll-free reservation number, is often higher than the one you'll be quoted by calling the local reservation office directly. Some local offices have special sales or unpublished discounts, and others—especially if it's the day you plan to rent the car—will negotiate a better rate or an upgrade based on availability.

▶ **Check rental-car rates on the Web.** You'll rarely save money and almost never save time calling a car-rental company's toll-free reservation number for rates rather than searching on the Web. General discount booking sites like Expedia.com and Orbitz.com allow you to comparison shop, and they sometimes list Web-only deals. You can also score good rates using a bidding site, like Priceline.com, but these deals often come with restrictions and require that you pay up front.

▶ **Look to local, independent car-rental agencies for good rates.** You can often find these places by using on-line search engines. And if it's not a very busy period, you can also just take your chances and book a rental car when you arrive—most local agencies have courtesy phones in airport terminals. Avoiding the national chains and renting through local agencies can save you big bucks, particularly in touristy areas like Florida and California, where competition is stiff. The potential downside is that local agencies sometimes have limited hours or infrequent shuttle service, a limited car selection and high insurance costs (which doesn't much matter if you have your own auto policy that covers rental cars); they rarely provide roadside assistance.

▶ **Reserve an economy car even if you want a larger vehicle.** Economy cars are usually the cheapest to book, but they're also the first category of vehicle that agencies usually run out of. When you have a guaranteed reservation for a car size that's not available, the agency must upgrade you to a better vehicle. And even when the size you reserved is available, agencies frequently will try to entice you to upgrade by offering you a better deal than you would have gotten had you reserved the larger car in the first place. The catch, of course, is that the success of this strategy depends on supply and demand—during busy times, such as holidays and vacation periods—it might turn out that trying to upgrade proves prohibitively expensive, so don't try this unless you know you'll be content if you end up in an economy-size vehicle.

▶ **Read the fine print on weekly rates.** A national chain recently offered a great weekly rate of $119 for a midsize car, but the promotion had a big catch: The daily rate was $69.99, and the contract's fine print stated that renters had to keep the car a minimum of five days to qualify for the weekly rate. Otherwise, the rate reverted to $69.99 a day. If a customer returned the vehicle after only four days, the charge would be more than double the weekly rate. If you come across a weekly rate like this, make sure you'll be able to keep the car for the duration of the rental, or negotiate a better daily rate before you leave the counter.

▶ **Never "prepay" for rental-car gas.** You know the routine: The rental agent asks you whether you want to purchase the gas already in the tank for a "reduced" price or return the car with a full tank. Simple answer: Never, ever buy the gas in the car. The reduced price rental agencies offer is usually within pennies per gallon of the going rate, and unless you coast in with a completely empty gas tank upon return, you wind up paying for gas you don't use. Be sure to return the car with the tank full, though, because the refueling fees are exorbitant.

▶ **Think before you pay for rental-car insurance.** In most cases, if you have personal car insurance or are paying with a major credit card, there's no reason to pay for additional insurance on your rental car. Know what your personal car-insurance company or your credit card issuer cover before you leave home.

RENTAL CARS AND THE WEEKLY RATE SCAM

Greg and Linda thought they were getting a great deal on a rental car for a long weekend in Orlando, Florida. After doing much research on the Internet, Greg found a weekly rate from a major agency that was less than what other agencies were charging for a mere two-day rental. Of course, he only needed the car for four days, but his plan was to pay for the entire week and turn the car in early. Linda, pleased by Greg's resourcefulness, suggested the couple upgrade to a suite at their hotel, using the money they saved on the rental car. But after four days of carefree fun, they returned the car and were shocked when they were handed the receipt: A weekly rental that was supposed to be $169 had turned into a bill of more than double that amount. What happened?

▶ FODOR'S FIX

Rental agencies are smart about pricing and timing—usually smarter than the customer. After years of drawing business by offering attractive weekly rates, rental agencies found that many renters were taking advantage of the weekly rates, but not keeping the cars the entire week. To maximize their profits, the companies changed the terms of the weekly rates to snare unsuspecting customers like Greg and Linda. The fine print on most weekly deals defines a week as at least five days; if you fail to keep the car for at least five consecutive days, the contract automatically reverts to a preset daily rate—and it's usually an inflated rate meant to penalize the customer for breaking the contract. (Of course, it's hard to defend any rental policy that actually penalizes you for returning early.)

The Bottom Line: Illogical corporate policies aside, Greg and Linda had an unpleasant surprise simply because they failed to read the contract before they signed it. Had they read it, they would have realized the trap they were falling into and could have negotiated a rate better than the punitive one they were forced to pay simply because they returned their car "early." The lesson here is to make sure you read all of the fine print before signing—good deals can still be had, but be sure you have all the facts before committing. Unfortunately, in Greg and Linda's case, there is little that can be done because rental agencies are famous for using the "it's-in-the-computer-there's-nothing-I-can-do" excuse.

FOR ROAD WARRIORS

▶ Buy your European car where it was manufactured. Some automakers, among them Saab, Volvo, and Mercedes, offer deals where you can pick up your car at a number of European cities, use the car to travel around the continent, and then drop the car off at any of 10 or 20 locations, where it's then shipped back to the United States. You won't necessarily save money on these deals, but you'll be able to enjoy your own new vehicle on your vacation instead of a rental car.

▶ Don't take a sport utility vehicle on long road trips. Of all the types of automobiles on the road, SUVs are among the least practical for long trips, despite the fact that they're spacious. Poor SUV gas mileage is an obvious and costly drawback for long trips. SUVs can be harder to navigate and park in areas with which you're not familiar, such as congested cities. And although you can fit a lot of luggage in the back of an SUV, potential thieves can see the contents (unless you have smoked or dark-tinted windows).

▶ **Consider renting a car, even if you're starting at home.** If you lease your car, or have some other reason to avoid putting a lot of miles on your own vehicle, you may want to consider using a rental car for long road trips. A rental car with unlimited miles can pay for itself if you drive it for a couple of thousand miles instead of using your own vehicle.

▶ **Watch a great road movie before your trip.** There are loads of great movies out there that involve road trips, and it can be great fun renting one before you embark on a journey. A few favorites, of varying artistic merit: *Easy Rider, Two for the Road, National Lampoon's Vacation,* and *Road Trip.*

▶ **E-mail yourself any important documents.** Before you leave, send yourself an e-mail containing your itinerary, any important travel information, a calendar or "to do" list, and contact information of friends, relatives, travel resources, and the like. If you include credit card numbers or other valuable information, consider disguising them in a way that you can decipher but others can't. E-mail yourself this document, and keep this as "unread mail" during your trip. You can always access this document whenever you need to from your laptop computer, or from a hotel's business center, a Kinko's, or some other place with public Internet access. Just remember that most e-mail services keep unopened mail for only limited periods, so resend this document to yourself periodically if you're going to be gone a while.

▶ **Don't overplan.** Although a little research and preparation can go a long way, remember that one of the best ways to experience an auto vacation is by giving yourself the chance to be spontaneous. One strategy is to set up two or three potential itineraries and then vary your actual route according to whim and maybe even weather. Another, if you're feeling adventuresome, is to reserve hotels on some nights but leave others open—it's a good idea to check rates and availability of hotels in a few places you might stop along the way, however, just so you know roughly what to expect if you show up without a reservation.

▶ **Make a list of attractions and events along your route.** You can help to plan your road-trip itinerary by researching attractions that fall roughly within your route, and by finding out if any notable events are planned in areas you might be passing near. Knowing these things can also prepare you for unpleasant surprises—an impending event or attraction may cause hotel rooms to book up fast or roads to clog with traffic.

▶ **Confirm car-rental and hotel reservations well before your arrival.** Especially in a world where travel reservations are often made on-line, it's worth remembering that mistakes happen. Computers foul up, reservationists press the wrong key—any number of snafus can arise. It's wise to confirm your car-rental and hotel reservations, going over the exact dates and rates, with a human voice and well before you arrive, so that you'll have enough time to remedy any error should it occur.

AN OUNCE OF PREVENTION

▶ **Gas up when you're down to a quarter tank.** It can be tempting to go as long as possible between refills, but it's a great idea to get used to refueling your car whenever it's down to about a quarter tank. Particularly when you're traveling in unfamiliar territory, you never know exactly how far you are from the nearest gas station—waiting until the indicator is on Empty (or below) puts you at great risk of running out of fuel before you can find a gas station. Also, engines run more efficiently when there's more than a couple of gallons in the tank.

▶ **Make sure your spare tire is in good shape.** Routinely check on the condition and pressure of your spare tire, as well as your vehicle's four primary tires. If you're not used to changing a tire, do a test run before you leave home for a long road trip. Make sure that the lug nuts on your tires can easily be removed (mechanics sometimes overtighten them), and keep a pair of work gloves near your spare, as changing a tire can be a messy job.

▶ **Have your car checked out before the big trip.** How long has that red engine light been flashing on your dashboard? Are your windshield wipers smearing the glass instead of clearing it? When's the last time you had your oil changed? You've probably been putting off seeing a mechanic, figuring that you can live with these seemingly minor issues. But the last place you want little irritations to turn into major headaches is on the road, far from home. So take your car in for a checkup before you leave.

▶ **Get regular oil changes.** It's easy to forget to change the oil when you're on the road, away from home. But especially when you're far from your home mechanic, it's a good idea to keep up with regular maintenance. Depending on the make of your car (check with you mechanic or your auto manual), you should schedule an oil change every 3,000 to 5,000 mi.

▶ **Keep backups of important car parts and fluids.** For long trips to unfamiliar places, it's a good idea to keep extra coolant, windshield-washer fluid, hose tape, jumper cables, oil and transmission fluid, fan belts, and fuses. These items are particularly useful if you drive a car that's relatively exotic or uncommon.

▶ **Be prepared for bad weather.** Keep an umbrella, poncho or waterproof windbreaker, cap, and sturdy gloves in your car. These items will prove indispensable if you break down or need to check under the hood or change a tire during a rainstorm.

AIRPORT INS AND OUTS

▶ **Avoid on-site, long-term airport parking lots.** The official, long-term lots at most airports cost more than off-site lots and aren't necessarily more convenient. They often fill up quickly, so finding a space can take plenty of time, especially as many airports have reduced their long-term parking as a security measure following 9/11. On the other hand, a growing number of off-site lots offer valet parking, which saves you having to search for a space and then remember its location on your return. Also, the shuttle buses at many off-site lots run as or more often than at on-site lots, and they're often less crowded.

▶ **Use long-term airport parking rather than an airport shuttle.** You might assume that if you're going to be parking your car for two or three weeks you'll save money using public transportation or an airport shuttle or limo service to reach the airport. In fact, especially if you're traveling more than an hour to the airport, the round-trip cost of airport shuttle vans, taxis, or even commuter trains and buses can be pricey, and these services can take several hours' longer than driving your own car. Additionally, many off-site parking lots can arrange oil changes, car washing, and other maintenance services while you travel.

▶ **Don't be so cheap you miss a bargain.** In San Francisco, New York, Los Angeles, and other cities, cabs to the center of town cost $30 or more, and shared-van and bus services cost from $10 to $17. But remember that if you're splitting expenses with a traveling companion, the cost of a taxi might be only a tad more than the cost of the alternatives (which usually take longer and can be less comfortable); with three or more people, a cab can become a bargain.

▶ **Look for on-line discounts on airport parking.** Several nationwide companies offer Web-only deals and coupons good for long-term airport parking, both on- and off-site. Airportparkinglots.com guarantees the lowest off-site rates at more than 50 U.S. airports plus several in Canada, Europe, and Australia—just print out the no-obligation rate quote and present it to the lot. Discountairportparking.net provides a similar service at many airports, only you can guarantee your reservation by paying up front for the first day's parking. Parking Company of America (www.parkingcompany.com) and AviStar (www.avistar.com) both offer significant on-line discounts at the on-site lots they have at dozens of major U.S. airports.

▶ **Try using a competitor's coupon to park at the airport.** Just like many supermarkets, airport parking lots often honor competitors' coupons.

▶ **Rent a car to save on airport transportation.** Especially in cities like Denver and Los Angeles, where the airport is a 30-minute drive from downtown, it can be cheaper to rent an economy car than to take a cab or even shuttle bus into town—and you may get frequent-flyer miles this way. And using your car instead of a cab for trips during your visit may increase your savings. When pricing this option, be sure to factor in the cost of parking the rental at your hotel.

CABBING IT

▶ **Offer to share a cab with a stranger.** You can often save money, and possibly make a new friend, by asking around at the airport taxi stand if others in line are headed to the same area that you are. This works more effectively in some cities than in others, and always check with the driver first to see just how much sharing a ride will save versus going it alone.

▶ **Write down your hotel name and address on a slip of paper.** In places where you don't speak the language, jot down the name, address, and phone number of your hotel on several pieces of paper, along with the same information for any restaurants, attractions, or other sites you're planning to visit, and present these to cab or bus drivers as you travel. Be sure, if appropriate, to write this information in both the local alphabet and your own.

▶ **Always record the badge or medallion number and name of your driver.** In the unfortunate event that you must dispute a cab charge or leave an item in the cab, having the information will prove invaluable. Also, be sure to ask for a receipt, and jot down the cab company's phone number if it's not already printed on the receipt.

▶ **Act relaxed and knowledgeable when you get into a cab.** Most cab drivers are honest, but the deceitful ones are less likely to take you on a circuitous, and therefore more expensive, route if they believe that you're familiar with the local roads. It's not a bad idea to study a map before you use a cab, and even to discuss the best possible routes with your driver before you set off.

▶ **Avoid unlicensed taxis.** So-called "gypsy" cab drivers are sometimes legit, but you generally have no way of knowing this before you hop into the vehicle. And if you are overcharged or mistreated, you have little chance of disputing the incident. At airports or other places with taxi stands, only use authorized cabs. And if you're unsure, ask a hotel doorman or airport ground-transportation employee for information on which cab companies in the city you're visiting are reputable.

BEATING BOREDOM, FATIGUE, AND CAR SICKNESS

▶ **Avoid traveling by car on an empty stomach.** Crackers, bread, sports bars, and other easy-to-digest and mild foods are good snacks for long car rides, as motion sickness is much more likely to occur when you have an empty stomach. Eating rich or spicy foods can also exacerbate the problem, as can smoking. On the other hand, keeping hydrated with water or juice often helps to ward off car sickness.

▶ **Keep your eyes on the horizon to avoid motion sickness.** If you suffer from queasiness during car rides, try to get as much fresh air as possible, sit in the front seat, and avoid looking out at the window at nearby objects as you pass them. It's much better to fix your eyes on the horizon or a distant object.

▶ **Rest often during long road trips.** It may sound counterintuitive, but you're more likely to make better driving time—and to arrive safely—if you take frequent breaks when traveling long distances. pull off the road, get out of your car, and stretch every two to three hours, you'll actually increase your alertness and endurance. On the other hand, if you drive four or five hours without stopping, you're more likely to become fatigued and unable to continue safely without stopping for a long break or even an overnight. Breaks are also important when traveling with kids—stopping to toss a ball around or play a game helps to stave off boredom and restlessness.

▶ **When resting in your car, choose a lighted area.** A rural back road in the country may look like the perfect place to pull over and catch some z's during a long drive, but it's actually much safer to pull into an established, popular rest area, truck stop, or even a motel or department store parking lot. Just as you wouldn't leave your car full of valuables in a desolate place, no matter how scenic, you shouldn't doze off in a parked car unless you're at a designated rest area and or some other place with good security and high visibility.

▶ **Keep a small pillow and a blanket in your car.** When embarking on a long road trip, it can be refreshing to pull over for a short nap—especially in cooler climes, keep a waterproof blanket and pillow somewhere in the car.

EMERGENCIES

▶ **If possible, remain with your car in case of an accident or emergency.** If you're in an accident, no matter how seemingly minor, wait with your car until authorities arrive, even if the other driver insists on leaving or offers to cover the damages. In the end, your insurance company is going to care about only one thing in determining the fault in an accident: the police report. Never admit fault to another driver, and avoid confrontation. It's best to remain calm and wait patiently for a police officer.

▶ **Create an "emergency" kit for the trunk of your car.** There are some items that you should always have in your car: a blanket, first-aid kit, flashlight with extra batteries, Swiss Army knife, matches (in a resealable bag to keep them dry), jumper cables, flares and reflectors, sturdy and warm gloves, crackers and bottled water, and a supply of relevant road maps.

▶ **Keep flares or reflectors in your car.** These are invaluable in the case of a breakdown or accident, especially if you're pulled off onto the narrow shoulder of a busy highway. If you have room under the front seat, store them there; otherwise, keep them in the trunk in a waterproof container. But be sure flares are kept away from children.

▶ **Keep a first-aid kit in your car.** You can buy an inexpensive, prepackaged car first-aid kit at many department stores, but you can also create your own.

Some items to consider: topical cream for cuts, scrapes and bug bites; sunburn lotion; heartburn medication; necessary prescription and over-the-counter drugs and allergy remedies; contact lens solution; ointment; tweezers; Band-Aids and bandage tape; pain relievers; and scissors or a Swiss Army knife. Periodically check that medications are current.

▶ **Try the pump at a station that appears closed.** Next time you're rolling down the highway on fumes, your tank on its last few drops of gas, don't fret if the first gas station you pass appears to be closed. Many gas stations with automated pumps, which you activate using your credit or debit card, remain open 24 hours, even when the station is closed.

▶ **Enroll in a roadside assistance plan.** Before you embark on a long trip, check to see if your car's warranty if still in effect, includes emergency roadside assistance, which typically covers towing, changing flat tires, and retrieving keys that have been locked inside cars. If you don't have such a plan, consider joining AAA, which offers this service.

CAR TRAVEL WITH KIDS

▶ **Pack car games for kids.** Long car rides can feel even longer if the kids traveling with you have nothing to keep them entertained. You don't have to invest a lot in games for the car—books, audiotapes, clipboards, action figures, toy animals and vehicles, sticker books, coloring/activity books, dolls, colored pencils (you might want to avoid markers and pens, as they stain car seats if they're dropped while uncapped), and notepads can all be used to fun effect.

▶ **Think snowsuits when car-seat shopping.** Bulky winter coats or snowsuits have to fit inside the car seat, so make sure the seat can be adjusted to accommodate the clothing.

▶ **Install car seats correctly.** This may sound like obvious advice, but the National Transportation Safety Board (NTSB) estimates that four out of five car seats are improperly installed in vehicles. Contact the National Highway Traffic Safety Administration, a division of the U.S. Department of Transportation, or your state's department of traffic safety for locations of Child Safety Seat Inspection Stations.

▶ **Put a pillow between two quarrelsome kids.** Also make a hard and fast rule: no touching each other. If you have three children, place the most mild-mannered one in the middle.

▶ **Let your kids use the road maps.** Give the kids road maps and have them help navigate during a drive. They can estimate distances and learn some geography. Generally speaking, the more involved children are in a trip, the less antsy they'll be. And if they hold the maps, the less likely you'll hear, "Are we there yet?"

▶ **Make some choice rules.** If kids squabble over who gets to sit in what seat, who gets to choose a campsite, or who gets to play the Britney Spears CD first, put their names on a list and rotate the top name each day to decide who gets first choice when.

▶ **Pack a ball.** A game of catch recharges kids of almost every age and takes up almost no space. If you have Little Leaguers, make it a baseball and bring a mitt. Shop toy stores before the trip to find unique and diverting balls.

In the Air

The airline industry has changed dramatically in recent years. Since the late '90s, it has become increasingly common to book airline tickets on-line, using a variety of methods. A downturn in the economy has forced airlines to eliminate routes, reduce fleets, and cut jobs, creating more overcrowding on planes and fewer ways to get from place to place. And massive airline-security overhauls have greatly altered the process of getting through the airport not to mention the flying itself.

Not all the changes in the airline industry are inherently bad for consumers, but it is more important than ever to learn some reliable strategies for booking flights and getting quickly in and out of airports. In some cases, such as for trips shorter than 500 miles, it sometimes makes more sense—both time-wise and economically—to drive or take a train or bus rather than fly. But for the most part, airplanes continue to be the quickest and most economical way to get you where you're going.

Cutbacks and consolidations may continue to reduce the number of airlines out there, in the long run if not quite soon. But for now, a sharp drop in air traffic has forced airlines to cut fares on many routes, especially those where a low-cost, lower-frills airline offers competition. Several of these alternative carriers—Southwest Airlines, Frontier, JetBlue, Spirit, and Midwest Express among them—offer a terrific value between select U.S. cities. But you don't have to fly them to take advantage of their great fares, as they often force some of the major airlines, with a greater variety of routes, to drop their fares, too. The biggest tip of all is to shop around, whether by going on-line, by having a travel agent go to work for you, or by phoning different airlines to get a sense of the going and cheapest rate. If you keep your dates and times flexible and plan ahead, you can end up flying as cheaply now as any time in history.

Flying, if not necessarily a pleasure, remains an amazingly safe and relatively affordable way to access even the most far-flung corners of the globe. There's something exhilarating about boarding a plane from your home airport and stepping off on a continent two or three oceans away—making a journey that would have taken our forefathers weeks or even months. It wasn't all that long ago that the idea of an Atlantan weekending in San Francisco seemed inconceivable, or at least completely extravagant. But not any more.

Talk of long delays and invasive security pat downs and searches have become almost the stuff of legend in recent years, but major inconveniences at most airports are actually quite rare—and avoidable. If you plan well, exercise common sense, and arm yourself with a few insider tips, you can steer clear of many of the pitfalls.

BUYING A TICKET

▶ **To save money, fly on a holiday.** Just as the most expensive fares tend to be on the days or weekends on either side of a holiday, some of the least expensive are on the holiday itself especially Christmas and Thanksgiving.

▶ **Do your fare research midweek, late at night.** This tends to be the time when you'll find the cheapest fares.

▶ **Know your flight type.** "Nonstop" goes from city A to city B without stopping. A "direct flight" stops, then flies on but does not require a change of planes. "Connecting" means that you will change planes. And a "through flight" requires you to change both your plane and your airline.

▶ **Fly on "your" important dates.** Many airlines will upgrade your seats on your birthday (with proof of ID), anniversary, honeymoon, and so on. Agents sometimes upgrade first-time fliers as well.

▶ **Always consider flying from secondary airports.** Smaller, secondary airports are often used by discount airlines and therefore offer better fares; furthermore, in many cases, they're smaller and less chaotic than a region's main airport(s). In New York City try MacArthur (Long Island) or Hartford, in Boston try Manchester or Providence, in Miami try Fort Lauderdale, in Chicago try Midway, in L.A. try Orange County or Burbank, and in San Francisco try Oakland, San Jose, or Sacramento.

▶ **Try flying on a Tuesday or a Thursday.** These two days typically see the fewest air passengers. You're more likely to end up on an uncrowded flight, and therefore to have more room to spread out. And in many cases you'll get cheaper fares (assuming you have a Saturday-night stay over) on these days than others.

▶ **Try not to book at the last minute.** Despite the much-publicized "last-minute" fare bargains available on the Web, the closer you book to departure, the greater the odds that a mistake or a glitch can foul up your plans.

▶ **Pick the flight with the best on-time record.** Major U.S. airlines are required to publish in the computer reservations system a one-digit code for each flight that indicates how often it arrives on time (within 15 minutes of schedule. A code "6" means that the flight arrived punctually between 60% and 69% of the time, a code "3" 30% to 39% of the time. When choosing flights with similar schedules and times opt for the one with the higher on-time rating.

▶ **In winter, make connections in through a warm-weather city.** If you're flying from Phoenix to Boston with a choice between a connection in Dallas and a connection in Chicago, choose Dallas. Even if this option takes slightly longer, you're much less likely to encounter the winter weather–related delays that plague northern cities all winter long.

▶ **Beware pricey intercity airfares in Europe.** You can often get the best deals from London's numerous discount travel agencies or "bucket shops."

▶ **Look to Europe's no-frills discount airlines.** A wealth of cheap, bare-bones discount airlines have started up in Europe in the past few years, and many of these offer inexpensive flights between key European cities. It's not a bad idea to recommend this to your travel agent, too.

▶ **Be aware of the pitfalls of e-tickets.** Many flights that require you to connect from one airline to another cannot be booked as a single e-ticket. On multiairline flights, check when making your reservation whether your e-ticket will work, or play it safe and book using a paper ticket.

▶ **Request a special meal.** On flights with meal service, ask for a special meal when you reserve your seat. Vegetarian, vegan, sodium-free, and kosher meals are often better than the drab food served to the economy-class masses—and they're often delivered before the other meals.

▶ **When using an e-ticket, always carry a hard copy of a receipt.** In the event that something goes wrong, you'll have a much easier time remedying the situation if you have paper documentation of both your itinerary and your purchase. If you bought the ticket on-line, print out any e-mail confirmations or on-screen "receipts." And have the credit card with you that you used to buy tickets on-line.

▶ **Flying early in the day? Book a seat away from the sunrise side of the plane.** You'll be less likely to be bothered by the intense glow of early morning sunlight.

▶ **Don't sit over the wing if you love seeing clouds.** Window seats directly over the wing offer the worst viewing from your window.

▶ **With kids? Don't book a seat in an exit row.** Only adults may sit in these seats—if you try this, you and/or just the kids will be moved to a different seat.

▶ **If you're completely flexible, book a flight that you think will be crowded.** It may sound crazy, but if you can deal with arriving late (possibly even the next day), try to get yourself onto a flight that will end up over-booked. These are especially common around holidays and on Fridays and Sundays. If your strategy pays off, the ticket agents will ask for volunteers to give up their seat and fly on the next available one, and they'll reward these passengers with all sorts of perks: typically a future round-trip ticket or $200 or $250 voucher, a first-class upgrade, and possibly even some free drinks coupons.

▶ **Book mid-morning to early afternoon flights.** These are sometimes slightly less crowded, and if the flight is delayed or canceled, there's usually still time to rebook and get out that day.

▶ **In summer, plan to arrive before 4 PM.** Late-day summer thunderstorms can cause havoc with your travel plans.

▶ **Keep abreast of fares even after you buy the ticket.** Especially if you buy an air ticket many weeks in advance, check periodically to see if the fare has come down. You'll often have to pay a fee of $75 or $100 to rebook your flight, but this charge may be worth it if the fare has dropped by more than this amount.

▶ **If you're traveling with a group, negotiate a discount.** Are you and a large group of friends heading somewhere, or are you planning a family reunion? If more than 20 of you are planning to fly to the same place, contact the group sales departments of a few airlines and have them submit bids for your group. You can expect to get a fare at least one-third lower than the going published prices for individual travelers.

Shopping On-line

▶ **Book on a reverse auction site.** So-called "reverse-auction" sites, built on the name-your-own-price concept pioneered by Priceline.com, are best if you have a lot of flexibility and don't particularly care which airline you fly; last-minute tickets can be a good buy. However, if a specific itinerary or earning frequent-flier miles in a particular program is important to you, go elsewhere. Notable reverse-auction sites include Cheapfares.com, Hotwire.com, and Youpriceit.com.

▶ **Play the bidding game smartly.** Priceline.com and similar on-line booking services don't let users submit repeat bids using the exact same criteria. For example, you can't start at $100 for an LA to NYC ticket and then keep "working your way up" to a price the booking service will accept. If you have to fly on particular dates to or from a town with multiple airports and want to make sure you pay the lowest possible fare, test the waters by listing just one airport for each town on your first bid. List the ones you prefer first, in case the bid is accepted. If it's not, add airports as you raise your bid.

▶ **Don't bid too low.** Before you go to a bidding site, visit a traditional site to research the best fares and the associated taxes and set yourself a bidding limit of no more than 10% or 15% below that.

▶ **Read the fine print when booking on-line.** Internet booking services often present you with a choice of alternative airports "near" your destination. On one service, for instance, Chicago's Midway airport is listed as an alternative airport for flights to Grand Rapids, Michigan, which is a three hours' drive away. Additionally, don't mistake the airport at which a discount flight is actually terminating for one where you'll switch planes.

▶ **Don't rely solely on the Web for booking flights.** Fares on the Internet aren't always the lowest. Travel agents may still be able to get you a better price, simply because it's their business to know their way around the reservations thicket. However, if you've checked fares on the Web and then go to a travel agent or call the airline directly, you'll be able to recognize a good deal when you're quoted one.

▶ **Look at an airline's Web site to get the best seat.** Many airlines post schematics of their planes on-line, and even allow you to choose seats. You can get a sense of the plane's layout and its exit rows this way. If you're traveling alone or as a couple on a plane with a two/three seat configuration, opt for a seat on the "two" side—this will at least ensure that you won't get stuck in the dreaded "middle" seat of a "three" section.

▶ **Try sites operated by individual airlines.** Don't assume that Orbitz, Travelocity, Expedia, or another site that lists several airlines' airfares will always offer you the best deal. You may just find the cheapest fare on an airline's own Web site. Airlines often offer special deals not available elsewhere, or give you bonus frequent-flier miles to induce you to use their site. Also, you can't book flights on many smaller or discount airlines, such as JetBlue and Southwest Airlines, on Orbitz, Travelocity, or Expedia—you need to visit their sites directly.

Consolidators

▶ **Learn the ins and outs of consolidators.** Consolidators have contracts with airlines that allow them to sell tickets up to 50% off the published fares. Consolidators sell tickets to travel agencies or directly to the public. There are hundreds of consolidators; not all are reputable. There are some drawbacks to consolidator fares. You usually can't change dates and times after you buy the ticket, and you might fly an indirect route with multiple stops. Consolidators can be a great option when you can't meet an airline's advance purchase requirements and for international coach flights. You can save the most money on flights to Asia and South America, but there are also some good deals to Europe and other continents. They're often not the most economical option during the off-season, however, such as to Europe in winter, when regular commercial fares are already quite low.

▶ **Pay consolidators with a credit card.** Many airline consolidators offer a nominal discount to customers who pay with cash, however, if your credit card issuer provides travel insurance or any other protections it may be wiser to forego the discount. Additionally, credit card firms will cancel charges if you report a problem within 90 days.

▶ **Don't be rushed when booking through a consolidator.** Most consolidators are high-volume shops with thin profit margins; their agents may be in a hurry to book the transportation and move on to the next customer. Ask questions and read the fine print. Ask if you can get a refund, reserve seats, order special meals, collect frequent-flier miles (it depends upon the consolidator's contract with the carrier), and find out what the charges are for cancellations or changes to your itinerary.

▶ **Use a travel agent to buy from a consolidator.** Most full-service travel agencies can buy consolidators tickets for their customers. Savvy agents have relationships with the good ones and deal regularly with them.

▶ **Consider a consolidator instead of trying for a bereavement fare.** Unfortunately, serious abuses of bereavement policies have forced some airlines to revise their policies and require more stringent managing of the policy by airline personnel. Obtaining a bereavement fare can involve a lot of hassle (proof of emergency documentation and other limits), and the price isn't always better than what you'd find by buying a ticket through a consolidator.

Frequent Flier Do's and Don'ts

▶ **Don't cash in frequent-flier miles for a cheap flight.** If you're getting a fare much below $250 or even $300 for a round-trip domestic flight in the United States or Canada, you're probably better off paying this fare and saving your miles for a trip that costs more than this, such as a last-minute or high-season flight.

▶ **Get a credit card with an airline rewards program.** You might be surprised by just how many credit cards can be used to earn points good for airline tickets—it's not just cards that are affiliated with specific airlines or travel programs. Many other cards out there award points that can be used to buy products in special "rewards" catalogs, and these products often include airline tickets.

▶ **Beware of restrictions on travel with frequent-flier miles.** Only a certain number of seats on certain flights are set aside for travelers cashing in frequent-flier miles—don't be caught off guard. If you're planning to use your miles for travel during the holidays or other busy times, find out which blackout dates apply, and book your reservation as early as possible. Attempting to use miles for a flight that's just a week or two in the future can prove nearly impossible, especially during busy periods.

▶ **Transfer miles to a friend of family member.** Different airlines' rules vary on the transferability of frequent-flier programs, but many of them have loosened the rules in recent years and now allow you to transfer miles to a spouse, partner, or member of the immediate family. And you can also cash in miles to buy a ticket in virtually anybody else's name. This can be especially handy if you have miles about to expire but no plans to travel soon yourself.

▶ **Make sure frequent-flier miles have been credited.** If you wait until your next statement or even several days after you fly before noticing that you haven't received frequent-flier credit for a flight, it might already be too late to get credit from the airline. Check as soon as possible after your flight, either on-line or by phone, to see whether your account has been updated.

SMOOTH SAILING AT AIRPORTS

▶ **See if your airline offers remote check-in.** This service, offered by some airlines in a number of cities, can save you plenty of time. With this system, e-ticketed passengers can log onto the airline's Web site up to 24 hours before departure (but no less than 90 minutes ahead) to confirm their flight and seat, answer the security questions, and print out a boarding pass. When you get to the airport, you can proceed to security with your pass and go directly to the gate to check in.

▶ **Arrive as early as you can to the airport.** The average wait time at check-in counters alone has increased considerably since 9/11. To be totally safe, especially on busy flying days or with busy airlines, arrive 2 hours ahead of time for domestic flights and $2\frac{1}{2}$ to 3 hours ahead for international flights. Hate waiting around in the airport? It beats missing your flight.

▶ **Use car services, not taxis, to get to the airport.** To avoid being stranded during peak hours and in peak travel seasons (e.g., a Friday afternoon in July in New York City), consider booking two cars from different car services rather than using a taxi to get to the airport. You can request that one company send a car 30 or 45 minutes before you actually need it to reach the airport on time; and request that the other company send one at the exact time you need it. If the first one arrives on or close to schedule, call and cancel the second car from your cell phone. If not, call the second company to be sure its car is on the way, and call the first company to cancel. Either way, you'll get a car when you need one.

▶ **Assume that the plane will be packed.** In recent years, airlines have cut many routes, resulting in higher load factors than almost anytime in history. This makes it all the more important to arrive at the airport, and your gate, as early as possible, and to anticipate possible delays.

▶ **Factor rental-car return time into your schedule.** People have been known to miss their flights because they underestimate how long it will take to return their rental cars. If you need to be at the airport two hours before a flight and you're also returning a car, get to the agency 45 minutes to an hour earlier than you hope to get to the terminal. Better yet, phone your car-rental agency (the actual local office, not the national toll-free number), and ask exactly how far they are from the terminal, how often shuttles run, and how early they suggest you return your car in order to make your flight. Or do this when you pick up your car.

▶ **Check in early so you don't lose your seat.** Just because you've arrived at the airport and you booked a particular seat when you bought the ticket, it doesn't mean you're guaranteed that seat. If you check in late (different airlines have different requirements, but checking in at least 45 minutes before departure is recommended), you won't lose your place on the plane, but you may lose your seat assignment.

▶ **Check your flight status.** Many airlines have systems in place to e-mail, page, or phone you with the updated flight status a few hours before departure. If this option isn't available, before you leave for the airport, check the status of your flight.

▶ **Be polite.** When you make your reservation find out if there is space in first class. This will at least give you an idea of the potential to upgrade. The earlier you check in the higher your name will appear on a wait list. If you're on a less crowded flight, your odds of getting an upgrade increase.

▶ **Increase your chances for a first-class upgrade.** Relatively few passengers actually pay full fare for first-class tickets—more often these seats are given to an airline's top customers. But you can also score an upgrade simply by smiling pleasantly, asking politely, and perhaps schmoozing with the gate attendant a bit. Dress well, try to be unassuming (bribes or a self-important tone will rarely get you what you're looking for), and give it your best shot.

▶ **At airports that have them, use skycaps.** Checking your baggage curbside outside the airline terminal can save you hassles and waiting in long lines. Try to use this option when possible—skycaps issue boarding passes, so once you've checked your bags, you can usually proceed directly to your gate for check-in. Be sure to tip skycaps $1 per checked bag.

▶ **Know what airline you are traveling on.** In these days of code-sharing, appearances can be deceiving. Your ticket may have been issued by one airline but one or more of the legs may actually be on a different airline.

▶ **Be smart about snacks.** Although you once saved money by packing food and drink from the supermarket in your carry on to tide you over during delays, these days goodies must comply with the TSA's guidelines (see www.tsa.gov), or they'll be confiscated—a big waste of both money and time. It might be easier, if not more economical, to eat in the terminal before going through security screenings or to pick up refreshments at the gate afterward. If you opt for the former, just remember that lines at food counters can be long—plan your time accordingly, particularly when you have a connection.

▶ **Where available, use automated check-in computers.** Many major airlines now have computer kiosks near their ticketing counters where you can check in quickly and conveniently. You'll be asked some simple questions to identify what flight you're on, and asked to swipe your credit card (for identification purposes, not in order to charge you), and to declare how many bags you're checking. The computer will then print out your boarding pass, and airline staff will quickly tag your luggage. The kiosks are as easy to use as an ATM, but because many passengers are wary of them, lines still form at the staffed counters. If you have curb-checked your bags or are carrying on, you'll likely bypass the lines.

▶ **Know where you are going.** Be certain you know your departing terminal, otherwise the longest leg of your trip could be from terminal A to terminal F.

▶ **Buy a one-day pass to an airline's VIP lounge.** If you don't belong to an airport club, you can often get a one-day pass for between $35 and $50. In exchange, you will get a measure of tranquility plus free snacks and drinks, magazines and newspapers, and phones, typically with free local calls. Personal computers may be available, or you can hook up your own laptop. And the staff can help with seat assignments and other matters.

▶ **Shop duty-free.** If you're flying internationally, you can avoid paying sales taxes, V.A.T., and other local taxes by shopping in the duty-free area. Be aware that you may still owe customs duties when you arrive in your home country, however. And before you buy anything major, know the prices in town and at home. Just because you buy something duty-free doesn't make it a bargain.

▶ **Look for kids' play areas in airports.** Some airlines have set up play areas on their concourses, with playhouses or ball crawls. You can sometimes find video games as well. Chicago O'Hare has a Kids on the Fly learning space in Terminal 2 equipped with a play hel-

AIRLINE VOUCHERS: LET'S MAKE A DEAL

Clark had finished up a three-day business trip to Chicago and was waiting to board his flight home from O'Hare when the announcement was made: volunteers were needed to give up their seats in exchange for a free travel voucher and a later flight home. Excited by the prospect of a free ticket, Clark agreed to give up his seat on an overbooked flight for a travel voucher he could use toward a future family vacation.

As it turned out, the "travel voucher" was not for a round-trip ticket but only a $200 credit that could be used toward the purchase of a ticket. Furthermore, the voucher had to be used within a year of the date of issue, was nontransferable, and had no residual value if the ticket purchased with it cost less than $200. After learning the restrictions placed on the use of his voucher, Clark wondered whether he could have gotten a better deal from the airlines for the inconvenience of having surrendered his seat.

▶ FODOR'S FIX

Although Clark might have held out for more money, how much the airlines are willing to offer depends on how oversold the flight is and how desperate they are to free up some seats. Airlines know that a certain percentage of ticketed passengers will be no-shows, so they routinely overbook their flights to maximize their profits. Occasionally, however, every ticketed passenger shows up for the flight, and that's when the "let's make a deal" begins. The airlines' first tactic is to offer a standard travel voucher to volunteers willing to take a later flight, which usually solves the problem. But if it is a peak travel time—Thanksgiving or Christmas, for example—and nobody wants to give up a seat, problems can arise.

The Bottom Line: Before passengers are denied boarding on an involuntary basis the airlines usually up the ante considerably to get more volunteers. This is because there's no worse PR nightmare than having to deny boarding to confirmed, ticket-holding passengers. In some cases, the travel voucher offer can approach $1,000—in addition to complimentary dinner and a hotel room if passengers are forced to stay overnight. Again, exactly how much you can get depends on the circumstances of the flight, but even if you agree to get bumped for the initial offer, ask for an upgrade to first or business class on the later flight home. Although it might not be part of the offer, a savvy gate agent will likely give you the upgrade if there is room—and if you are savvy enough to ask for one.

icopter and a mock cargo plane that kids can climb. London Heathrow has playrooms in each of its four terminals.

Security Issues

▶ **Don't offer to watch another traveler's bags.** Similarly, don't ask somebody to watch yours. It's tempting, when you have a bunch of bags and you simply must use a rest room or go to the ticket counter, to ask a friendly looking traveler near you to watch your stuff. The problem is, airport security actually asks people not to watch strangers' bags, so you're putting others in an awkward position by asking them to do so. And in a world where airline security is paramount, you're taking a big chance watching a stranger's bags anyway. Keep your own bags with you at all times. Or check your bags for total airport freedom.

▶ **Do your bit to keep the skies safe.** Never carry anything onto an airplane for another person, and report any unattended bags.

▶ **Keep cool during security screenings.** Especially since 9/11, no passenger is immune from what may seem like annoyingly invasive searches, at the airport security screening area, the ticket counter, and at the gate before check-in. The best thing you can do is grin and bear it—asking why you've been chosen or appearing grumpy just gives the security staff reason to be suspicious, and to spend more time checking through your bags. Keep in mind that passengers who pay for a ticket with cash or buy a one-way ticket are more likely to be taken aside for questioning; try not to take it personally.

▶ **Don't carry on items that set off metal detectors.** All kinds of items that may seem unassuming can set off the detectors and cause delays—and possibly inconvenient or embarrassing searches. Items to be aware of: keys, belt buckles, loose change, pens, watches, jewelry, aluminum foil, cigarette cases, metal-underwire bras, metal collar stays, button-fly jeans, nail clippers, shoe shanks, and steel-toe boots.

▶ **Charge your electronic devices.** You may be asked at security to turn on a laptop computer, portable CD player, or other gadget to prove that it is what it seems.

▶ **Store film inside clear canisters.** Storing film in dark canisters requires that hand-inspectors at airport security open each container. If you use clear canisters, inspectors can easily see that it's film inside each one and not something else, and they're much less likely to open each canister, thus delaying you and the passengers behind you.

▶ **Take care with unexposed film at security.** Not all X-ray machines damage all unexposed film—slow or moderate-speed film that passes through just one or two scanners is very unlikely to be damaged. However, high-speed film is susceptible to damage (usually in the form of a stripe or line across your pictures), as is any film that's run repeatedly through machines. If you're concerned, play it safe and request a hand inspection of your film.

▶ **Don't worry about X-ray machines damaging your computer.** Because airport X-ray machines do not create a magnetic pulse, they should not harm computer equipment, videocassettes, audiotapes, exposed film, or other gear. Keep in mind, however, that although state-of-the-art scanners won't harm computer hard drives or floppies, there's a chance that an outmoded scanner you might find in some small overseas airport—using old technology—might have an effect. Request hand inspection if in doubt.

▶ **Walk through security with empty pockets.** Carrying change, pens, cell phones, portable stereos, and other equipment through security only causes unnecessary delays and increases your likelihood of being frisked or searched thoroughly. Place all these items inside your carry-on bag before approaching security.

▶ **Wear slip-on shoes when flying.** Avoid boots or high-top shoes and sneakers. Shoes that are big or high enough to potentially conceal a weapon are a red flag when passing through airport security. You'll often be delayed and asked to remove your shoes, and possibly to undergo a full search of your clothing and luggage. Also, shoes with large metal buckles or other metal elements may set off security-screening devices. Simple sneakers, shoes you can slip off easily (mules, loafers, etc.), or dress shoes are your best bet.

▶ **Don't leave home without a government-issued photo ID.** Airlines strictly enforce the requirement that every traveler have one. A driver's license works; some travelers feel more secure with a passport, even if all their travels are domestic. As solid identification, you can do no better. On international trips, a passport is mandatory.

▶ **Book your ticket using the name on your ID.** Just married? If you were ticketed using your spouse's last name but your ID remains in your maiden name, bring your marriage license to back up your explanation. Does the name on your ID differ from a nickname or middle name you prefer to be called? Avoid hassles and make sure that the ID matches the name on your ticket or e-ticket confirmation.

▶ **Remember that only ticketed passengers may pass through security.** Airports no longer allow nonticketed passengers to proceed to the gate to wait for arrivals. Let anybody you're picking up at the airport know that you'll meet them just outside the airport security area or, better yet, in the typically less chaotic baggage claim area.

Delays, Strikes, Bumping
▶ **Know of alternate routes and airports.** In the event that you miss a flight, it's canceled, or some other ob-

stacle arises, it helps tremendously if you've already jotted down a couple of alternate routes, both on your intended airline and some others. And it can be useful to know the names of nearby alternate airports.

▶ **Be prepared in the event of an airline strike.** If there's a strike, passenger traffic will move to other airlines and you can expect additional terminal traffic and delays at check-in. The most important thing is to get to the airport early and have your proper documents in hand. Once a strike situation has been announced, contact your travel agent or airline immediately. And even if a strike is announced as possible in the future, ask for a paper rather than an electronic ticket, as it will then be easier to work with any other airlines handling passenger rebookings.

▶ **Know your rights if you're bumped.** Fewer than one in 10,000 passengers with reservations are ever bumped. If it does happen, know that the U.S. Department of Transportation has rules about compensation you're entitled to: nothing if the new flight is scheduled to get you to your destination within one hour of your original scheduled arrival time; $200 (maximum, or the one-way fare), if you'll arrive between one and two hours late (one to four hours for international flights); $400 (maximum, or twice the one-way amount), if you'll be more than two hours late (more than four hours internationally). You always get to keep your original ticket for use on, or credit toward, a future flight.

▶ **Act quickly if your flight is canceled.** Don't wait for the gate agent to help. If you're a member, go to the airline club or call your travel agent and/or the airline's 800 telephone number. The airline can be more helpful with weather conditions or equipment updates, and your travel agent will probably be faster making reservations on your scheduled carrier, or another carrier.

▶ **Bumped? Canceled?** Ask to fly on another carrier. Your airline might have canceled all its flights and say its hands are tied due to weather, etc., but the airlines have ticket-sharing arrangements and can put you on another airline's flight if they're running and there's room. You might just have to ask, because they likely won't offer.

▶ **Know the cost of flying standby.** Most airlines now charge a $100 fee for flying standby. Although many will still let you, don't expect to hop onto an earlier flight or catch a later one than planned for free. The clerk can legitimately enforce the charge.

▶ **If you miss your flight, be patient and try to relax.** The gate agents' first responsibility is to get the flight off safely and on time. If you are bumped because you were late, they'll get around to helping you after the plane has departed the gate.

▶ **Get some stress relief if you're stuck at the airport.** There are more services available at airports than ever before—consider getting a back and neck massage to relieve a little tension. Or just go for a walk. Let someone on your flight or an agent know you're leaving the area in case your flight status changes and you need to be found.

▶ **Call your hotel if your flight is delayed.** It's one of the last things you may think of when faced with the chaos and uncertainty of a delay, but your failure to do this could result in your reservation being dropped because your hotel believes you to be a no-show.

▶ **Pack diversions in your carry-on in case of delays.** If you have kids in tow, carry on some light reading, portable stereos with headphones, video games, cards, and snacks. These are handy in the terminal and on the plane.

Baggage

▶ **Keep important items in your carry-on.** Never travel without a small bag of essential toiletries (toothbrush, deodorant, hairbrush or comb, aspirin or pain reliever, etc.), along with important papers—your tickets, a credit card and some cash, a copy of your itinerary, and any additional travel documents or valuable papers. (Just be sure toiletries comply with TSA rules.) Keep this bag under the seat in front of you, and use the overhead bin for larger bags containing less crucial items.

▶ **Don't check your bag if you can help it.** If you can fit all your clothing and travel gear into one carry-on (most airlines allow one small additional bag, pocketbook, or laptop-computer case), you won't have to check luggage, which saves you time checking in and leaving the airport. You won't have to worry about the airline losing your luggage, and you'll pack more efficiently if your space is limited.

▶ **Keep your bags in sight.** Except for when you hand them over at check-in at the airport, never, never let your bags out of your sight, not even for an instant. It's astonishing how many people make this mistake—and never see their bags again.

▶ **Check that bag tag.** Be alert at the airline check-in counter when the three-letter baggage tag is attached to your bag. Is the correct tag attached for your destination?

▶ **Remove old luggage tags.** Old tags may look good on your ski jacket, but at check-in, if an old tag remains, you're just asking to have your luggage sent to the wrong airport.

▶ **Label your bags clearly, inside and out.** Always make sure your current address, phone number (including cell phone), and e-mail address are filled out clearly on luggage tags. Place tags or cards with your contact info inside your luggage, too, in case the external tags are lost. If you're planning to stay at one address during your travels for more than several days, consider including that address on your bag tags, too. If someone picks up your luggage by mistake, they'll know where to find you in town.

▶ **Board as early as is permitted if you have large carry-on bags.** There's seldom enough overhead storage space on a filled-to-capacity plane to accommodate every passenger. If you're traveling with a carry-on that's too large to fit under your seat, wait near the boarding area, so that you can be one of the first in line when your section of the plane boards. In coach, the rear of the plane always boards first, so if you regularly travel with large carry-on bags, it's not a bad idea to book a seat toward the rear of the plane, since you'll be almost assured room in the overhead bins. Just keep in mind passengers in the rear of the plane board first and debark last.

▶ **Carry a photo of your checked bags in your carry-on.** It can help to identify your own bag on the odd chance that you can't. More important, if your luggage is lost by the airline, you'll have an easier time describing the bags in question to the lost luggage office.

▶ **Make certain your carry-ons comply with airline regulations.** They vary from airline to airline, so check when you make your reservation.

▶ **Know your rights in the event of lost luggage.** Federal regulations now require that all U.S. airlines be liable for a minimum of $2,500—per passenger—for bags lost on domestic flights. On international flights, you'll be reimbursed $9.07 per pound of luggage—that comes to an average maximum of about $640 per bag. Items not covered include computers and electronic equipment, jewelry, cameras and camcorders, and photographs.

▶ **Resolve lost baggage issues immediately.** If your luggage is not on the flight, don't leave without speaking with the appropriate airline staff and getting written acknowledgement of the lost luggage. Get the name and direct phone number of the person who takes your report, and make sure they're legible, if handwritten.

ONBOARD

▶ **Before boarding remove inflight necessities from your carry-on.** Once you're in the air, unless you have an aisle seat, it can be difficult for you and inconvenient for fellow passengers to retrieve articles from your carry-on bag if you've stowed it in the overhead bins or even under the seat in front of you.

▶ **Grab a pillow and blanket as you board.** It can be very difficult to find these items once the plane has taken off, so even if you don't anticipate needing these, it's a good idea to snag one as you get settled into your seat.

▶ **Read the emergency card in the seat pocket.** Chances are that nothing is going to happen, but you should know what to do if something does. Be sure to locate your nearest emergency exit, and pay attention, especially if you fly infrequently, to the safety program presented by your flight crew prior to takeoff.

▶ **Bring moisturizer on the plane.** Airplane air is dry and uncomfortable. Pack a 3-ounce bottle of hand lotion in your 1-quart resealable bag, and possibly even a 3-ounce spray bottle of water to spritz your face occasionally.

▶ **Use a children's car seat on flights.** Although most airlines allow children under two to fly free or for reduced rates if they sit on an adult's lap and do not occupy their own seat, children are safest in FAA-approved car seats aboard planes. Some airlines offer up to a 50% discount on the extra seat needed for car seats, which you should ask about when booking.

▶ **Be courteous about reclining your seat.** Some passengers feel it's their absolute right to throw their seat back into a reclining position the minute they're allowed to, while others consider even the occasional and polite use of a seat recliner to be rude and invasive. At the very least, recline your seat back gently and slowly, so the person seated behind you is prepared. You should also avoid reclining during meals, when seat trays are in use.

▶ **Don't expect fellow passengers to switch seats.** You can ask—politely—but be aware that some passengers make a point of reserving aisle or window seats well ahead of time and for very specific reasons. It's certainly reasonable to ask a passenger to consider trading with you in order for you to be closer to a traveling companion, and especially if your seating assignment prevents you from sitting with a child. But ask only once, and respect the wishes of a fellow passenger who would prefer to sit in his or her assigned seat.

▶ **Remove your shoes once your plane takes off.** Your feet swell at high altitudes, making your shoes a tighter fit during air travel than when on the ground. Slipping out of your shoes, and loosening belts or other tight-fitting clothing, can greatly improve your comfort level in the air, especially during long trips. (But be considerate of the passengers around you—stinky shoes are better left on—you can always untie or loosen them instead of removing them completely.)

▶ **Dress comfortably.** Smart but casual, loose-fitting clothing is your best outfit for air travel. The temperature on a plane changes frequently, so the trick is to layer. Wear short sleeves, even in winter, and pack a sweater or light jacket in your carry-on even in summer.

▶ **Dress well.** There's no reason to dress to the nines for an airplane flight, but do avoid sweatpants, jogging gear, sleeveless T-shirts, and other super-casual garb. If you make a small effort to look your best, you're more likely to be treated respectfully by others, and you'll feel better.

▶ **Bring a sleep mask.** Nothing says "do not disturb" more effectively than wearing a sleep mask while flying. Most fellow travelers will leave you alone, and you may even sleep more effectively.

▶ **Share your armrest.** There's no getting around it— those tiny armrests on planes, especially in coach, are simply too narrow for two adults to fully rest their arms simultaneously. But you'll have a more pleasant trip if you try to avoid hogging too much of the armrest, and politely remind your neighbor to do the same, if it comes to that. Making a pleasant request generally beats sitting and fuming throughout the duration of your flight. Surrender the inside armrest if you have the aisle or window seat on a three-seat (or more) row. It's a giving gesture to the person crammed between you and some other stranger.

▶ **Stay in your seat until your turn to leave the plane.** It's amazing how uncomfortable passengers look when they get up out of their seats and stand, hunched over beneath the overhead baggage bins, for 5 or 10 minutes while they wait to leave the plane. Standing up isn't going to get you out the door faster. Why not sit back, relax, and wait to stand up when there's actually room to do so?

AFTER YOU LAND

▶ **Do look back.** Never, never leave a plane without casting one last glance backward to see whether you've left anything behind in your seat.

▶ **Always save your boarding pass.** If you're not properly credited for frequent-flier miles for a trip, or if some other dispute arises following a flight, your only true proof that you actually traveled someplace is your original boarding pass. This document can come in handy months after you've completed your travel—it's a good idea to keep your boarding pass indefinitely.

▶ **Be careful opening your toiletries after a flight.** Ever open a bottle of hair gel or shaving cream after a flight only to have the contents shoot out all over you and the bathroom? Changes in air pressure during flight can cause all kinds of things to become unsettled. Always open any pressurized or airtight canister or container gently after you've just flown. And to be safe, consider keeping shampoo, hand lotion, and similar items in a resealable plastic bag so that if the pressure forces their caps loose during your flight, the mess will be limited.

▶ **Know your rights as a passenger.** The Federal Aviation Administration (FAA www.faa.gov/passengers, 866/835–5322) has rules concerning liability for lost luggage, compensation for delays, airline security, and other issues. You can also check with the FAA for information on what passengers may carry through airport security.

FIGHTING JET LAG

▶ **Know the common symptoms of jet lag.** Most travelers try to make the most of their limited time overseas, yet fail to take into account the leap in time zones they make in a matter of hours. It can take your body's internal clock several days to catch up to that leap, and in the meantime, you are likely to experience the disruption of your sleeping and waking cycle known as jet lag. Symptoms of jet lag include sleepiness during the day, insomnia at night, poor concentration, confusion, hunger at inappropriate times or lack of appetite, and general malaise and irritability.

▶ **Adjust your internal clock.** Several days (at least four) before departure, gradually shift your sleeping and eating times to coincide with those at your destination. Once you arrive, adopt the local time for your daily routine.

▶ **Curtail coffee.** For 12 hours before, as well as during, your flight, avoid overeating and caffeine. Although caffeine can help keep you awake longer, it makes you wake up more often once you do fall asleep and so reduces total sleep time.

▶ **Avoid or limit alcohol inflight.** Airplane air dehydrates passengers, and altitude changes can quicken the effects of alcohol. A cocktail may relax you, but it's also apt to dry you out, and possibly even worsen symptoms of jet lag.

▶ **Drink plenty of water when you fly.** With the dry air in planes, water is your great weapon against fatigue, dehydration, and combating that overall feeling of staleness. Just remember that water from the airplane lavatories is not meant for drinking, and the cups aboard planes tend to be small: bring your own supply of bottled water.

▶ **See if melatonin is for you.** Consider taking the nonprescription drug melatonin. Research suggests that the body uses this hormone to set its time clock. Because melatonin seems to control when we go to sleep and when we wake up, a number of scientists advocate supplements to alleviate jet lag. Some (but not all) studies suggest that taking 5 milligrams of fast-release melatonin prior to bedtime for several days after arrival in a new time zone can ease the transition.

▶ **Get outside.** After arrival, spend a lot of time out in the sunlight, which will help your body reset its natural time clock to coincide with your new surroundings.

On the Water

You can nap on planes and overnight on trains, but there's really only one form of transportation that can comfortably double as a world-class hotel accommodation: the cruise ship. In the past few decades, and especially recently, cruising has evolved from a relatively elite leisure pursuit enjoyed predominantly by the wealthy into one of the world's most popular and accessible forms of travel. There are still ultraposh ships sailing the seas that charge top dollar and provide plush staterooms and fancy food, but other ships offer almost unbeatably affordable opportunities to tour a part of the world you might never otherwise see.

Not only have cruise vacations become attractive to every kind of budget in recent years, they've also become more appealing to a wide range of tastes. Megaships built in the past decade are like minicities, complete with shopping arcades, numerous restaurants, spas and health clubs, multiple swimming pools, and snazzy casinos and nightclubs. But other cruises emphasize education, offer a more intimate ambience and easy pace, or focus more on ports of call than leisure time at sea. Smaller ships often access ports and scenery that larger ships could never hope to navigate.

Surveys show that cruises have among the highest consumer satisfaction ratings of any type of vacation. Most travelers seem to have a pretty good time no matter the ship they choose or its itinerary—but there plenty of things to keep in mind to ensure that you make the most of your time at sea. Ships and cruise lines not only vary greatly in price, size, amenities, and ambience, the list of destinations and itineraries is vast. Options range from three- or four-day jaunts between South Florida and the Bahamas to weeklong and two-week cruises in the Caribbean, Europe, Mexican Riviera, and Alaska to much longer cruises that ply Asian, African, and South American seas.

Whether you're a first-timer or an inveterate cruiser, it pays to spend a little time researching the different cruise options available. Better yet, find a knowledgeable travel agency that specializes in cruises. With a bit of legwork out of the way, you'll be free to appreciate what many travelers consider to be the most relaxing, and exhilarating, vacation experience out there.

BOOKING YOUR CRUISE

▶ **Test the waters.** If you're new to cruising, try booking a short trip—maybe a three- or four-day sail to the Bahamas or Key West and Cozumel out of Florida, or a four-day cruise down the Southern California coast to Baja. Short itineraries may include stops at one or two ports of call, or none at all.

▶ **Consider a cruise to nowhere.** If you're a first-time cruiser unsure about committing to a longer trip, ask your travel agent about a short "cruise to nowhere." There are no ports of call and no real itinerary. You set sail, float at sea, and return home. That's it. These cruises last between two and four days, usually over a weekend, and they cost just a few hundred dollars. The level of luxury will be the same as on a longer cruise.

▶ **To save money, arrange your own flight to your port of embarkation.** You can often find a much better airfare than that offered by your cruise line's air-sea department. Just be certain to book an early enough flight to ensure that you'll have ample time to get from the airport to the ship, and keep in mind that you'll be responsible for your own transportation between the airport and the cruise terminal.

▶ **For peace of mind, book your flight to your embarkation point through the cruise line.** There's a good chance you'll pay more for a flight arranged through your cruise line's air-sea department, but you'll also be guaranteed to make your cruise. If your flight is canceled or delayed, the cruise line will make the necessary arrangements to get you to the ship as soon as possible, even if it means flying you to the next port of call.

▶ **Know the single-supplement charge to go it alone.** Some ships are better geared toward single travelers than others, and many charge single supplements—a higher surcharge for a single traveler who books one cabin. The single-supplement will have you paying anywhere from 125% to 150% of the published cabin rate based on double occupancy. On request, some lines will pair a single traveler with another, so that you can each avoid the single supplement.

▶ **Cruise through your honeymoon.** Most cruise lines offer special perks for honeymooning couples, from breakfast in bed to a special cake to free champagne. You may also be given a credit for the ship's casino or other activities, a complimentary massage in the ship's spa, or some other upgrade or perk. Always let your cruise line or agent know that this will be a honeymoon cruise (or even a major anniversary or other important celebration).

▶ **With a reluctant first-timer? Cruise Alaska.** Trying to get a spouse, friend, or family member to enjoy a cruise with you? Certain destinations have more appeal to first-timers than others. Alaska often appeals to folks who aren't wild about the tropics, or who want to mix education with relaxation on their travels. Cruise ships offer access to parts of Alaska's Inside Passage that you simply cannot get via other transportation. And these ships often attract a more adventuresome and cerebral crowd than party-oriented cruises to the Bahamas or up and down the Mexican Riviera.

▶ **Know your prospective fellow passengers.** You've found what appears to be the perfect-size ship and a dazzling itinerary, but what about the crowd that will be sharing your vacation? It's worth finding out who they are: some ships and itineraries draw certain age groups and styles. A good cruise travel agent can tell help you to figure this out. The ship brochure is another clue. If the people being depicted look like people you'd like to know, you may well find sympatico fellow cruisers. Or vice versa.

▶ **Plan a cruise for your whole tribe.** Cruises are ideal for multigenerational trips because they generally provide activities for all ages in a self-contained setting and a variety of accommodations to suit varied budgets. Most ships offer kids' programs, which free up time for the adults in the group to pursue their own interests. Other activities—such as poolside games and shore excursions—are often perfect for kids and adults to spend time together.

▶ **Negotiate a group discount.** Planning a cruise for a large group of friends or family members? Work with your travel agent or directly with the cruise line's group sales department for a perk—if you book at least 15 cabins, you should be able to score a discount of one free cabin, or you might be able to secure other discounts, such as shipboard credit or free parties.

▶ **For the best group discount, approach more than one cruise line.** Let each line know that you're negotiating with the competition, and have each group sales department provide a written offer.

▶ **Ask about discounts for senior citizens.** Several cruise lines offer reduced rates for senior citizens (sometimes only on certain sailings), and seniors may be able to take advantage of local discounts ashore.

▶ **Be flexible on dates.** Some sailing dates are more popular than others. If a sailing is "soft"—that is, not all cabins are booked—cruise lines lower the price in order to fill the ship. So leaving just a week later can get you the same cruise—same ship, same itinerary—for a lower price.

▶ **Consider booking an off-season cruise.** Many itineraries are based on seasons—Alaskan cruises are typically offered from May to September; European and Caribbean cruises are usually between November and April. Off-season sailings always cost less, but even within the off-season, prices for different departure dates can differ considerably.

▶ **Figure out if your cruise line is a good citizen.** A cruise-ship brochure can help you figure out if your cruise line is a good corporate citizen. Some lines trumpet their respect for the environment and charity to environmental causes. Others have very high-profile recycling programs. Of course, it's not just altruism that drives the cruise lines. They believe it's good business because many passengers care about a cruise line's environmental record.

▶ **Ask prospective cruise lines for a video.** You can take a virtual tour of many ships by watching videos. Produced by the cruise lines, these videos are promotional in nature. But like brochures, they can tell you a lot. With their extensive onboard footage, they give you a look inside before you ever board—so you can get a sense of what the ship looks like and see if it appeals to you. These tapes usually cost $10 or so, but you can sometimes borrow them from your travel agent, and, if you buy them, some cruise lines will credit the cost back to you if you book their cruise.

▶ **Watch the weather.** Hurricane season is from about June 1 through November 30 in the Caribbean, with greatest risk for a storm from August through October.

► **Consider trip-cancellation insurance.** Weather, technical problems, and financial difficulties—unfortunately, each of these can lead to the cancellation of a cruise. If you've purchased an insurance policy that covers cancellation, you're covered. If you didn't buy insurance but you did pay via credit card, you may have another avenue of recourse—contact the credit card company and see if they'll advocate for you.

► **Join an alumni club.** After your cruise, join the line's alumni club. You'll receive newsletters with notice of discounts on future cruises, some as much as 50% below brochure prices.

► **Know the line's policy on late passenger arrivals.** Whether you book your own flight or book it through the cruise line's air-sea department, read your cruise line's policy carefully to find out what your responsibilities and entitlements are if a flight delay or cancellation forces you to miss your sailing.

► **Consider booking a pre- or postcruise tour.** These short trips in or near the city from which your cruise originates and/or terminates will allow you to bypass the throngs of passengers racing from the airport to the cruise terminal on the day of departure. Best of all, however, these trips extend your vacation and give you a sense of enjoying two trips in one—it's especially nice if somebody in your party is more of a landlubber than a seafarer.

Working with a Travel Agent

► **Use a travel agent who's an expert in the field.** Just as there are all kinds of doctors with finite specialties, there are travel agents specializing in virtually every style of travel—and many of them are cruise specialists. A specialist not only knows the ins and outs of the industry, he or she can often get you cabin upgrades and provide 24-hour service in case of travel snags.

▶ **Know how to pick a cruise specialist.** A reliable travel agent with experience booking cruises can be your best friend: one who works regularly with few cruise lines may be able to negotiate a more favorable deal for you on several carriers versus those travel agents who work closely with one cruise line, who often know the inside scoop down to the floorplan, but can't offer deals on others. It's always good to ask if your agency has partnerships with certain cruise lines, and to keep clear of agents who seem to steer you persistently toward these in hopes of netting a big commission.

▶ **Review a travel agent's cruise qualifications.** The most qualified travel agents are members of the Cruise Lines International Association (CLIA); those who are CLIA Accredited Cruise Counsellors and Master Cruise Counsellors have had extensive cruise and ship-inspection experience. If you opt for a cruise-specialist agency, make sure it's a member of the National Association of Cruise Oriented Agencies.

▶ **Favor agents who ask you questions.** A good cruise agent will ask you many detailed questions about your past vacations, your lifestyle, and even your friends and hobbies. Never book a cruise with an agent who asks only a few cursory questions before handing you a brochure.

▶ **Get help when choosing a cabin.** With some lines it's hard to get cabin assignments in advance, and if you've never sailed on a particular ship before, it can be difficult to know ahead of time whether your cabin is in a convenient and less noisy location. This is where booking through an agent with extensive cruise experience, especially one working with the line you're interested in, can be invaluable. He or she is also better able to contact the cruise line directly and get you moved to a better cabin in the event that you've been assigned an undesirable one.

▶ **Be loyal.** With luck, after you've taken a couple of cruises, and maybe dealt with a couple of travel agencies, you'll find one you like. If you become a frequent customer, many agencies, especially larger ones, will keep you informed of special deals and last-minute discounts. Notification may be by newsletter, fax, or maybe even e-mail. So get on the list.

▶ **Be cautious about using an Internet agency.** There are hundreds, if not thousands, of travel sites on the Web and many of them specialize in cruises. You'll find agency sites as well as cruise-line sites, along with full-service travel sites like Travelocity.com and Expedia.com. Although the Internet is terrific as an information-gathering tool, you can't develop the one-on-one relationship with a Web site that you do with an agent. Sometimes you will indeed find great bargains on-line, and some sites even let you book your tickets on-line. But most travelers find that a good agent who has experience working with the cruise-line industry can get the same—if not better—bargains as those spotted on-line.

▶ **Choose an agency with a 24-hour client hot line.** All kinds of things can happen just before or during a cruise that could require assistance from your travel agent. Agencies that have 24-hour hot lines can be invaluable when crises arise.

► **Never consider unsolicited over-the-phone offers.** Occasionally, con artists will buy a direct-marketing list and call people blindly, offering a "special deal" on a cruise. If anybody phones you to discuss a deal on a cruise, don't listen, don't indulge the caller, and don't feel that you must be polite. Just hang up.

► **Don't let yourself feel rushed.** Even if you're nearly certain that you've found the perfect cruise, or your agent has sold you on a great trip, resist the temptation to book immediately. Cool off, go back home and go over your brochures and other research materials one last time, and sleep on it. Any agent who pressures you to act immediately shouldn't be trusted.

Choosing the Right Ship and Itinerary

► **Above all other factors, choose the right ship.** Some say the most important aspect of a cruise is the destination or itinerary. Others say it's the cruise line. But they're wrong. The most important choice you'll make when booking a cruise is the ship—this will be your home for seven days or more. The ship you choose will determine the comfort of your sleeping quarters, the quality of your food, the quality of your entertainment, and the ports you'll visit. Also, each ship attracts a certain crowd. If you don't like your ship, you won't like your cruise.

► **Do your homework.** Check cruise-lines' brochures and videos, and, to get other points of view, go to the library or on-line to check out cruise guidebooks that include ship portraits and to read travel articles about the ships you're considering. There's a wealth of information out there on most cruise ships, and a little research can go a long way toward choosing the voyage that's right for you.

▶ **Choose a cruise line with varied dining options.** It used to be the standard rule on cruise ships that you were seated at the same dinner table at a set time with the same waiters and guests every night of your cruise. Now, on many lines, you'll find smaller, more numerous dining areas known as "restaurants at sea." This allows you to vary your dining schedule, try different restaurants, and dine with different guests. However, these kinds of meals are not usually included in the total cost of the cruise—you'll typically pay a surcharge of $5 to $20 for each meal.

▶ **Make a list of your favorite activities and interests.** Narrowing down which cruise suits you best is much easier if you, and any friends or family members you will be traveling with, compile a list of the things they enjoy doing. Are you seeking a full slate of onboard activities or seeking privacy and relaxation? Will you want to go on organized sightseeing tours while on shore, or laze away at the beach? Is evening entertainment a high priority? Haute cuisine or informal dining? Fancy staterooms you'll want to spend time in or simple cabins you're using only as a place to sleep?

▶ **If you're a nightlife maven, consider a larger ship.** On most smaller ships, evening entertainment is decidedly low-key, but today's modern megaships often have pulsing discos, over-the-top Las Vegas–style shows, cavernous casinos, and other after-dark diversions.

▶ **If you have mobility concerns, book a cabin near an elevator.** A traveler who uses a wheelchair or faces any other challenges related to getting around easily might be most comfortable on a ship whose public rooms are clustered on one deck. Ideally, choose a cabin that's mid-ship and so relatively close not only to the elevator but to public areas. And be sure not to book a cabin with upper and lower berths (where one bed folds out from the wall above the lower one, sort of like bunk beds).

▶ **Avoid older ships if you have disabilities.** Generally speaking, the older, smaller ships cause the most problems for people with limited mobility. Older ships have more lips between the doorways, for example, and fewer flat-to-level entrances to go on decks.

▶ **Single? Look for special singles sailings.** Cruise ships are generally a great place to meet people, and many single travelers have found cruise vacations well suited to their lifestyle. Making the choice between a large or small ship depends on your exact needs. Larger ships have more people on board, more singles, and more activities, while a smaller ship may sail to a remote and exclusive island where champagne parties are held in the surf. Windjammer, a small-ship cruise line, offers six to eight singles cruises a year. Other ships offer gay- and/or lesbian-themed cruises that can be fun for singles hoping to meet others of the same sex.

▶ **Consider a ship's size.** The biggest ships, registering 70,000 tons or more, are cities at sea. These boats have the best amenities and can feel less crowded than smaller vessels, but they're also prone to long lines to disembark or to board tenders bound for shore. If that's not your style, consider a midsize ship, carrying 1,000 people or so and registering 30,000 to 50,000 tons, or an even smaller, yachtlike ship that carries just a few hundred passengers and registers 10,000 to 25,000 tons (sometimes even less). They're cozier, and what they lack in facilities they make up for in intimacy—although sea sickness is more likely on these.

▶ **Splurge for a balcony room.** It used to be that only the most expensive staterooms on the best ships had cabins with balconies, but much has changed during the ship-construction boom of the past decade or so. Plenty of ships now offer standard cabins with balconies—on Disney ships, for example, nearly half the rooms have private balconies; on Royal Caribbean's Voyager of the Seas, the number is nearly two-thirds. There's nothing more pleasant than breakfast on your balcony amid sun and salty breezes.

▶ **Avoid cabin fever by picking a cruise with many ports of call.** If you hate being cramped in your room, or in any sort of confined space, you might want to avoid certain kinds of ships and itineraries, but you can still have a great time on a cruise. Try to pick an itinerary with as many ports of call as possible, so you'll be guaranteed lots of time off the ship. And you might think twice about spending a lot on an expensive cabin if you're going to be roaming around the ship most of the time.

▶ **If you're a hands-on traveler, consider a small ship.** A small ship is ideal for couples or friends who really like to explore together, being close to the environment as well as to each other. Small is a smart choice, in fact, for those who share an enthusiasm of any sort—for particular places, pastimes, pursuits, or plain old learning—in general.

▶ **Consider a ship's pools and deck layout.** Most ships have a pool, but the quality and size of the pool can make or break a sunshine cruise. Avoid large ships with small pools, where on a hot day the pool can seem like an overcrowded bathtub. Make sure there are enough pools and hot tubs on deck to accommodate your, or your family's, needs.

▶ **Study a deck map to decide on a cabin.** Your comfort depends largely on your accommodations, which can vary greatly on a ship. With so many cabin categories—outside and inside cabins, cabins with full or partial ocean views, cabins with full tubs or tiny shower stalls—it's wise to consider your exact needs.

▶ **To avoid motion sickness, choose a cabin near the ship's middle.** Aft (rear) and forward cabins tend to rock more when seas are choppy, as do lower cabins. The closer your cabin is to the ship's center of gravity, the less rocking you're likely to experience.

▶ **Consider your cabin's proximity to public areas.** If noise isn't important to you but convenience to dining rooms or nightclubs is, then go ahead and book a cabin near the public areas. But keep in mind that cabins near dining rooms, nightclubs, theaters, and casinos— as well as cabins near stairwells and engine-room bulkheads—tend to be the noisiest.

▶ **Honeymooning? Don't plan on leaving the day after.** Cruises may be the perfect honeymoon getaway, but keep in mind that most seven-day cruises depart on Saturday or Sunday (almost never on Monday), so you may need to plan for a departure the day of or after your wedding.

PREPARING FOR YOUR TRIP

▶ **Anticipate the extra costs.** Cruises aren't truly all-inclusive—extras, such as beverages, shore excursions, spa treatments, onboard video games, laundry and dry cleaning, Internet-usage fees—can add up. Cruising is still an excellent value, but be sure to factor in all related costs.

▶ **Find out about your cruise line's gratuities policy.** Some ships automatically add a gratuities surcharge to the total cost of your cruise, meaning that you don't have to tip individual staff during your cruise. Others suggest general guidelines for tipping different staff members at the end of your cruise. Make sure you bring along enough cash to tip accordingly, and unless you're very disappointed with your cruise experience, in which case you should speak with a staff member, try to tip at least the minimum the cruise lines suggest.

▶ **Don't overpack.** The average cruise-ship cabin is about 170 to 200 square ft, about half the size of the average hotel room. Although you can get away with a lot, you'll be much more comfortable in a cabin this size if you pack as lightly as possible, with just enough clothing—and variety of clothing—to get by.

▶ **Consider a ship's dress code.** One of the biggest differences among ships is how dressy things are onboard. By day, all ships are universally casual. (Resort wear is most commonly recommended.) However, at night it's a different story. On seven-day cruises, all ships have two casual nights (the first night and last night) and two formal nights, when a dark business suit or tuxedo or formal dress or gown is the order of the day. Dress on other nights varies widely depending on the ship.

▶ **Know the ship's electrical specifications.** This can vary a good deal from ship to ship, especially if you're sailing an international ship. Before you go, find out about electrical supply. What is the current and the plug style? Can you buy, rent, or borrow converters and adapters on board ship?

▶ **Ask what toiletries and amenities are in cabins.** Good things to ask about include: shampoos and conditioner, hair dryers, stationary and pens, beach towels, and irons and ironing boards. Also find out whether your ship has onboard self-service laundry facilities, and whether laundry detergent is available.

▶ **Make a list of important items to pack.** It can be expensive or even impossible to buy seemingly common household products at sea. Some often-forgotten, useful items include: alarm clock, camera and batteries/film, feminine hygiene products, insect repellent, backpack, maps and phrase books, money belt and/or document pouch, sandals, sports gear, sunglasses/clip-ons, and windbreaker/lightweight raincoat.

▶ **Bring along some cash.** There are circumstances which will warrant it, even on an all-inclusive trip. In casinos, for example, you trade cash for chips and tokens for slot machines. It's also more personal to hand tips directly to the person who served you, in cash, than to charge them to your shipboard account. You can plan to use ATMs at the ports of call for sightseeing money, but even then it's best to have a little cash in the event you have trouble accessing your money.

▶ **Look into details about your cabin's beds.** Bed configuration is key. On most newer ships, cabins come with two twin-size beds that can be pushed together. On some older ships, the beds are nailed to the floor and may be laid out in an L-shape configuration. Sometimes you can figure this out from cruise-line brochures, but it's safest to ask your cruise line or travel agent to confirm this information before you book.

▶ **Get a passport.** Think you don't need a passport? Not so. No matter what you hear from friends, family, or travel agents, and no matter what you read in the cruise brochure, *do* bring your passport—even if you're going to the Caribbean or Alaska. Not only does a passport verify your identity and nationality, but you'll soon need one when traveling by sea between the United States and several destinations for which other forms of identification (e.g., a driver's license and a birth certificate) were once sufficient. A passport—valid for 10 years—really is a good investment.

▶ **Check your documents.** With luck, you've been so busy preparing for your cruise that you haven't had time to worry about your tickets and your cruise documents. Then, a couple of weeks before your departure, they arrive. When they do, make sure to check your tickets over immediately and carefully. Usually, they're perfect. But mistakes do occur. If you've bought an air-sea package, check your airline tickets. Make sure you're ticketed for the right dates, from the right airport, and to the right destination.

ONCE YOU'RE ON THE SHIP

▶ **Make sure your cabin works.** Run the water in the sink and shower, flush the toilet, and turn on lights to make sure that everything works. Report problems right away.

▶ **Learn about your ship as soon as you check into your cabin.** Every cabin has a desk, and on that desk you'll find a folder or binder. This will be your bible for the cruise.

It's full of information on everything from ordering room service and using the shipboard telephone system to channel surfing on the TV.

▶ **Tour your ship.** On arrival, you'll find a deck plan of your ship in your cabin or with your welcome information. Tuck this in your pocket and set a course for checking out the ship. Begin by taking the nearest elevator to the top deck. Go to the front of the ship (the bow) and walk toward the back (the stern). Once you've reached the stern, take the stairs or elevator down to the next deck and walk all the way to the bow, passing through all of the corridors and public rooms. Continue this front-to-back, back-to-front exploration until you've covered all of the public decks.

▶ **Make appointments and reservations early.** As soon as you're settled onto your ship, consider booking a massage in the spa, or making dinner reservations at some of the alternative restaurants that are common on many newer ships. These types of activities and meals fill up quickly.

▶ **Check your dinner assignment.** One of the first things you should do on boarding the ship is find the maître d', who typically sets up shop in one of the ship's public rooms (usually not the dining room). Now is the time to double-check your dining-room assignment and to change it if you didn't get the seating you want. The maître d' will have a layout of the ship's dining room, showing the location and configuration of every table. He or she can tell you where in the dining room your table is and how many people will join you for dinner. Make sure you get what you want, whether it's a table for two or a no-smoking table.

▶ **Make the most of days at sea.** On almost every cruise there are days at sea, when the ship doesn't stop in any port of call. Cruise ships, with their expansive outdoor facilities, have plenty of ways to keep you entertained (including sundecks that stretch three football fields long and multiple swimming pools). You'll find that days at sea also are perfect for enjoying the great indoors. Your ship undoubtedly has many indoor attractions in addition to the spa, restaurants, and shops you saw on your initial tour—some have video arcades, shopping boulevards, and caviar-and-wine bars.

▶ **Beat the rainy-day blues.** Life on a cruise ship when it rains doesn't have to be a drag. It's a vacation, after all, and sometimes it's nice to have a day to play couch potato. Even a standard cabin can be a cozy place to pass some time. Recently released movies are run continuously on TV. Many ships have a collection of videos you can view, as well as onboard libraries. There's also the card room, where you'll find decks of cards and board games. Games and books are usually free to borrow. And you can order room service for free.

▶ **Know where to find privacy.** Cruise ships can feel crowded. If you want privacy, both on and off the ship, consider these suggestions: book a cabin with a private veranda and book a table for two in the dining room. When the outdoor buffets are in full swing, eat inside—the indoor restaurants are often half empty.

▶ **Try a midnight whirlpool.** At least once during your sailing, slip into your bathing suits and head to the upper deck in the middle of the night. Ease into the whirlpool and enjoy the bubbles under the stars. You've just turned a 2,000-passenger megaship into your own private yacht.

▶ **Get teed off on deck.** Besides putting greens, miniature golf courses, and golf simulators, some ships carry onboard pros. And virtually every major line has a shore excursion program for golfers, who can tee up while everyone else is on a bus.

▶ **Bring the running shoes.** It's easy to feel cramped onboard even the largest ships, especially if you're at sea for a few days. However, you can usually find a place to stretch your legs. For jogging there are generally two options. Most ships have a wraparound promenade deck, which is also ideal for a light stroll. On other ships there are specially designed and dedicated tracks, sometimes covered with a high-tech cushioned surface. Keep in mind that some smaller ships may have no place to jog at all. Other fitness facilities may come with fitness instructors. There may be aerobics classes, stretch classes, and group jogs. Some fitness programs run all day.

▶ **Enjoy dinner in your cabin one or two nights.** Most cruise ships offer complimentary 24-hour room service, which ranges from light snacks and breakfast to full meals on some luxury ships. Some passengers who prefer informal attire order room service during a cruise's formal nights. It's also a good option if you've enjoyed a large, late lunch during your shore visit and only need a light snack at dinner.

▶ **To contact home, send an e-mail.** Improved technology has made it easier than ever to phone home during a cruise, but calling can be pricey. You'll typically pay from $4 to $18 per minute for calls back home from your cabin. E-mail is much more cost-effective, if still pricey. On many ships you'll pay several dollars per outgoing and incoming e-mail, and additional for file attachments. Not all ships with e-mail services allow Internet access, so confirm in advance if you want to go on-line during your cruise.

Health and Safety

▶ **Know your ship's medical facilities.** Information about medical care aboard ship is usually buried in the fine print in the back of brochures. No government body or international treaty governs medical care aboard cruise ships. Each cruise line is left to its own devices, and some lines are better known than others for the quality of their medical care. If you have any concerns, book a cruise line that has a reputation for medical readiness at sea—and buy travel insurance that includes coverage for pre-existing conditions.

▶ **Don't forget a sufficient supply of medication.** Bring a supply of prescription drugs and medications extensive enough to last a few days longer than your trip and return home. Place all medications in your carry-on—never in checked baggage. Carry a written list of medications and their dosages on your cruise. And be sure to bring along the phone number of your home physician.

▶ **Ask about a cruise line's health standards.** If you have concerns about whether you'll contract a virus on a cruise, ask your cruise line how they rank and how you're protected. The Centers for Disease Control (CDC) Web site (www.cdc.gov) posts many details about sanitation standards and the latest news on the topic of vessel sanitation.

▶ **Be wary of shady characters around ports of call.** Many cruise passengers are hassled by local businessmen who aim to swindle visitors or lure them to shops where they get a commission. Bypass them, and head for a taxi with a company phone number or credential printed on it or a legitimate, local tour operator.

Shore Things

▶ **Book shore excursions early.** You usually book shore excursions on board ship, and most people wait until the shore-excursion talk before making their reservations. That's a mistake. The shore-excursion talks are well attended, and once the presentation ends, everybody lines up—it's easy to get shut out of the trip you want. Don't book anything you're unsure of, however: Shore-excursion tickets are often nonrefundable.

▶ **If you're independent, avoid organized shore excursions.** You can often visit the same places and attractions offered through your ship's shore-excursion programs for less money on your own, but you will need to plan ahead of time. This is a great option if being on a cruise ship already has you yearning for time away from crowds. Take along a travel guide to your port of call; there you can hire a local driver to take you around to the attractions that interest you—and the flexibility can make your exploring more pleasurable. Just be certain to get back to your ship on time.

▶ **Book a shore excursion to unfamiliar ports.** Shore excursions offer plenty of advantages over simply wandering around a port by yourself. You'll usually be led by an experienced guide, you'll have the opportunity to mingle with other passengers, and you're guaranteed to make it back to the ship on time (in the very unlikely event that your group is delayed and misses the ship, the cruise line will make arrangements to get you as quickly as possible to the next port of call).

▶ **Remember that itineraries may change.** Cruise lines reserve the right to change their itineraries for virtually any reason—often this happens because of weather conditions. You may end up calling on the same ports as planned but on different days, a port may be dropped at the last minute, or a new one may be substituted. If you're making your own private arrangements for shore activities, such as a personal tour or a trip to a local spa, make sure you call and cancel or change your reservation if the ship changes its itinerary.

Kids' Stuff

▶ **Ask about children's discounts.** Most cruise lines charge children under age 12 third- and fourth-passenger rates or children's fares when they're traveling with two adults in the same cabin. These rates tend to be about half—or sometimes even less than half—the lowest adult fare. On certain off-peak sailings, children may be permitted to travel free.

▶ **If you're traveling with your family, start small.** No matter how enthusiastic you are, don't book your entire brood on one of the megaships the first time out. Massive ships like Voyager and Explorer of the Seas can seem irresistible on paper, but the behemoths run only weeklong excursions, and seven days can be an eternity if you discover halfway through that the adventure isn't for you. If you haven't been at sea before, consider a three- or four-day jaunt to start; if you love it, you can always go back.

▶ **Go when other families will be on board.** Whether you're traveling with teens or young children, it's important to make sure other kids will be on board. You don't want to be the only family with kids on a couples-only cruise. Search the brochures and videos for images of children. Timing is also a factor—summer cruises, holiday cruises, and cruises during major school holiday periods (Christmas, Easter/spring break) will have more children on board and, it's likely, more children's activities planned.

▶ **Look for separate programs for each age group.** Younger groups may have a clubhouse, a pirate ship, storytelling, or arts and crafts. Older children may be able to access science and educational programs and computers and undertake detailed art projects. Programs for teens might revolve around movies, sports activities, or dances.

▶ **Check out the children's programs' staff-to-child ratio.** Especially if you have very young kids, it's best to find a children's program where this ratio is no greater than 1 to 3.

▶ **Evaluate the supervision and activities.** The best programs have supervised activities throughout the day and include meals. Some ships provide facilities for children and child care but no organized activities.

▶ **Ask about baby-sitting and day care.** Some ships provide day care and group baby-sitting for younger children at no extra charge, while most charge a nominal hourly rate. On many ships, private baby-sitting is by arrangement with crew members (at a negotiated price).

▶ **With younger kids, get the first dinner seating.** If your ship offers two dinner seatings, the earlier of the two is preferable for families with younger children (in fact, some cruise ships actually assign guests with children to the earlier seatings). Some lines will not permit children to eat alone in the dining room. If your kids are picky eaters, choose a line that offers special children's menus. And if you'll be needing a high chair, request it in advance.

▶ **Find out about age requirements.** Some cruise ships don't allow infants aboard, period; others require a minimum age, anywhere from 4 to 18 months.

▶ **Check facilities.** If your ship does allow toddlers and infants, find out exactly what the cruise line provides (some supply diapers, formula, and baby food free of charge) and plan accordingly.

▶ **With a baby? Get a cabin big enough for a crib.** Many cruise-ship cabins are tiny, and you'll need one large enough to accommodate you and your child's crib comfortably. Make your request well in advance.

▶ **Book an outside cabin opposite an inside cabin for your family.** Side-by-side outside cabins cost more than a combination of an outside cabin across from an inside one. Sure, those occupants of the inside cabin won't enjoy a view, but this can be an ideal compromise if you're traveling with kids, or even with another couple, and you wish to save money. And you could always switch cabins partway through the trip, so you each get to experience the outside cabin, and plan to congregate more as a group in the more pleasant outside cabin.

► **Look for a ship with a no-adults teen club.** A cruise is an ideal vacation for families with teens. Parents can rest assured that the kids are in a safe environment on board, and yet the teens can roam independently and find plenty of cool things to do. Look for a cruise ship that has an exclusive program for teens—ideally this includes a private club room where no children or adults are allowed.

Riding the Rails or the Bus

Travel by train, and even its usually pokier cousin, bus, might just be the most relaxing way to get where you're going. As with flying, you leave the "driving" to a professional and get to sit back and enjoy the scenery from your seat—but you don't have to endure a long and complicated check-in process, random security pat downs, and the often time-consuming process of searching among several airlines for the cheapest ticket. Best of all, the scenery from a train or bus can, depending on the route, remain engaging throughout your trip, while scenery from a plane typically isn't too exciting except when preparing to land.

Using your own car may offer you more freedom on a vacation than using a bus or train, but you then must drive yourself, and contend with possible traffic jams and tricky directions. And if you'd prefer to use a car wherever you're going, just rent one once you arrive—most major bus and train stations, at least in cities, either have rental-car agencies on-site or are fairly close to one. Of the two options—trains or buses—you'll usually enjoy the best scenery on a train, and you won't as often encounter the overbuilding, billboards, and sprawl that mar the roadsides of so many highways, at least in densely populated parts of the world.

One final advantage to traveling by train or bus is that there's far more potential to meet new friends during your travels than when you're flying or driving. In some parts of the world, trains encourage a spirit of camaraderie among travelers—people often notice one another's luggage or the guidebooks they're reading, and strike up a conversation. There's a relaxing pace to train and bus travel; especially on trains, you can move about to some degree, carry on a conversation without straining to hear over the groan of a plane engine, and actually take advantage of the many hours that it can take to get where you're going. A car trip can take just as long, and yet you won't have time to catch up on a book or work on your laptop computer.

However, you may be surprised to learn that train travel—especially for very long routes in the United States and Canada—can be more expensive than flying, considerably so. Bus travel usually costs half as much or less, and is thus far more economical, but it's also more likely to take longer. These are relatively uncomplicated forms of transportation that appeal to a broad cross section of travelers—there aren't as many things to think about and prepare for as with planning a plane or car trip. But there are a few tricks and ideas for making your bus or train journey more enjoyable.

TRAIN OR BUS?

▶ **Don't assume the train is faster.** Compare routes and whether the train or bus will put you closer to your actual destination. In some areas, a bus will go express and drop you closer to your actual stop than a train station. Given the chaotic nature of Amtrak, and the Odyssey-like travel times American train trips can take, spend a couple of minutes on the Web and see if traveling by bus makes more sense.

▶ **Take the train if you're the restless sort.** If you hate sitting for long periods or require extra seating space, try traveling by train. Train seating areas are usually less cramped than cars and airplanes, and it's much easier to get up and move about at regular intervals. Best of all, you don't have to stop for bathroom breaks—and often there's a dining car.

TIPS FOR A SMOOTH RIDE

▶ **Have luggage sent ahead to your destination.** This way, you'll be free to get out and explore a bit at each stop without having to carry your luggage. Do pack a small bag of reading material, toiletries, snacks, and other things you need to have by your side throughout the duration of your trip.

▶ **Get there early for your departure.** This is important because if everyone else gets there earlier than you, you won't be able to choose a good seat.

▶ **Allow enough time for connections.** Trains, particularly during the busy summer months, are highly susceptible to delays. If your trip involves a connection, try to allow at least three hours from the time of your arrival to the time of your connecting train's departure.

▶ **Bring a small pillow for sleeping in your seat.** On trains and buses, if you're hoping to sleep in your seat, a small pillow can be tremendously helpful. You might want to consider buying an inflatable pillow or cervical collar, which can be easier to store.

▶ **Buy earplugs for trips where you plan to sleep.** Some buses and trains can be very noisy, as can passengers. Earplugs are your best assurance of a restful nap.

▶ **Travel midweek to avoid crowds.** For most rail and bus service, especially intercity and international travel, you'll find less crowded trains and buses if you travel midweek. The exception tends to be commuter-oriented buses and trains, which get the most traffic during the week.

▶ **Secure baggage with a small lock.** Especially for night trains or other instances where you'll be sleeping, use a small bicycle lock or padlock to secure your travel bags.

▶ **Never leave baggage unattended in stations.** It's even riskier to leave bags unattended at a bus or train station than in an airport, where there tends to be better security. Even if you plan to step a few feet away for only a few minutes, don't ever lose hold of your bags.

▶ **Use a locker to store luggage while exploring.** Unfortunately, many U.S. train and bus stations have stopped renting lockers in light of security concerns, but you can still often rent storage lockers for a few dollars at stations in many European cities.

▶ **When sleeping en route, keep your money secure.** You're best keeping money, credit cards, and other valuables in a money belt or a concealed clothing pocket—any spot that's difficult to access while you're napping.

▶ **For kids, pack noiseless toys and games.** Fill your toy tote with items that won't make a lot of noise and bother other passengers: pencil and crayon sets, stickers, colored paper, and other crafts-oriented goods. Magnetic travel board games and puzzles are also ideal.

▶ **Bring an iPod and music or a book on tape.** Short of napping, tuning out those around you may be the best way to pass the hours during a trip of any length. Keep the volume of your headphones low enough that others can't hear what you're listening to.

▶ **Bring only what you'll need onboard.** Put the rest under the bus in the luggage compartment to maximize your legroom and general comfort.

▶ **Bring your own food, when it's permitted.** Healthy snacks such as grapes, cheese, and crackers are a necessity when rest stops proffering chips and sodas are all the choice you're given. Choose items that are not sticky (peeling oranges can be a mess) or overwhelm-

The Wilsons were proud Los Angelenos, having lived in Orange County their entire lives. The family car was their sole source of transportation, and they never found the need to take a taxi, a city bus, or even a train to get where they needed to go. So it was with some trepidation that they took a family trip to the city, one that caused them to leave their beloved car behind. But instead of learning the ins and outs of public transportation in a new place, Mr. Wilson decided he would avoid the hassle and rent a car when he got there—he was familiar with cars, and felt the convenience of having one at his disposal would make his vacation simpler and save time.

As it turned out, the car proved to be not a convenience but a liability and a headache. The hotel charged them an additional $30 a day for parking, and other parking lots around the city—when they were able to find them—were astronomically expensive. The added pressure of dealing with a car in a big city put an unnecessary burden on the family and wound up detracting from their vacation. Mr. Wilson was dumbfounded because he never imagined having a car could be so much trouble. In retrospect, he realized he should never have rented a car, but how was he to know? What should he have done differently?

▶ FODOR'S FIX

This is a case where a little research would have gone a long way. It sounds obvious, but don't go on vacation expecting your destination to be like home. The truth is that in most major metropolitan areas, traffic congestion makes using public transportation not only advisable, but downright necessary—it's often the fastest and most convenient way to get anywhere in town at any time of day. If you are going to a place you've never been, it's best to ask around and see whether anyone you know has been there, because firsthand advice from a familiar source is always the best kind. Secondly, check Web sites such as Fodors.com, whose Travel Talk section allows you to post destination-specific questions on a bulletin board where seasoned travelers offer advice and suggestions—all for free. You'll be able to find out details, often overlooked by travel guides, that will make your trip that much more enjoyable.

The Bottom Line: Whatever you do, be aware of all your options before deciding on a mode of transportation in a new place. Many municipal transit systems—both at home and abroad—offer daily and weekly passes that could save city-trotting tourists considerable money. But also be aware that, in certain instances, a family of four might pay less money using taxis, which usually charge a flat fee, than for buses or subways, which always charge per person. A tip for taking taxis in foreign cities: Bring a small notebook to write down the fare and negotiate a price in advance with a cab driver if you don't speak the language—Arabic numerals are almost universally recognized. That way, there will be no chance of you getting "taken for a ride" and winding up paying double for a fare that got lost in the translation (just be sure you agree upon the currency, too).

ingly saucy, making sure to include some protein. Also, forego the richer and aromatic foods, which are a better eaten in a stationary position, as to minimize indigestion. You'll feel much better when you arrive at your destination having eaten well.

▶ **If scenery is important, travel by day.** Booking nighttime train and bus trips can be useful depending on your schedule and other circumstances, but part of the joy of busing or training across country is enjoying the magnificent scenery out your window. If this is the main purpose of your trip, consider traveling only during the day and staying in motels or hotels at different stops along the way for your overnights.

TAKING THE TRAIN IN THE USA

▶ **Calculate point-to-point fares before buying a discount pass.** Depending on where you're going and how much train travel you have planned, it may be cheaper to buy individual tickets than to pay for a discount pass.

▶ **Mention AAA membership when booking.** Always mention any affiliations or memberships when booking train tickets; you'll often be eligible for discounts.

▶ **Try training it with kids.** With room for fidgety kids to roam about, travel by train can be a great alternative to cars for vacationing families—so long as you have the time and the trains to go where you need to go. Snack bars, rest rooms, and water fountains are infinitely entertaining for kids; reclining seats, overhead luggage racks, and even sleeping compartments on long-distance routes make travel hours relatively comfortable.

▶ **Look into kids' discounts on Amtrak.** Children ages 2–15 ride for half fare on Amtrak when accompanied by an adult paying full fare. Children under 2 ride free.

▶ **Ride the rails, then rent a car.** Traveling long distances by car and renting cars at different destinations along the way can be both more economical and more relaxing than driving your own car the entire trip. Many rail stations have on-site car-rental agencies, and other car-rental companies will deliver cars to you at the station.

▶ **Consider a rail trip for your honeymoon.** Don't overlook the romantic alternative of the railways for your honeymoon getaway. If trains ring your bell, the traveling itself can be a honeymoon highlight.

▶ **Check out TrainWeb.com if you're a rail enthusiast.** This extensive Web site has the lowdown on North American tourist and scenic railways, dinner trains, private railcar excursions, and train museums.

▶ **Compare Amtrak's deluxe or standard sleepers.** Amtrak has both deluxe and standard bedrooms for two in its first-class cars. Deluxe accommodations are on the upper level of a bi-level car. The private rooms are equipped with a sofa and armchair that convert to upper- and lower-berth beds. You get a sink and vanity, shower and toilet, reading lights, thermostat, and electrical outlets for your hair dryers, shavers, and so on. There's a hospitality hour for first-class passengers, and movies are shown each night in the lounge car. A standard bedroom, which might be on an upper or lower level of the car, has two reclining seats that convert to a bed, and a fold-down upper berth. There is no shower or sink in the room, but they are nearby.

▶ **Ask about student discounts.** Many rail lines all over the world offer special discounted passes for students, or in some cases offer reduced fares for any travelers under age 26. Always ask about student rates, and be sure to have a valid student ID when booking your trip.

▶ **Travel off-season.** From late fall through early spring, Amtrak offers U.S. passengers Explore America fares, allowing multiple stopovers in one, two, or three regions. Prices vary according to the number of regions chosen.

▶ **Consider commuter trains.** Amtrak may be the most popular service for intercity travel in the United States, but many regions also have more extensive and less pricey commuter rail service—especially New England and the Mid-Atlantic states. Commuter rail service is a great way to get from New York City to some of the great getaways on Eastern Long Island and in the Hudson River Valley.

▶ **Book an excursion train ride.** In many parts of the country—such as Durango, Colorado; Napa Valley, California; and Newport, Rhode Island—sightseeing trains provide passengers with a chance to take in magnificent scenery. Many excursion trains offer meals, and most of them are leisurely round-trip journeys that aren't intended to be the quickest or most practical way to get between two points.

Rail Passes

▶ **Have your rail pass validated before you board.** In most cases, you'll pay a service fee (about $5 to $30) if you wait to have your pass validated onboard. Never write anything on the pass itself—this could void it.

Instead, go to the ticket office of the first station you're traveling from and have the pass validated there.

▶ **Take care to keep your rail pass safe.** These passes are not refundable or replaceable if lost or stolen, so keep this in a safe place. You can buy railpass insurance, which will get you a refund for the unused portion of your pass after you return home.

▶ **Read the fine print for rail passes.** This pass will get you onto a train, but it won't guarantee you a seat. Also, some high-speed trains cost extra, so you may have to pay a supplement for using your pass with these services.

▶ **Research Amtrak's and VIA Rail Canada's passes.** The North America Rail Pass can be purchased by residents of the United States and Canada, as well as by other international travelers, and travel must include both countries. A second pass, the Northeastern North America Rail Pass, is valid for 15 days of travel in eastern Canada and the northeastern United States only, and it is sold only to international travelers who live outside both countries.

▶ **Check out VIA Rail Canada's discount passes.** VIA Rail Canada's Canrailpass allows 12 days of unlimited economy-class travel across Canada within a 30-day period. In addition, Via Rail offers the Corridorpass, good for 10 days of travel between Québec City, Montréal, Ottawa, Toronto, Niagara Falls, Kitchener, Stratford, London, Windsor, and all stations in between. It can be bought by anyone, but must be bought at least five days in advance.

▶ **Visiting from abroad? Get a USA Railpass.** This pass allows overseas visitors 15 or 30 days of unlimited travel nationwide. Fifteen- and 30-day regional rail passes can be purchased for the far west, western, eastern, and northeast areas of the United States; 30-day passes are also offered for rail travel along the East Coast and West Coast. These rail passes are sold in the United States at any Amtrak station, but to qualify you must show a valid non-U.S. passport.

BY TRAIN OUTSIDE THE USA

▶ Travel Europe high-speed. Some national high-speed train systems, which sees trains traveling from 150 to 190 mph, have begun to link up to form the nucleus of a pan-European system. On a long journey, you still have to change trains a couple of times as the national railways jealously guard their prerogatives. France, Switzerland, Italy, Brussels, the Netherlands, and Germany are among the nations offering this service. Remember that this service requires reservations and doesn't come as cheaply as conventional rail service.

▶ Know Europe's "class" system. Virtually all European rail carriers, including the high-speed ones, operate a two-class system. First class costs substantially more and is usually a luxury rather than a necessity. Some of the poorer European countries retain a third class, but avoid it unless you're an adventure-minded budget traveler.

▶ Buy a European rail pass at home. EurailPasses—available only from your home country—provide unlimited first-class rail travel for the duration of the pass in 17 European countries: Austria, Belgium, Denmark, Finland, France, Germany, Greece, Hungary, the Irish

Republic, Italy, Luxembourg, the Netherlands, Norway, Portugal, Spain, Sweden, and Switzerland (but not the United Kingdom). Price travel segments individually before deciding to get a pass.

▶ **Think carefully about your travel plans before picking a pass.** If you plan to rack up miles, get a standard pass. These are available for 15 days, 21 days, one month, two months, and three months. You will have to pay a supplement for certain high-speed trains. Other passes are available for travelers under 26, small groups of passengers traveling together, and travel in Eastern Europe.

▶ **Look up routes on-line.** In many countries, maps are not customarily provided to passengers. You may do best to consult a map on the Internet first or obtain one from a travel agent in your home country.

BY BUS IN THE USA

▶ **Have the exact change for local buses.** In many instances, you'll need to pay with the exact change when boarding the bus. Find out ahead of time the bus fare, and have the right change handy.

▶ **If you're with a group, consider a bus tour.** You need to have at least 25 people in your group, and ideally 30 to 40, but chartering your own tour bus can be cheaper than paying individual tickets for a bus tour, and it can be an excellent way for a bunch of friends, colleagues, or family members to experience a destination together.

▶ **Try to travel by bus with a friend.** The affordable yet somewhat cramped seats come in pairs, and the person beside you might as well have personal boundaries, social skills, and eating habits that you might not want to endorse, but that you can stand.

▶ **Sit with women.** If you're traveling alone by bus, don't choose a seat with an empty seat beside it. Sit down next to a woman or across from a family.

▶ **Make cell phone calls before you board the bus.** Otherwise, you might be asked to comply with increased no-chit-chat regulations designed to give all passengers a quiet ride.

▶ **Find out if food is allowed.** You might have to eat before you travel on some small, regional coach lines, which prohibit snacking.

▶ **Don't sit in the back.** It's where the bathroom is, and the ride can be bumpy back there.

▶ **Don't sit in the very front.** That's where everyone typically wants to sit , and if your bus is three-quarters full you'll likely have a seatmate, while those in the back won't.

▶ **Choose a good movie-watching seat.** Many buses show movies en route. If you're really interested in seeing one, don't sit in a seat with a screen directly overhead; sit a row or two back from one.

▶ **Ask what a "direct" or "nonstop" trip means.** Even when a bus is supposedly a "direct nonstop" there's usually a quick stop if the ride is over three or four hours. Sometimes passengers have time to dart into a convenience or truck stop to buy food or use the bathroom. Sometimes not. If you smoke, though, and the thought of seven hours, say, on a no-smoking bus (and they're all no-smoking: Federal rule) makes you edgy, call a ticket agent and ask if the "nonstop" bus actually will stop somewhere along the way. You'll have enough time to suck down a cigarette or two.

▶ **Don't worry about reserving for Greyhound.** Generally, no reservations are needed—buy your tickets before boarding (allow 15 minutes in advance in small towns, up to 45 minutes in larger cities).

▶ **For serious U.S. bus-touring, consider the Greyhound Lines Discovery Pass.** The Greyhound Lines Discovery Pass, a one-price ticket for up to 60 consecutive days of travel, can be used by both U.S. citizens and foreigners; it can be bought on-line, at Greyhound terminals and travel agencies throughout the United States, and at Greyhound-affiliated travel agents worldwide. International visitors are entitled to special discounted rates provided they buy the pass before they leave home, at the Greyhound International Office in New York City, and at a few other U.S. locations, or on-line.

▶ **Use a commuter bus or train to the airport.** In many cities, your cheapest fare between an airport and a city's business district or even many outlying areas is either a local commuter bus or even an intercity carrier. Trains, which usually provide faster service, are typically more costly but still usually offer service that's a fraction of the price of taxis, limos, and airport shuttle buses.

BY BUS OUTSIDE THE USA

▶ **Take the bus where it's the primary mode of transportation.** Although Americans tend to think of European trains as a means to get around, within several southern European countries—including Portugal,

Greece, parts of Spain, and Turkey—the bus has supplanted the train or is a comfortable alternative, as in Britain and Sweden. The bus is often quicker and more comfortable, with more frequent service than the antiquated national rolling stock. Be prepared for the bus to be more expensive. Competition among lines is keen, so ask about air-conditioning and reclining seats before you book.

▶ **Get written instructions/station names where signage is not in Roman letters.** This is the case in Russia and much of Asia, and using buses, trains, or subways here can prove extra difficult for foreigners. Get written instructions from your hotel clerk or a local to show the driver.

▶ **Choose the "class" that's right for you.** Many countries outside North America have classes of buses. Buses range from huge, modern, air-conditioned beasts with lead-foot drivers, bathrooms, and an occasional movie to something a little less new and a whole lot more sweaty and crowded, with three to a two-person bench. Ask your hotel concierge for the recommended tourist class bus, if air-conditioning and a seat to yourself is important to you.

▶ **Keep a close eye on your belongings on crowded buses.** Pickpockets like nothing better than to ply their trade in these cramped circumstances. Of course, most passengers are friendly and open to a chat to pass the time.

▶ **Prepare for delays at borders.** Even if the bus company has a tried-and-true international route, long lines at borders can happen due to traffic—and if each bus passenger must show a passport and pay an entry tax (carry a bit of local currency or small bills in U.S. currency).

▶ **Expect a squeeze on Central American local buses.** This means three occupying a seat meant for two on a retired U.S. school bus. It's perfectly fine to step into the aisle to let someone take a middle or window seat. Sometimes a bus won't depart until it's completely filled with passengers, both sitting and standing in the aisle. It's also common for vendors to hop on, shove their way down the aisle as they sell snacks or newspapers, and jump out the emergency exit at the back.

7

Seeing the Sights Day and Night

Let's assume you made it there. Whatever it took to get where you wanted to go in your travels, it's hard not to feel a burst of excitement that first day you arrive in a new place. One of the best ways to make the most of a vacation is to think clearly about your goals before you set off. Are you in dire need of some rest and relaxation—a break from your overscheduled daily grind? Maybe all you truly want is some time lazing on the beach or lying around the pool of your hotel.

On the other hand, if you lead a rather prosaic, predictable life in a town that's nothing like where you're going, you might want to pack a lot of activities in. You shouldn't feel obligated to run yourself ragged taking in the sites on your vacation, however. You don't want to return from your vacation exhausted and in need of another one. Be realistic about your needs, and be good to yourself.

Vacationing is not a competition or a scavenger hunt—it's not especially fulfilling to arrive with a checklist of "must-see" sites and knock them off one by one. If you want to make a list of "vacation goals," which includes places you hope to see and activities you'd like to pursue while traveling, go right ahead. But list the things that really interest you, not that you've been told are most popular. Don't worry about what others think: it's okay to visit Paris and never ascend the Eiffel Tower or visit Washington, D.C., without setting foot in a Smithsonian museum.

One of the most satisfying forms of sightseeing is the kind that involves no plan, no lists, and perhaps no formal attractions. Just hop in the car, rent a bike, or set out on foot to wander and see what comes your way. Venture down roads and lanes that look intriguing. Allow yourself to get sidetracked, or jot down the name of an interesting shop or attraction you stumble upon but would rather spend more time visiting another day. A formless, unplanned day of exploring can always be a terrific way for parents to interact with kids, or for old friends to catch up and share time together.

Activities are the meat of your vacation sandwich—getting there and home again is the bread. So make the most of your time during your travels, choosing activities and a pace for partaking of them that fits your exact needs and interests.

PLANNING AND LOGISTICS

▶ **Familiarize yourself with a general-overview tour.** If you're spending several days or weeks in a place, it can be very helpful to take a guided bus or walking tour as soon as possible after you arrive. This will give you the lay of the land, and will help you to decide what local activities and attractions interest you, and where they are in relation to one another.

▶ **When given directions, ask for distances and landmarks at turning points.** Also find out whether the route includes physical challenges like steep hills or bridges. If you need to know the location of the convention center or the nearest bank or restaurant, don't accept an answer such as "Oh, it's only three blocks away." The length of a block can vary greatly from one city to another—or even from crosstown to uptown— and what might be a charming stroll on a summer's eve becomes an unbearable trek on a sub-zero winter's day.

▶ **Make backup plans for inclement weather.** There's no reason that a rainy day should put a damper on your vacation. Consider the climate of the destination you're headed to, especially in terms of the time of year that you're going. And then plan realistically for the possibility that you'll have some rain—perhaps this will be when you go shopping or to a museum? If you're traveling with children, bring along games you can play, rent a video in your hotel room, or make a list of indoor attractions that you can enjoy regardless of wet weather.

▶ **Research the best hours to visit tourist hot spots.**
Okay, you've just got to see Stonehenge, but crowds can put a damper on your experience. Check your guidebook, the Web, or call in advance to ask about the best times to avoid crowds. Also ask about less-visited areas nearby.

▶ **Plan your activities realistically.** Look over a guidebook, tourism brochure, or Web site about the area you're visiting, and really assess the strength of its activities. Try not to plan a busy itinerary of sightseeing just for the sake of doing so—some places, like laidback beach locales or secluded countryside B&Bs—lend themselves to unscheduled rest and relaxation. Others have so many activity options that you can easily feel overwhelmed. Don't over-schedule or fret about seeing it all—you may get the hang of simply relaxing much more quickly than you'd imagined.

▶ **Carry a bit of change in local currency with you.**
You might find that little unexpected payments are required in order to gain admission to sights, like public parks, or in order to use illumination devices in churches (timed lights on certain parts of the interior or artwork).

▶ **Drop everything for an unforeseen adventure opportunity.** Even after you've logged lots of time laying out plans and possible itineraries, it's important to honor your whims and recognize a once-in-a-lifetime opportunity, should one come your way.

▶ **Ask local tourist boards about discount passes.**
Always check with the local office of tourism, either via their Web site or by phone (many have toll-free numbers) to find out if they provide discount passes,

coupons, or other package deals good for several or possibly even all of a destination's main attractions. Sometimes tourist boards also offer deals that include accommodations and attractions discounts.

▶ **Check "Best Of" issues of local publications.** Most regional magazines and newspapers produce "best of" editions once a year; this can be a great resource for the best-of-the-best selections for new restaurants, shops, or nightlife spots. Monthly city-focused magazines have annual editions that spotlight the best places in town as well, which give great insider information on fresh hotspots as well as perennial favorites. Both newspaper and magazine articles of this sort can generally be accessed on-line.

▶ **Plan your visit to coincide with an event or festival.** Arriving in a city during a major event can ensure that you'll have plenty to see and do. Keep in mind, however, that it may be difficult or costly to obtain hotel rooms at this time, and even airfares could be higher.

▶ **Vary your activities from day to day.** Visiting large art museums back-to-back can be taxing for even the most ardent culture vulture, just as shopping for six straight hours can wear out inveterate browsers. If you're someone who simply must pack a lot into every day of your trip, try to mix and match your activities. Spend a morning at a museum, and follow with a light hike or garden tour in the afternoon. Save a second museum for a different day, when you might also take a bus or boat tour.

▶ **Drop in on classes and tour groups.** Cooking classes and sightseeing tours are ideal. You may even meet locals in the classes. Sightseeing tours kill two birds with one stone: you might get to spots that would be difficult to get to on your own, and you might meet other travelers.

▶ **Don't over-schedule.** How much you try to see and do in one day depends entirely on the individual, but everybody will benefit by trying to be realistic. Think back to your last vacation—did you overextend yourself or visit so many attractions that you ended up not liking some of them? Resist succumbing to the fear that you may never return and so must see everything a destination has to offer, and instead focus on those activities and attractions that truly appeal to you. Take it easy—this is your time off.

▶ **Always call ahead to confirm hours and admission.** No matter how much you trust your guidebook, or how recently you've checked an attraction's Web page, call the day of your visit to make sure the place is open. Some museums open or close late or early at whim, or may close unexpectedly because of a staff shortage, a local holiday you're not aware of, a change in the budget, or for renovations.

▶ **Bring bottled water.** There is probably no product that travelers more underestimate their need for than water, which is sometimes unpleasant-tasting or unavailable at popular attractions. Drinking a bottle (or even two or three) is sometimes the difference between conking out halfway through a hike and trekking 2 miles farther than you thought you ever could. It's also a must at theme parks, for city strolls, and just about any place that gets lots of sun. And although you can often buy bottled water at convenience stores or museum or attractions shops, you'll pay dearly—if you're traveling by car, buy a case of bottled water at a discount store and keep it in your trunk.

▶ **Hire an English-speaking driver or private guide.** If you're not a fan of big tour groups, try this option. You'll get the guide's expertise in English—and his or her companionship. In some destinations, this request is par for the course and your request will be quite standard. And, depending upon where you're traveling, you may end up safer, too.

▶ **Pack a portable umbrella.** How many times have you been caught in a torrential downpour with neither an umbrella nor the appropriate outfit? Watch the weather the night before or morning of planned activities, or check with the front desk at your hotel. If there's so much as a slight chance of an afternoon shower, at least try carrying along a collapsible umbrella—the smallest of these fit easily in a backpack, shopping bag, or even a large pocketbook. In rainy destinations and upscale hotels, large umbrellas are often provided.

▶ **Wear comfortable shoes.** If there's one aspect of your wardrobe in which you should always let comfort and utility win out over style, it's shoes. Let your foot fetish go if you have a day of walking or exploring planned, and wear lightweight, breathable shoes or even sneakers that will make your feet comfy.

▶ **Put your feet first.** Sightseeing can be hard on your tootsies. Carry a small bottle of foot spray, a small foot-massage gadget, and a small tube or bottle of foot cream or gel and fresh socks. Then, during a bathroom break in the middle of sightseeing, give yourself a five-minute foot treatment and change your socks. When your feet are invigorated and refreshed (read: cool), so, too, is the rest of you.

▶ **Bring along just one backpack for the two of you.** There's no reason each of you should have to haul around a bag filled with your day's necessities (maps, guidebooks, cameras, bottled water, etc.). Use one sturdy and comfortable backpack for all your gear, and take turns carrying it. Just make sure that one person in your party is responsible for the whereabouts of that bag throughout the day—passing it from person to person makes it easier to misplace or forget.

▶ **Bring a map.** You can find all kinds of small, portable maps at bookstores and tourism offices (where they're typically free)—or consider tearing the map out of a guidebook. Whatever you use, never set out for a day of exploring without a reliable, reasonably well-detailed map of your destination. You may never have cause to consult it, and you might hate looking like a tourist when you do, but that little piece of paper might save you hours of frustration or steer you from a dangerous area.

▶ **Don't forget your cell phone or phone card.** If your cell phone works where you're going, carry it with you, even if you don't plan to use it and hate being bothered by incoming calls. Turn it off and use it only when you want or need to, but do try to keep it close at hand. It can be a lifesaver when you're trying to confirm a museum's hours, directions, or admission; need to make or change a dinner reservation for later in the day; or if you become lost or disoriented. If your cell phone doesn't work where you're going, purchase a phone card or carry along the appropriate change for local calls.

SPORTS AND THE OUTDOORS

▶ **If you love to fish, charter a fishing boat.** Hiring a boat, with crew, can be reasonably affordable for even two or three travelers, and it's ideal if you have a limited amount of time and are unfamiliar with the fishing where you're going. Prices vary by location and boat but usually run several hundred dollars per day or half day, so the more people you have in your party, the more ways you can divide the bill.

▶ **Hire an expert.** Are you an avid fly-fishing enthusiast who's visiting a place for the first time? Have you always wanted to hike a particular national park but are unfamiliar with local trails? You might be surprised how inexpensive it is to hire a guide, especially if there are several people in your party. Guides can usually help you to custom-design your itinerary, and they can be available for as little as a few hours or for as long as several days. Their expertise in a given field may end up saving you time and frustration—just be certain to find someone with excellent credentials in the activity you're planning to pursue.

▶ **In busy national parks, bypass the busiest areas midday.** Take this time to explore the park's more peaceful areas.

▶ **Don't rule out 18 holes at a private golf course.** Many of the world's top golf courses are closed to all but members and their guests, but depending on when you hope to play and how you couch your request, you might be fortunate enough to gain entry to what's normally an off-limits club. Many private clubs allow members of other private clubs to visit, and others will honor guests of certain hotels or passengers of certain cruise ships. Also some companies (yours?) have corporate affiliations. Avoid being heavy-handed or pulling rank—just ask politely, and try asking if you can play on a Monday or during the late afternoon on another weekday, when courses are least busy.

▶ **Research your sports interests in advance.** Whether you want to use a health club or play a round of golf, call ahead and ask about any deals such as reduced fees for certain days or times of day. You may save a bundle.

▶ **Rent sports gear rather than carrying your own.** If you're an avid golfer or skier, the idea of renting equipment may simply be beyond comprehension. But at least consider renting—sports gear is readily available at many golf, ski, and other sports venues, and equipment is often reasonably priced and in very good condition. It can even be a chance to test a brand or type of equipment you've always wanted to try. Then you will enjoy the freedom of not having to haul a giant golf or ski bag with you through airports, on shuttle buses, and in taxis.

▶ **Visit a farm.** Agricultural tourism is a rapidly growing industry, and visits to farms can be great fun for kids and adults. Many farms invite customers to pick their own produce, cut down their own Christmas tree, or enjoy fresh food made with locally grown or produced ingredients (from ice cream to apple cider). Hayrides and petting zoos are other popular activities. In addition to checking with tourist boards for names of farms open to the public, also consult the Department of the Environment in whatever state you're visiting.

▶ **Catch a minor-league game.** You might think of attending a football, baseball, basketball, or other game only when visiting a big city with a major-league team, but hundreds of smaller municipalities across North America offer lively minor-league games. Tickets are cheaper, stadiums are often more intimate, and many minor-league clubs throw fun or outlandish promotions, such as concerts and giveaways. Minor-league players are generally friendlier and more approachable than their big-league counterparts, and you might just catch a glimpse of the next superstar while he's still working his way through the farm system.

THE GREAT INDOORS

▶ **Find out when museums offer free admission.** Many large museums offer free or "pay-as-you-wish" admission one or two days per week, often for just part of the day (the first couple of hours in the morning, or a few hours late in the evening). Thursday and Friday evenings are common for this practice, but exact days can vary greatly—you might be able to plan your museum visits to get into several places free. Keep in mind, however, that most museums are nonprofit. If you are in a financial position to make a donation, it's always appreciated.

▶ **Plan a late-night museum jaunt.** Quite a few major museums extend their usual opening times by two or three hours one night a week. This can be a great time to visit a museum, perhaps combining your tour with dinner afterwards at a nearby restaurant. Sometimes museums offer special evening programs, such as lectures, wine-and-cheese socials, exhibit openings, or films.

▶ **Join the museum when you visit.** It's never a bad idea to ask about the costs and benefits of becoming a member of a museum. Sometimes the cost of annual membership isn't all that much greater than one day's single admission, and this membership might be good for two or several of you in your group. Obviously, it makes the most sense for attractions you're likely to visit more than once a year, but membership might come with an interesting newsletter or magazine subscription that will remind you of your trip long after you've returned home, as well as reciprocal benefits at museums in other cities and discounts at the gift shop—plus, you're donating money to what's probably a good cause.

ARTS AND NIGHTLIFE

▶ **Check the college scene.** Whether you're visiting a big city or a small town, if there's a college or university around, even a little one, find out what's happening on campus—either call, look for a college newspaper, or visit the school's Web site. Universities often have museums, and nearly all of them have performing arts venues that produce or host both local and sometimes professional plays and musical events. The commercial strips near college campuses often buzz with coffeehouses, bars, and eateries, too.

▶ **As soon as you get to town, find a coffeehouse.** If you're keen on nightlife, theater, concerts, and other evening activities, the local coffeehouse—even if it's a branch of a national chain like Starbucks—is like a de facto resource center. Here you'll typically find local alternative newsweeklies with events and entertainment listings, and you're likely to see postings for upcoming shows. Furthermore, coffeehouses are often in arts or gallery districts, near college campuses, or in lively shopping areas. And they can be a great social alternative to bars.

▶ **Consider visiting a bar or club on an "off" night.** If you're a die-hard disco bunny, hitting a nightclub on the weekend might be your best bet. But if your goal is more to meet others, people-watch, and get a feel for the local vibe, you may end up having a better time on a weeknight. Monday and Tuesday tend to be quiet in most cities, but on Wednesday, Thursday, and sometimes Sunday, bars and clubs often have special theme nights and draw sizeable but manageable crowds.

▶ **Look for half-price, same-day theater and concert tickets.** Many cities have booths or agencies that specialize in selling concert and theater tickets to performances that day. If you're flexible and open-minded about what you may see that evening, these can be a bargain and a fun way to experience a performance you might never have thought you were interested in. You may end up paying half the ticket price (or less) for a top show.

▶ **Consult your hotel concierge for hard-to-get tickets.** A good one can get you tickets to almost anything. Theater events and concerts often "sell out" well in advance, sometimes the day tickets go on sale. But rare is the show that has absolutely no available seats. You can check with ticket brokers and other agencies in the city you're visiting, and you'll often find last-minute seats, or put your hotel concierge to work on this: Just be prepared to shell out many times more than the ticket's face value, and be sure to reward your concierge with a $5 to $20 tip, depending on the show and the difficulty of getting you those tickets.

▶ **Catch a matinee.** Taking in a show or concert during the afternoon can be a nice change of pace, and it's an excellent way to see a performance if you're traveling with kids. Matinee shows are often less likely to be sold out and are less pricey, too.

▶ **Make sure you have the endurance for standing-room-only seats.** No matter how popular a show is, it's often possible to get last-minute standing-room-only seats. Make sure you really have the endurance to stand through a long performance before going this route, and consider that in some theaters, standing means that you'll be quite far from the stage. These seats are usually sold the day of performance, and are usually available by calling or showing up at the theater directly.

▶ **Don't be scammed.** Avoid scalpers and never pay more than 20% of a ticket's face value if you do use a scalper, no matter how tempted you are to shell out more. And be sure to examine the ticket carefully before any cash changes hands. On the other hand, you'll sometimes find people outside shows and concerts who honestly have a spare ticket or two because of a no-show; if they're selling this at roughly the ticket's real value, and you're satisfied that the ticket is authentic, go for it—in most places, selling a ticket at close to its face value is perfectly legal. Just remember: if a deal sounds too good to be true, it probably is.

▶ **Don't let velvet ropes or a snooty door policy ruin your night.** First off, ask yourself whether gaining admission is so important to you that it's worth waiting an hour in line or subjecting yourself to the arbitrary whims of the fashion police. Beyond that, if you insist on waiting, smile pleasantly at the bouncers, conduct yourself with aplomb (whining or acting desperate will likely be met with dismal results), and—yes—try (subtly) greasing palms. A discreet bribe of $10 or $20 will sometimes get you right where you want to go. Lastly, dress to impress—your outfit doesn't have to be expensive or fancy, but if you convey a sense of style and confidence, you're more likely to move quickly through the line.

▶ **To make new friends, ask the time.** If you're with friends or alone in a new town and out visiting clubs and bars, there are two questions that, when asked in succession, always make for excellent conversation openers. Ask "do you know what time it is?" and hide your watch, if you're wearing one. Then, after you're told the answer, ask "what time does this bar close?" It's an innocuous approach that needn't be used as or taken to be a cheesy pickup line; it's pretty easy to ask even if you're rather shy; and it immediately suggests that you're not local (which means that you'll often be asked back, "oh, where are you from?" or "are you visiting?").

▶ **Drink downscale.** If you're looking for the best or funkiest or offbeat happenings at night, don't look for the city's hottest club. You'll likely get another tourist trap. Instead, ask around at smaller watering holes, as the people there are probably locals, and probably know what's really hot.

▶ **Look for free-admission and open-bar teasers.** Many nightlife promoters try to fill their clubs up early by offering free admission or one- to two-hour open bars early in the evening—usually around 9 or 10 PM. This can be a good way to check out a place before having to commit to an exorbitant cover charge. You can often find out about these deals in local alternative newsweeklies and other nightlife-oriented papers.

Brenda and Leslie decided to leave their suburban Cincinnati lives behind and spend a fabulous weekend exploring glamorous New York nightclubs. The first night out they arrived fashionably late at the West Village hotspot where some of their favorite celebrities had been spotted only a week before. After waiting in line for more than two hours, they finally approached the door only to be told by the bouncer that there was a private party that night and the club was not open to the public. Most of the other famous clubs in town seemed to be hosting private parties, too, and they wound up partying not with the A-List but with other tourists at overcrowded bars in Times Square. Their weekend of glamor turned into a run-of-the-mill couple of days they could have had back home. Was their timing bad, or is there something else going on here?

▶ FODOR'S FIX

This is simple case of the "when in Rome" syndrome. Although Brenda and Leslie are two lovely, single thirtysomethings, New York City—like Rome, London, Paris, and most any other world capitol—has its own set of rules regarding nightlife. The "private party" excuse proffered by the bouncer is a standard device used to gently turn people away who don't have the "right look" for a particular club. Although the women had an appropriate look for the clubs back at home, their outfits didn't pass muster with the bouncers, whose job it is to ensure a hip-looking crowd.

The Bottom Line: The women should have taken their fashion cue from the queue—that is, note how the other people in line were dressed and see whether they "fit in." Or, earlier in the day, they could have asked their hotel concierge to put them on the club's guest list and then stopped by any chic local boutique, asked advice, and bought appropriate (read: hip) club wear. In the end, once you do achieve the right look—and anybody can with a little effort—you need to arrive at hot clubs as early as possible and be patient. Unless you are part of the celebrity A-List, your appearance will be scrutinized, but the right clothes, the right attitude, and the right timing go a long way toward getting you in. And, as a last resort, a little harmless chitchat and a $20 pressed into the hand of a bouncer might be just the thing that gets you on the other side of the velvet rope.

SPAS

▶ **Book treatments before you arrive in a city.** Even if the spa is located at your hotel, you may have trouble getting the treatment you want when you want or maybe even at all.

▶ **Don't think that spas are just for women.** About 80% of spa goers are female, but men are a fast-growing market. Many spas have special treatments and programs designed specifically with men in mind.

▶ **Visit a hotel's spa even if you're not staying there.** An incredible number of hotels, and not only high-end luxury ones, have opened spas in the past few years— they're becoming as commonplace as swimming pools. The vast majority of these hotel spas offer day packages for nonguests, and often these deals include use of other hotel facilities, such as health clubs, pools and sundecks, tennis courts, and even business centers.

▶ **Jump-start your fitness program with a spa vacation.** If you really want to enjoy the full spa experience, consider staying at a resort or hotel that's geared entirely or largely around spa activities. Destination spas are self-contained environments. All guests are there precisely to enjoy the spa experience, and because of that, you'll usually find a sense of camaraderie. If you're looking to begin a weight-management program, embark on a fitness regimen, or make other lifestyle changes, a destination spa is best. You'll be totally immersed in an atmosphere of wellness along with other like-minded people, away from the temptations found at most resorts.

▶ **Think about the type of spa that suits your style.** Spas come in all shapes and sizes but can be broken down into several key categories with different emphases: luxury pampering, nutrition and diet, sports conditioning, holistic health, medical wellness, and mineral-spring treatments. Some spas focus on more than one of these areas, and deciding what your own interests and goals are will greatly enhance your spa experience.

SHOPPING

▶ **Don't get tied up in chains.** Unless you live in a rural area and have little access to national chain shops when you're at home, on your vacation try to avoid shopping districts and malls packed with the usual chain shops. Seek out neighborhoods, often downtown arts and/or entertainment districts, which cultivate a local retail scene with plenty of independent shops. You're more likely to find places that stock locally made arts and crafts, too.

▶ **Spend less.** Knowing what items are sold for less in your vacation destination means you can shop without the imported and inflated prices you'd pay at home. If your shoes are made in Spain, for example, it's likely that they'll be cheaper if you buy them there. Designer clothing, housewares, linens, silver, and art are just some of the additional items that can cost less outside the United States.

▶ **Look beyond outlet shops to find the best deals.** What began as a way for shops to unload last season's fashions; discontinued merchandise; and less popular colors, sizes, styles, and models—at cut-rate prices— has blossomed into a lucrative side industry in recent years. Most outlet stores do offer some deep-discounted items and great deals, but they also frequently sell merchandise designed expressly for outlet shops, and they sell items that are no cheaper than those in regular shops. Don't assume everything you find in a chain shop is a bargain.

▶ **Don't assume you'll save at duty-free shops.** Sure, it's tempting to buy anything that piques your interest in a duty-free shop, especially if you're trying to dump currency that you won't be able to use back home, or if you're bored and killing time at an airport or on a cruise ship. But avoid buying easy-to-find goods—liquor, candy, some jewelry, electronic goods, compact discs— unless you're really sure how a duty-free shop's prices compare with those at home.

▶ **Save shopping for a rainy day.** Some destinations, such as beach resorts, have attractions you can appreciate only on sunny days. Shopping is a good backup activity when the weather is less than perfect.

▶ **Check the Web before pounding the pavement.** If you're planning to visit a notable shop during your vacation, especially one with a brisk mail-order business, check the company's Web site before you arrive. Many shops have on-line coupons that you can print out and present when you shop, and others have Web-only offers or advertise upcoming sales. It's also a good way to get a sense of the merchandise and prices before you actually visit the store.

▶ **Carry an extra bag in your luggage.** Know thyself. If you plan to hit the stores, pack an extra soft-sided bag in your suitcase. This can also make it easier to deal with customs if you're traveling abroad and need to show the goods you've purchased.

▶ **Ask salespeople where to shop.** People who sell stuff tend to also know where to buy it. Go into the kind of shops you like, ask the salespeople for their recommendations on the best places to buy shoes or scarves or whatever it is you want. Hit up a half dozen stores and you'll probably start getting a good idea where to look for things, and where to find items you weren't even looking for.

▶ **When possible, pay with a credit card.** It's easier to dispute charges, to be credited in the event that you must return an item, and to document any case of unfair business practices or consumer fraud, if you paid with a credit card. This is less important on minor purchases, and you may actually get a better price if you offer to pay cash on smaller items.

▶ **Know when to haggle.** In some cultures, you're expected to haggle or dicker over the price of local goods, in other cultures it's an insult to offer any less than the asking price. Sometimes it depends simply on what you're shopping for. Find out, by consulting a guidebook or even checking with your concierge or local tourism office, when and to what degree haggling is appropriate. And no matter how aggressive the seller is, always set a fixed price in your head and stick to it.

▶ **Buy what the locals buy.** Sometimes items are sold to tourists that locals, who know better, would never touch. In an unfamiliar place, it can be hard to spot a markup unless you shop where locals do. When buying edible souvenirs, like coffee, for example, go to grocery stores and see which brands of coffee locals really drink—and you'll get the lower price they'd pay.

▶ **Travel globally, buy locally.** Be sure the items you want to purchase were made in your destination by carefully reading the tag or asking the salesperson. How sad will you be to discover the Moroccan slippers you've purchased in Marrakech were actually made in Taiwan?

▶ **Make sure it's legal to bring your purchases home.** Many countries ban the exportation of antiquities, products made from endangered species, and other items. And your home country may also ban the import of some products, and can also impose a hefty duty on some others. Know this information before you pay for an item.

▶ **Ask about tax refunds.** In many countries, the local or national taxes you pay on certain goods will be refunded to you at customs, as long as you fill out the proper forms, save your receipts, and document your purchases. Check with the tourist board of the destination you're visiting, and for major purchases, double-check with the merchant you're dealing with.

▶ **Consider shipping home your purchases.** The variety of shipping services available today makes sending your purchases home rather than carrying them very attractive in some places. Many merchants have special volume deals with certain shippers, and places that specialize in antiques, art, crafts, and other delicate items usually know best how to pack your goods carefully. Not having to lug around pottery or artwork can easily justify the shipping costs. And if the merchant in question doesn't usually ship items, ask for the name of a good shipping service in town—chains like Pak Mail and Mail Boxes, Etc. are very reliable in the United States.

THEME PARKS

▶ **With a group? Consider a theme park.** Most parks have been planned specifically to appeal to a broad range of interests, so apart from wild rides there are gentle ones that please young children, older travelers, and more sedate types. Plus, many attractions in many theme parks are completely accessible to people who use wheelchairs or who have other disabilities.

▶ **Go with discounts.** The local tourism boards almost always have coupons for the big theme parks—and many people are eligible for corporate deals through their company, school, or credit card company. If you go after 4 PM, many parks charge almost half price; if you go in the off-season, your discounts will be even better. Check around for deals before you fork over your money.

► **Save money with a multiday pass.** Theme-park admission can be pricey, but multiday packages are always available, and these often include additional benefits, such as accommodations, transportation, or even some meals. Some packages include early entry to the park.

► **Visit the theme park after it rains**—especially if you have a multiday pass. You'll find you'll have the place to yourself if the weather's iffy.

► **Set up meeting points at the beginning of the day.** If you're visiting the park as a group—or even with as few as three or four people—start out every day with a couple of different rendezvous points and times, just in case you get separated accidentally.

► **Split up according to your interests.** Any number of variables, from taste to age to endurance, can influence which travelers in a group want to go one way and which prefer to go another. It can be nice for everyone to divide your group into smaller posses and split up to pursue your separate interests.

Health and Safety

There's nothing more miserable than getting sick or scammed while you're away from home. Some simple precautions—from having the appropriate immunizations and knowing how to blend in with the locals—can make your travels healthier and happier.

PLANNING TO STAY WELL

▶ **Don't go wild, unawares.** You don't have to brave an unchartered landscape to have an Indiana Jones–type adventure. Consider destinations with a tourism infrastructure or English-speaking guides. Pick a place that's got what you want, in a palatable package. For example, thanks to its generally high safety and health standards, Costa Rica is popular with travelers looking for the rain forest and wildlife. Most of the health problems you might associate with the tropics are rare or nonexistent in Costa Rica (though they do still exist somewhat in neighboring Nicaragua), and the country's most popular destinations have plenty to offer families with kids.

▶ **Do a little homework.** Buy a guidebook and get familiar with your destination from home. Talk to other travelers you know or visit Fodors.com Travel Talk on-line forums to communicate with others based there or just back. Know the risks associated with your destination: are they comparable to the ones at home? Will they require new purchases, like a money belt that you wear under your clothes or a hard-core bug repellant? Also, research who you'll need to get in touch with if something goes wrong. With this important information handy, you'll have more time to relax and enjoy your trip.

▶ **Visit travel health Web sites.** Some of the best include Tripprep.com and Medicine Plus at www.nlm.nih.gov/medlineplus. The latter gives details about the causes and symptoms of illnesses and provides definitions of medical terms and information about first-aid treatments and disease prevention. You'll also find information about prescription drugs. The Centers for Disease

Control and Prevention Web site, www.cdc.gov/travel, explains the health risks associated with almost every country on the planet and what precautions to take.

▶ **Assess your health insurance.** It's likely that your existing policy won't cover you internationally. A short-term international policy with evacuation coverage is a wise investment if you plan to cross the border for an extended period of time.

▶ **Talk to your doctor.** Get a checkup, look into your last batch of shots including your MMR (measles, mumps, and rubella immunization) and tetanus, and discuss your travel plans ahead of time. Consult with your doctor about any drugs or vaccines recommended for your destination. Your doctor or a travel medicine expert can also recommend additional items that may be needed in a travel medical kit if you plan to spend an extended amount of time in remote areas.

▶ **Know the words for "I'm sick" in the local language.** This and other related phrases found, learned, or simply highlighted in a dictionary will help you in a pinch.

▶ **Pack a mini medical kit.** Reflect on your health, your habits, and your destination, and then anticipate what you might need to bring along in case you get a regular old illness (a blister, a stomachache, a sunburn) or an illness endemic to your destination.

THE ESSENTIAL TRAVEL MED KIT

Obviously, you shouldn't pack your entire medicine chest, but you also don't want to skimp when it comes to necessary or potentially lifesaving supplies. What bare medical necessities to bring? Although the contents of your medical kit will vary depending on where you're headed, most travel medicine experts agree that there are some items that ought to be in nearly every traveler's black bag.

▶ **Prepackaged antiseptic towelettes, bandages, and topical antibiotics.** The more you're out and about, the more likely you are to get a few scrapes. There's no sense letting a minor scratch develop into a major infection, especially if you're traveling to a remote area.

▶ **Flashlight.** Although not necessarily a medical supply, a flashlight is necessary for many situations, from unlighted city streets to midnight trips to the bathroom in jungle resorts run on generators.

▶ **Pepto-Bismol and Imodium.** Rich food or bad food can give you stomach troubles. Plan for them by bringing these tablets along.

▶ **Moleskin.** Although not lifesaving, this adhesive padding can be the key to preventing the activity-limiting blisters that are likely to develop as you trek from site to site.

▶ **Sunscreen.** A sunburn is not only annoying but also cancer-causing. It can also hamper your skin's ability to perspire, which is essential for preventing your body from overheating in hot climates.

► **Motion sickness drugs.** Dramamine tablets and Scopamine patches can relieve a lot of discomfort if the boat crossing is rougher than expected or the bus ride is wickedly bumpy.

► **Thermometer in a sturdy case.** The best way to assess whether you have an infection needing a doctor's care is to take your temperature to see if you have a fever.

► **Pain killers.** Such pain relievers as Tylenol, Advil, or Nuprin can come in handy for treating headaches, joint pain, and fever.

► **Hydrocortisone 1% ointment or cream.** The alien bacteria you may encounter when you go swimming in the sea or other natural bodies of water can trigger itching or a rash, which this cream can counter. It can also help relieve those unbearable symptoms of a poison ivy rash.

► **Allergy medicine.** If you are an allergy sufferer, take along some antihistamines: your allergies may not be acting up at home prior to departure, but changes in altitude and a different clime at your destination may trigger even an occasional allergy. Of course, if you have food allergies, reactions to bee stings, or other specific conditions requiring medications, make sure you have an ample supply before you hit the road.

► **Special ointments.** If you are a woman prone to yeast infections, over-the-counter creams for these infections, such as Monistat or Gynelotrimin, should also be in your medical kit. And if you are a person who suffers from athlete's foot or jock itch, don't forget an antifungal cream.

▶ **Repellents.** A mosquito repellent containing DEET (N,N-diethylmetatoluamide) is especially critical if you are traveling to tropical areas where malaria, yellow fever, dengue, and other mosquito-borne diseases are likely to lurk. Skin-So-Soft and Naturapel are two DEET-free repellants for areas without malaria. You could also pack mosquito coils.

▶ **Antimalarial drugs.** These are also essential if you are traveling to an area where malaria is prevalent, such as Africa, central and northeastern South America, India, and southeastern Asia. You will need a prescription for an antimalarial.

▶ **Water purification tablets, packets of oral rehydration salts, and Cipro or Bactrim.** As many as half of all travelers experience the dreaded traveler's diarrhea. Water purification tablets (found in sporting goods stores and pharmacies) can help prevent it, and oral rehydration salts (found at pharmacies) and the antibiotics Cipro or Bactrim are used to treat it. You need a prescription for the antibiotics, which should be used only to treat—not prevent—traveler's diarrhea.

▶ **Condoms.** These can be lifesaving, no matter where you travel—and they may not be available everywhere.

SHOTS AND MEDICINES

▶ **Check with the Centers for Disease Control and Prevention (CDC).** Ask about health risks and get information on vaccinations, drinking water, cruise ship sanitation details, and many other health issues. Call the hot line for international travelers at 877/394–8747 or visit the CDC's Web site at www.cdc.gov/travel. This is especially important if you plan to visit remote regions or stay for more than six weeks.

▶ **Don't put off getting your shots and medicines.** Some preventative inoculations, like those for hepatitis B, require three shots over a period of six months. You must get the first two within a month of each other before you travel; the third can usually be administered after your return home. Drugs that prevent malaria—antimalarials—also require you to take them before you leave for an affected area. Be sure to do your research, though, as some antimalarial drugs are more effective in some parts of the world than others and some have unpleasant side effects.

▶ **Watch out for mosquitoes.** Malaria, dengue, and yellow fever are carried by mosquitoes, so in areas where they are prevalent, take precautions and consider antimalarial pills for malaria or get a yellow fever vaccination in advance. There is no dengue vaccine. Carefully use insect-repellant topical sprays with DEET and wear long pants and long-sleeved shirts from dusk to dawn, when biting is prevalent. Depending upon your lodging conditions, you may want to bring mosquito coils and a mosquito net for sleeping; you could even take it a step further and have the netting dipped in permethrin insecticide.

▶ **Never pack prescription drugs in checked bags.** If your luggage is lost, you may not be able to get what you need in Vacationland to stay well. Instead, carry them onto the plane with you, in their original packaging; they might otherwise arouse suspicion at customs. Be sure to pack enough of any medication you take to last a few days longer than the entire trip.

▶ **Bring an extra prescription written generically and noting potency.** Have the generic drug name indicated in case your brand isn't available. You may also ask your doctor to write the potency information, as this may vary from country to country.

▶ **In your carry-on, pack extra eyeglasses or contacts.** In luggage to be checked, never pack prescription drugs and valuables.

MEDICAL ASSISTANCE

▶ **Consider signing up with a medical-assistance company.** No one plans to get sick while traveling, but it happens. Medical-assistance company members get doctor referrals, emergency evacuation or repatriation, 24-hour telephone hot lines for medical consultation, cash for emergencies, and other personal and legal assistance. Coverage varies by plan, so review the benefits of each carefully: International SOS Assistance Emergency (www.intsos.com) provides evacuation services and referrals for people traveling more than 100 miles from home; WebMD (www.webmd.com) is a medical information site that discusses providers of medical coverage, evacuation and trip-cancellation insurance, and the types of policies available to supplement your regular health insurance while you're abroad.

EXTREME DESTINATIONS

▶ **Visit your doctor before you book your trip**. Get a checkup first so you know that your body can survive the trip you have in mind. Tell your doctor exactly what your plans are and if they include high altitudes, scuba diving, or extreme climates.

Altitude

▶ **Climb carefully.** Altitude mountain sickness—which causes shortness of breath, nausea, and splitting headaches—may be a problem when you visit Andean, Himalayan, and other high-altitude countries. The best way to prevent it is to ascend slowly. Spend a few nights at 6,000–9,000 ft before you head higher. If you must fly straight in, plan on doing next to nothing for your first few days. If you begin to feel ill, local traditional remedies are a good way to go—in Chile, for example, there's an herbal tea made from coca leaves. Over-the-counter analgesics and napping also help. If symptoms persist, return to lower elevations. Note that if you have high blood pressure and/or a history of heart trouble, check with your doctor before traveling to the mountains. If a gradual ascent is not possible, acetazolamide may be used prophylactically. The CDC reports that dexamethasone and nifedipine also may be carried for emergencies.

Beat the Heat

▶ **Avoid becoming overheated or dehydrated.** To avoid losing too much water and salts from excessive perspiration, allow your body to get used to hot weather slowly by gradually boosting the amount of time you spend in the hot outdoors each day and planning outdoor activities and tours in the morning or evening when it's not so hot.

▶ **Drink lots of water before, during, and after your jaunts outdoors.** Don't rely on thirst to tell you when to drink; people often don't feel thirsty until they're a little dehydrated. If you're exerting yourself, drink about a quart an hour. Also, refrain from drinking alcoholic beverages, which cause you to lose more fluid.

▶ **Wear a hat, long but lightweight clothing, and sunscreen.** It should go without saying, but these strategies really help your body to cope with high temperatures. Choose a hat with a broad brim and wear loose, lightweight, and light-color clothing. Don't assume that shorts and sleeveless shirts are the way to go—take a look at what the locals are wearing. It's likely they're wearing long pants or skirts and long-sleeve shirts to protect themselves from the sun. Whatever you wear, slather all exposed skin with a good high-number sunscreen—a sunburn will hamper your skin's ability to perspire and keep you cool.

▶ **Plan to rest frequently while exerting yourself.** Visit an air-conditioned space or try cooling off with a cold shower or bath.

▶ **Know the telltale signs of dehydration.** These include crying without tears, a dry tongue or mouth, no pooling of saliva under the tongue, sunken eyes, no sweat under the armpits during a fever, dizziness, lightheadedness, or headaches. Especially look out for signs of dehydration in children—vomiting and diarrhea can quickly reduce their body fluids to dangerously low levels.

▶ **Avoid heat cramps.** Heat cramps stem from a low salt level due to excessive sweating. These muscle pains usually occur in the abdomen, arms, or legs. When children say they can't take another step, investigate if they have cramps—sometimes they really mean it. If you have heart problems or are on a low sodium diet, get medical attention for heat cramps. Otherwise, stop all activity, and sit quietly in a cool place and drink clear juice or a sports beverage. Then, don't do anything strenuous for a few hours after the cramps subside. See a doctor if heat cramps persist more than an hour.

▶ **Watch out for heat exhaustion.** Your body's response to an excessive loss of both water and salt is to emit warning signs, which may include heavy sweating, pallor, muscle cramps, tiredness, weakness, dizziness, headache, nausea or vomiting, fainting, fast and shallow breathing, and a fast and weak pulse. Heat exhaustion can progress to heat stroke, which can be deadly. Seek medical attention immediately if your symptoms are severe or last longer than an hour, or if you have heart problems or high blood pressure. In the meantime, be sure to rest, drink cool fluids, and, if possible, take a cold shower or recover in an air-conditioned site.

▶ **Listen to your body's pleas to cool down.** Heat stroke occurs when all your body's means of coping with heat shut down, allowing your body temperature to quickly soar. Heat stroke can kill or cause permanent disability if not dealt with immediately; watch for signs of heat stroke in yourself and your companions. These may include high body temperature (above 103°F or

39°C); red, hot, and dry skin (no sweating); rapid, strong pulse; throbbing headache; uncontrollable muscle twitches; dizziness; nausea; confusion; and unconsciousness. These signs warrant immediate emergency medical attention. Until such medical care arrives, cool the victim rapidly with shade, cold water from a hose, a fan, ice cubes, or air-conditioning. Give fluids to the conscious victim, and prevent choking during vomiting by turning the victim on his or her side.

Enduring the Cold

▶ **Know the myths and facts of hypothermia.** It does not have to be below freezing for you to get hypothermia: This potentially fatal decrease in body temperature occurs even in relatively mild weather. Symptoms are chilliness and fatigue, followed by shivering and mental confusion. The minute these signs are spotted, get the victim to shelter of some kind and wrap him or her in warm blankets or a sleeping bag. Ideally another member of the party should climb into the sleeping bag, too. If practical, it's best for both people to be unclothed, but if clothing remains on, it must be dry. High-energy food and hot drinks also aid recovery. To avoid hypothermia, always carry warm, dry clothing, avoid immersion or exposure to cold water or rain, and keep energy levels up by eating high-calorie foods like trail mix.

▶ **Shorten your exposure time.** Frostbite is caused by exposure to extreme cold for a prolonged period of time. Symptoms include the numbing of ears, nose, fingers, or toes; white or grayish-yellow skin is a sure sign. Frostbite victims should be taken into a warm place as soon as possible, and wet clothing should be removed. The affected area should then be immersed in warm—not hot—water or wrapped in a warm blanket. Do not rub the frostbitten area, as this may cause permanent damage to the tissues. When the area begins to thaw, the victim should exercise the area, to stimulate blood circulation. If bleeding or other complications develop, get to a doctor as soon as possible.

Water Sports

▶ **Don't fly within 24 hours after scuba diving.** Find out where the closest decompression chambers are ahead of time, just in case.

▶ **Don't skimp on scuba diving training.** Resorts often offer guests introductory scuba instruction in a pool, followed by a shallow dive; some hotels have on-site dive shops. All shops or resorts should offer instruction and certification according to the standards set by either the National Association of Underwater Instructors (NAUI) or the Professional Association of Diving Instructors (PADI). Prices will vary place to place, but the quality of a program should not.

▶ **Don't swim alone in unfamiliar waters.** Similarly, never swim too far offshore; most beaches, except for the big, public U.S. ones, have no lifeguards.

▶ **Anticipate someone getting seasick.** Have them look out at the horizon, offer them Dramamine, or consider pulse-point bracelets, which some travelers swear by.

TUMMY TROUBLE

▶ **Prepare at home to avoid illnesses related to food and water.** These diseases range from the common traveler's diarrhea and the preventable hepatitis A to more serious afflictions like food poisoning, cholera, Typhoid fever, and parasites. These can be avoided in some part by knowing what exactly to expect in the way of local eating habits, how you'll select your meals ahead of time, and by giving your body a chance to adjust to the new environment and develop some immunity.

▶ **Think twice about consuming suspect food.** Locals eating it may have developed immunity to sicknesses you aren't prepared for or may carry the very illness you're trying to avoid. Commonly suspect foods include street food or food made in unlicensed restaurants (this might apply to a few places or an entire country) where hygiene standards aren't enforced; raw foods, including peeled fruit and vegetables that have been handled and/or washed, such as salads; cooked food that has been allowed to cool; shellfish and fish derived from water with high levels of toxins; and undercooked meat.

▶ **Avoid the curse of all travelers.** Traveler's diarrhea, caused by eating contaminated fruit or vegetables or drinking contaminated water, is the most prevalent form of illness away from home. Depending upon where you're going, avoid ice, uncooked food, and unpasteurized milk and milk products (including ice cream—sometimes made from powdered milk reconstituted with untreated water), and drink only bottled water or water that has been boiled for 10 minutes, even when brushing your teeth. Mild cases may respond to Imodium (known generically as loperamide) or Pepto-Bismol, both of which you should bring with you but can be purchased over the counter; paregoric, another antidiarrheal agent, sometimes requires a doctor's prescription. Make sure to stay hydrated.

Food Poisoning

▶ **Know the symptoms.** Both the stomach flu and food poisoning are caused by microbial invasions that trigger inflammation in the lining of the stomach and intestines. Stomach flu tends to be set off by viruses passed directly from person to person, while food poisoning is usually caused by bacteria harbored in food or drink. But the end result is often the same—an unpleasant bout of diarrhea and vomiting that lasts a few days, with or without antibiotic treatment.

▶ **Focus on avoiding dehydration.** Don't worry about whether or not you have stomach flu or food poisoning. Either way, you can manage either by drinking more fluids, such as bottled, boiled, or treated water, or weak tea. You can also drink fruit juice (diluted with safe water) or clear soup.

▶ **Stay hydrated.** Drink plenty of purified water or tea—chamomile is a good folk remedy. If your diarrhea continues for more than a day, drink some safe water mixed with oral rehydration salts after each loose stool. Packets of these salts are available from most city stores or pharmacies, and you should carry a supply when you travel. Drink bottled water or other safe, bottled fluids. If necessary, follow this rehydration recipe: $\frac{1}{2}$ teaspoon salt and 4 tablespoons sugar per quart of water.

▶ **Seek medical care if symptoms persist.** These include dehydration; severe diarrhea (three or more loose stools during an eight-hour period), or uncontrollable vomiting. Vomiting or diarrhea that shows no signs of abating after a day or two or blood in your vomit or diarrhea are not normal. Severe diarrhea in a cholera-prone destination is a reason for an immediate doctor's visit. Most cholera cases are mild. But a serious case can prompt the rapid loss of large amounts of fluid, which can be deadly in just a few hours. Other possibly serious signs include severe abdominal pain (or pain emanating from one section of the stomach), a fever greater than 102°F (38.9°C) and dizziness or confusion.

▶ **Give your body time to heal itself.** Fortunately, your body usually quickly resolves most bouts of food poisoning without the aid of any treatments; vomiting and diarrhea get rid of most offending substances, and your immune system takes care of the rest. After just a few days you could be back touring, or returning home with most of your fond memories intact. It might take the pressure off to change your plans to those that keep you close to a bed, air-conditioning, a toilet, and medical services. This might mean forfeiting part of your trip and parking yourself in a city hotel or heading home.

PESKY PLANTS AND ANIMALS

▶ **Inquire which animals are threats in your destination.** Some animals, especially rodents, carry dangerous diseases. If you are bitten by a wild animal, it's important to see a doctor as soon as possible. Many animal bites require a tetanus shot and, if the animal could be rabid, a rabies shot. In other places, wildcats, bears, or monkeys can cause serious property and personal damage. Take all warnings seriously, including two big ones. Don't feed wild animals (they can confuse you for the food or become less able to fend for themselves) and use bear boxes where they're provided.

▶ **Know how to avoid and treat snakebites.** Snakes will do everything to avoid you, but in the event you have a run-in and are bitten, act quickly. If it's a harmless snake, ordinary first aid for puncture wounds should be given. If the snake is poisonous, remain as still as possible so as not to spread the venom through the body; lie down, keeping the wound area below the rest of the body, and have another person seek medical help immediately. The Brazos River Rattlesnake Ranch offers step-by-step emergency instructions at ww.wf.net/~snake/firstaid.htm.

▶ **Take care in deer-infested areas.** Lyme disease is a potentially debilitating illness caused by a virus carried by deer ticks, which thrive in dry, brush-covered areas. When walking in woods, brush, or through fields in areas where ticks may be found, wear tick repellent and long pants tucked into socks. When you undress, search your body for deer ticks—which are no bigger than a pencil point—and remove them with tweezers and rubbing alcohol. If you find a tick, save it if possible and watch the area for several weeks. Some people develop a bull's-eye-like rash or flulike symptoms; if this happens, see your physician immediately. Lyme disease can be treated with antibiotics if caught early enough. If you are traveling with pets, be sure to check them as well: Humans have been known to catch the disease by coming into contact with ticks from pets. See some illustrations of the deer tick and the tick-removal process at Lymediseaseinformation.com.

▶ **Familiarize yourself with poisonous plants.** Knowing how to recognize poisonous plants is half the battle. In new places, ask about which plants to avoid and never eat unfamiliar berries or leaves unless a local guide can confirm they're safe. If you touch poisonous plants (poisonous ivy, poison oak, or poison sumac), wash the area immediately with soap and water. A variety of ointments, such as Calamine lotion and cortisone cream, may relieve itching. The American Academy of Dermatologists has produced a useful primer at www.aad.org/pamphlets/PoisonIvy.html that includes pictures of local dangerous weeds, gruesome photos of plant-poison sufferers, and prevention and treatment tips.

PLAYING IT SAFE

▶ **Keep your passport with you at all times.** Many hotels ask for it upon check-in; however, all they really need are foreigners' passport numbers or a copy of the passport document page. Make photocopies of your passport in advance for this purpose, and give another to your family at home, and keep a third copy with you, separate from the original in case it gets lost or taken.

▶ **Know how to replace lost traveler's checks.** Bring the addresses of offices that handle refunds. Lost or stolen checks can usually be replaced within 24 hours. To ensure a speedy refund, buy your own traveler's checks—don't let someone else pay for them: irregularities like this can cause delays. The person who bought the checks should make the call to request a refund.

▶ **Don't wear a headset.** It gives someone a chance to catch you with your guard down. (On the other hand, sometimes music is good company on long trips and late at night, when you're trying to get to sleep in an unfamiliar room.)

▶ **Don't try to access your money belt while wearing it.** Once you fish for your bills, everyone will know you're a tourist. And once you're pegged as a paranoid tourist, you're a sitting duck. Your best bet is to stash "walking around" money in your front left pocket (crooks tend to go for the right one), in a bag, in your shoes—scattering your money around is better than stashing it all in one place. And carry whatever you carry at home or, better yet, use what the locals are carrying—just make sure it can close tightly. Use your money belt for extra traveler's checks or cash that you'll carry if you don't have an in-room safe.

▶ **Don't wear a fanny or waist pack.** Only tourists wear fanny packs (and someone can grab your arms while an accomplice rips off your pack). You'll stand out immediately. One Fodor's editor—who was dragged by her purse from a motor scooter in Palermo, Italy—swears by a money pouch that hooks to bra straps and hangs down inside the front of her shirt. She stores only a little money in her purse, to cover casual spending.

▶ **Know the local scams.** It's common for travelers to be overcharged for a taxi trip, to have a bag lifted or a pocket picked in a crowded bus terminal, and to get a bad exchange rate. Some places have specific rackets—check your guidebook. Gypsy children flanking tourists in Rome are a notorious example.

▶ **Make a business-card size currency converter chart.** Store it with your money to avoid getting short-changed.

▶ **Get your bearings before you head out.** You'll call attention to yourself as a tourist if you're bewildered and reading a map on a street corner or from behind the wheel of a slowly moving car. If you know where you're going ahead of time, you can walk with an air of confidence and purpose that deters bad guys.

► **Be alert for high-crime areas.** You should know where the bad parts of town are before you find yourself in them. Know about those tricky kinds of neighborhoods or places that are safe by day and become less friendly at night. The same goes for places that may take kindly to locals, but not visitors.

► **Head out in groups, if possible.** Use your common sense and take a taxi or the advice of your hotel staff about where to go and what to do, if you must go it alone.

► **Be cautious in remote places.** Some destinations contain open roads and beautiful scenery but few well-traveled places to stop and enjoy the view. You'll be tempted to stop and look while driving, which is dangerous. Always lock your doors, even in small towns where nothing seems likely to go wrong. And never leave your belongings in plain sight in the backseat.

SHAKY DESTINATIONS

► **Check out the U.S. government's travel advisory Web site.** If you are planning a trip abroad and have concerns about the safety of the destination. Current travel warnings are listed by country on-line at Travel.state.gov. Note that this advice is probably the most conservative you'll encounter. (Even Cancun seems dangerous by these descriptions.) Fortunately, nearly every country is listed, so it's a good way to begin to assess the safety situation. Always check back with the State Department for updates before departing.

▶ **Carry the American Overseas Citizens Services hot line numbers.** It's 888/407–4747 or 202/501–4444 from overseas.

▶ **Know where the U.S. Embassy is in your destination.** Even if you aren't going to a far-flung or potentially dangerous destination, always keep a list of local embassies with you, complete with phone numbers and dialing codes. Let the embassy know you're there and give them a copy of your itinerary, and leave a copy of the list of embassy numbers with friends or family at home.

▶ **Don't make your American identity especially obvious.** Do your best to blend in with the locals.

▶ **Check in regularly with someone at home.** Tell friends when they can expect your calls and give them a copy of your itinerary. And don't forget to call.

▶ **Make sure you will have access to your money.** Are ATMs available? Is your ATM pin number four digits (six digits is uncommon in some places) and wired for your destination? Are traveler's checks or credit cards widely accepted? These are things you'll want to know before you go.

▶ **Find out if your cell phone will work in your destination.** If not, you can rent one in many foreign countries or get a prepaid phone card to make calls home.

NOT ONLY FOR SOLO WOMEN

▶ **Follow the women-and-children rule.** If you see women around, especially women with children, you've got less to worry about. This is critical at night. If all you see is men, men, men, high-heel it out of there.

▶ **Don't speak to creeps—in any language.** If you're dealing with an unsavory guy who speaks English, don't say hello back. Shake your head or shrug your shoulders and say "No English." If he says "Speak Italian?" say "French, no." If he says "Speak French?" say "German, yes." However, do learn such key phrases as "Help" and "Get lost" in the language of the country you're visiting.

▶ **Make like you're hitched.** Whether you're married or not, straight or not, consider wearing a wedding band. If a man bothers you, say you're meeting your husband soon, or pat your belly to indicate you're pregnant.

▶ **Never look at maps in public.** Memorize them in advance, or look at them in a café or your hotel room. In many cities you can buy credit card-size street and transportation maps—which you can glance at inside your purse, so no one knows what you're doing. Or sketch a rough map of major streets and write down the exact addresses and directions for places you're going, to avoid the map problem altogether. You might also want to bring a compass to help you get your bearings when you're lost, or just for navigating labyrinthine streets.

▶ **Consider going first-class on trains.** If you're nervous or simply want to relax, stick with first-class, sit in a corner, and don't meet anyone's eye—keep your stuff on the seat next to you and scowl a lot.

▶ **Trail other women in bazaars.** They don't even have to know. One Fodor's editor, tired of being stared at in Calcutta, walked closely behind a woman with kids, which quickly put an end to the stares. Another time she asked a middle-aged woman if she could walk with her. The lady graciously obliged, and even bought her an orange.

▶ **Sit next to older women or a couple.** To avoid unwanted propositions, put yourself "in the orbit" of an older woman or a couple. Their presence may help deter sleazy offers and comments.

▶ **Wear sunglasses to avoid scrutiny.** People look away when they can't make eye contact.

▶ **Go high- and low-tech.** A cell phone can be invaluable, to call—or threaten to call—the police. But a whistle can be just as effective at warding off trouble.

▶ **Time your last stop of the day carefully.** Arrive in cities by midafternoon, long before it gets dark. If you arrive early, you've got more time to find a decent hotel and get your bearings. At night, however, stores shut down, streets become deserted, and hotels get full. The last thing you want to be is stuck without a place to sleep when it's late, you're tired, and you don't know your way around.

SAFETY AFTER DARK

▶ **Don't use a car when you're clubbing.** If you do, don't drink or else designate a driver. If you must drive, play it safe, try to park in a secure lot or garage where you won't be towed or ticketed the next morning in the event that you don't drive your own car home or back to your hotel at the end of the night. Feeling that you must move your car might compel you to try driving when you clearly should take a cab or get a ride from a friend instead.

▶ **Always carry a local cab company's phone number.**
Whether you're headed to a bar or a show, even if you drove your own car or are planning to get a lift from friends, always have a cab company's phone number handy. One of the best things about having a night on the town is potentially one of the worst: you never know quite what's going to happen. Be prepared that your original transportation plans may fall through—and make sure you have enough money with you for cab fare.

▶ **Alternate alcoholic drinks with nonalcoholic ones.**
A lot of club goers end up consuming more booze than they'd intended simply because they drink quickly or feel most comfortable always having a drink in hand. If you're planning a big night out, you can go easier on your body and even save money by ordering one non-alcoholic drink, or even two or three, for every one that contains alcohol.

▶ **Know how to avoid a hangover.** All those silly sayings about which types of alcohol can or should not be mixed, or what never to follow with what, are mostly myth. Obviously, the best way to avoid feeling like you've been run over by a truck the morning after a night of clubbing is simply to drink in moderation. But if you do end up getting tipsy, opt for the tried-and-true remedies: take one or two (but no more than the recommended dosage) pain relievers before bed, drink at least three glasses of room-temperature water before you fall asleep, and try having a light snack (avoiding overeating, and spicy or rich foods).

▶ **Don't accept drinks in bars from strangers.** Unless you see the bartender make the drink, follow this simple, common-sense variation on the advice your parents probably gave you as a kid: don't take candy from strangers. If you're in unfamiliar territory, around people you don't know, it's important to keep your wits about you. Scam artists and other ne'er-do-wells often appear to be the most charming people in a bar.

Eating

Eating out is a major part of every travel experience. It's a chance to explore flavors you don't find at home. (And the walking you do when sightseeing means that you can dig in without guilt.) In fact, culinary biographies like Ruth Reichl's *Tender at the Bone,* Jeffrey Steingarten's *The Man Who Ate Everything,* and Tony Bourdain's *A Cook's Tour* treat the relationship between food and place as if they're as inseparable as peanut butter and jelly. And they'd be right.

If you think about it, ingredients and cooking methods evolve from a landscape and sociocultural history that's site specific; particular dishes and preparation techniques, like spices, tell us something about who settled a place—or who tried and failed. Through the simple (or confusing) act of taking meals on a faraway trip, we're actually taking part in the history of a place.

This is probably why it's not recommended that you throw in the towel and visit all the recognizable eateries. McDonald's and TGI Friday's may have planted their flag in many an American's Vacationland, but the inability of these chains to offer anything other than their familiarity to travelers makes them much less compelling than what the locals are serving—unless you seek their recognizable comfort or the sometimes interesting way the menu is amended.

Food is comforting after all, and it can be a tad scary to trade that in for the new, the mysterious, and the mind-boggling. Eating while on vacation can be a pleasure (for one, we forfeit our kitchens and often can't cook for ourselves). It's a commonplace ritual and a sensory experience that's likely to be remembered years later, and likely inquired about as soon as you return home. The following tips aim to demystify the process of eating your way around the world. *Bon appétit.*

SAVING MONEY

▶ **Eat at the counter.** Note that in cafés, bars, and some restaurants in Paris, it's less expensive to eat or drink standing at the counter than it is to sit at a table. Some other destinations honor this method, too.

WHAT TO DO FOR THAT TABLE FOR TWO

While on vacation, Brad and Jennifer wanted to dine at Château le Cher, one of the fanciest restaurants in town. They'd heard marvelous things about it from friends who had been there, but when they called to get a reservation they were told that nothing was available for the week they were in town. Not ones to give up so easily, they immediately contacted the concierge at their hotel and explained their situation, hoping he might use his contacts to get them in. The concierge said he tried but was unable to get them a table, and instead suggested another restaurant, which he claimed was equally good. Not willing to take a chance on an expensive restaurant they had never heard of, Brad and Jennifer instead dined at a chain restaurant near the hotel: It wasn't fancy, but they knew what they were getting and it didn't break their bank. Still, they couldn't help but wonder whether there was anything more they might have done to get a table at the Château le Cher. Was there?

▶ FODOR'S FIX

First of all, Brad and Jennifer need to know that you don't necessarily need a reservation to get a table at many popular restaurants, even the hottest ones in town. Even if you've tried to get a reservation for a certain date and were told that the restaurant was booked solid, try calling back again the day you wish to dine there to see whether there were any cancellations for that evening. Be sure to remind the reservationist that you called already—mentioning that you have just one night in town won't hurt, either—and if there is still nothing available, ask to have your name put on a waiting list and pass them your cell phone or hotel number. Although it might have less glamorous connotations, many restaurants allow guests to eat at the bar or in a cocktail lounge, partaking from the same dinner menu, without a reservation. It's always worthwhile to ask. If you must have a table, when you arrive at the restaurant that night, introduce yourself to the host or maître d', tell them how much you are looking forward to the evening, and ask if you may wait in the bar should a table become available. Settle in, order a drink, and remember to be patient. Keep a good attitude and share your situation with your bartender, who might be able to help; by sitting tight, the restaurant is more likely to find a way to accommodate you. But know it's a gamble and that you might not get a table.

The Bottom Line: Be aware that some concierges have ulterior motives in suggesting a restaurant: It's not uncommon for a concierge to receive some form of remuneration, anything from a free dinner to a cash payment, from restaurant owners for sending business their way. Although this practice is officially frowned upon, it still takes place, even at some of the world's most renowned hotels. And remember that if the concierge succeeds in getting you the coveted table, a big thank you—and a tip (about $10)—is in order.

▶ **Get a cheap meal at happy hour.** You might be surprised just how much free food you can find at certain bars during happy hour. Not only do bars frequently offer great drinks discounts at happy hour, they sometimes set up hors d'oeuvres buffets, dole out pizza and sandwiches, and pass around big bowls of nuts and snacks.

▶ **Don't pay for an expensive hotel breakfast.** Of course, if it's included, by all means, indulge. However, hotel restaurants can be expensive and mediocre; ask the concierge or staff about the neighborhood's bagel shops, cafés, and coffee places.

▶ **Check out the local supermarket.** That's especially true if you're staying put for a while or have a hotel with kitchenette. You'll get better prices here than at hotel shops, and you'll get a good look at cultural habits by seeing what the locals purchase.

▶ **Have a picnic.** The proliferation of inviting prepared-food shops, chichi delis, boulangeries, and the like mean that you can cobble together a veritable feast without forking over a tip. Find a special sanctuary—a bench overlooking a canal, a low stone wall in a park, a shady and grassy spot under blossoming trees—and bring your Leatherman or other multipurpose slicing-and-bottle-opening tool.

▶ **Don't assume you can use your credit card.** Know before you go. It's always fun to be surprised—but not when you can't cover your check. Some countries don't have the phone lines required to run a credit card processing machine or prefer not to wait for reimbursement from companies—although invariably some of the top-notch places or hotel restaurants do. If you must use credit, call ahead or have your hotel investigate on your behalf which restaurants take cards.

▶ **Plan a whole day around sampling different foods.** Rather than having an entire meal at any one restaurant, move around and snack here and there. The idea isn't to get uncomfortably full, but to expose yourself to different kinds of restaurants, gourmet shops, markets, and even snack stands. For obvious reasons, you might want to incorporate a bit of walking into this plan, and you should also try doing this on a weekday, as restaurants are less crowded then, and more willing to let you drop in for just an appetizer or dessert. Not only is this a fun activity for food lovers, it has the inevitable effect of introducing yourself to several different parts of town.

▶ **Ask about special dinner prices.** If you can be flexible about when you dine, you can take advantage of early bird specials or pre- or post-theater special menus.

▶ **Don't treat roadside food everywhere with scorn.** There are definitely some places you should avoid it entirely and other places where it's perfectly fine. Just make sure you've done some basic research, read your travel guide, and know the difference.

HOW TO GET WHAT YOU WANT

▶ **Start at the top.** Plan to take in a really good restaurant or two. A trip is a time to kick back and savor the pleasures of the palate. Read up on the culinary scene before you leave home, and ask friends who have dined there. Then reserve a table as far in advance as you can, remembering that the best establishments book up months in advance. Note that some restaurants require you to reconfirm the day before or the day of your reservation. Then again, some really good places will call you, so make sure to leave a number (perhaps your hotel?) where you can be reached.

▶ **Investigate whether your destination is vegetarian friendly.** Vegetarian visitors to Vietnam will find it easy to travel here. Since the country's largely Buddhist, a religion that shuns eating living things, you'll find a variety of delightful dishes to try. On the other hand, some countries have yet to really figure out what counts as vegetarian. On a trip to Peru, a veggie traveler tried to content herself with rice and salsa (even the beans had lard), but grew frustrated, and asked for a vegetarian *sopa* (soup). While the broth may have derived solely from veggies, floating within the bowl was a solitary chicken foot.

▶ **Get a reference.** If you have a business colleague based in your travel destination or friends who just returned from a trip there themselves, ask them for their firsthand advice on where to go and where not to.

▶ **Let the concierge know what you want in a restaurant.** You get what you ask for. Make sure he or she understands whether you want to dine with other visitors or seek a place with plenty of locals. If you want to experiment with cuisine, make that clear, too.

▶ **"Take a bite of butter."** That's *Gourmet* editor-in-chief Ruth Reichl's advice. "And if it tastes like the refrigerator, leave." Put another way, give a new place a test run. Have an appetizer or a hard-to-wreck entrée and see how well a place rates before bringing someone important or a group of finicky eaters.

▶ **Order what other diners are eating.** Kindly ask the diners at an adjacent table what they're eating or, lacking language skills, carefully point to the meals of others while politely nodding, so your food server can effectively interpret.

▶ **Eat where locals do.** This might not be such a big surprise, but many tourist destinations, even in big cities where there are lots of choices, have tourist traps where the food is mediocre (or worse) and the prices are unreasonably high. There's a reason New Yorkers don't usually eat in Times Square, for example. You'll almost always have a better meal—and at a price that's right—when you eat where the locals do. If you can't land a local newspaper or travel guide, ask the hotel staff where they'd go for a special meal, or seafood, or a cheap meal, or the like.

▶ **Eat at the bar.** It's a more casual and relaxed way to enjoy a high-end or even moderately priced restaurant; you can chat with the bartender or chefs and learn more about the restaurant, the local dining scene, or other local topics, and also with your fellow diners, who may be interesting people or have good tips on what's going on in the area; and you can generally show up without reservations and get a seat fairly quickly. The only downside to bar dining is that smoking may be permitted. If that matters to you, find out the policy before you sit down.

▶ **To get good service, be nice.** "It's nice to be nice" and no one appreciates it more than a food server, who will easily distinguish you from the bossy, finicky, overly entitled diners filling up the restaurant. A simple "How are you?" or willingness to ask questions (not too many!) about a dish before it's served can help predispose your server to act friendly and eliminate disappointments with your food choice.

▶ **Know what local reviewers say about a place.** Unless you're traveling way off the beaten path, many restaurants in any given city are written up in guide-books, newspapers, and magazines. Short of dining with a local who knows the ropes, these can be essential for finding a place to eat in a country where the language is unfamiliar and the cuisine mystifying.

▶ **Speak up if something's wrong.** If something is incredibly, and inedibly, salty or burned or has meat in it and you're a vegetarian, politely let your server know. The server wants you happy, since you're the primary source of his or her income, and may offer another meal in its place or perhaps a free dessert, as a gesture of good will.

Ordering

▶ **Get a traveler's picture dictionary.** Sold in many travel stores, these laminated books more resemble children's primers than tools for traveling adults. But before you make fun, consider it's a sound way to communicate without learning to read a tough language like, say, Tamil. (One such book is Dieter Graf Verlag's *Point It,* sold for about $8 at Flight 001 in New York; www.flight001.com.) You simply flip to one of the many pages dedicated to food items, politely get your food server's attention, and point.

▶ **Ask for help deciding what to eat.** Ask, "If I could only eat here once in my life, what should I order?" Food servers will usually have lots of great advice when you put it to them that way. (Although you could simply ask what's popular, you might not approve of the local clientele's selection.)

▶ **Sample the cuisine your destination is known for.** Or, if you're a serious food-lover and know what to expect, find out what chefs are locally famous. A terrific way to learn about a place is to eat there.

▶ **Beware "American" food.** Some places do a pretty poor imitation of pretty basic American dishes. Don't blame them: Local ingredients and cooking styles don't often lend themselves to creating an exact replica of, say, a thick, juicy hamburger.

LOCAL CUSTOMS

▶ **Don't eat with your left hand.** In many countries, this is offensive, as is using it to pass food. Always observe local manners and taboos. Is yours a destination where no implements or napkins are used, but a sink is nearby (southern India)? Where pointing or piercing food with chopsticks is downright rude (Japan)? Or perhaps you're going to Bangkok, Thailand, where the fork is not sent to mouth, but is held in the left hand and used to push food to the center, where it is scooped with the spoon and eaten. Make it your business to know the eating customs before you go—or enlist someone to teach you when you arrive.

▶ **Don't try to lunch at 3 PM.** Many restaurants close between lunch and dinner, either to "change kitchens," restaurant-speak for what happens when a place accommodates a different menu at dinner, or for traditional reasons, like to observe a siesta. In other words, know when to eat. In addition to off hours, be aware that both breakfast and dinner might start earlier or later than you're used to. If you don't know the hours and customs of the place you're going, you may find yourself cranky and hungry while waiting for mealtime to roll around again.

▶ **Ask what's included.** In a Mexican restaurant in nearly any U.S. city your first basket of chips and salsa is usually free. In upscale French restaurants, the chef will often send out a complimentary *amuse bouche* (a small treat from the kitchen; literally a "mouth teaser") before or between courses. In Portugal, the lavish dishes of cheese, olives, spreads, and bread put before you are not free. If you're in any doubt about what's included, ask first. It's hard to get something that you've eaten taken off the bill.

▶ **Make lunch your big meal.** In many countries, from Egypt to Costa Rica, lunch is the main meal of the day, when a larger array of entrée options is proffered and portions are big. Although some restaurants will cater to American customs, smaller places may not.

▶ **Don't enforce your strictest diet plans on vacation.** How will you truly know that New Zealand is the Land of Milk and Honey if you eat just celery sticks? Let yourself have a scoop of the nation's world-renowned Hokey Pokey ice cream and just plan to have a good walk home and a light dinner later.

▶ **Eat internationally.** Many cities have an international district where you eat your way across the world without having to travel there. One such example is the neighborhood of Newtown, in Sydney, Australia, where you can affordably work your way through the cuisines of four countries in one block.

▶ **Know how to tip.** Some countries expect a tip from Westerners but not from locals. Others expect a bit of change left over from the bill. In China, a tip of 3% of the bill is fine; in New York City, food servers expect 20%. To keep up with the rules, consult your travel guide.

FOOD AND WHINE: EATING WITH KIDS

▶ **Prep their palates.** Warm your kids to the idea of foreign fare by exposing them at home to some of the food they may experience on their trip. French or Thai food is less daunting when it's delivered in a familiar setting or comes out of a take-out box.

▶ **Bring comfort food.** If you're traveling to a location where your child's favorite food may not be available, mention this to your kids while planning your trip—then take along a familiar treat to help ease the withdrawal.

▶ **Pack snacks.** Restaurants and roadside stands seldom seem to appear when you need them most. Avoid snacks that melt, crumble, stick, or dribble down chins. Instead, fill zip-top plastic bags with unsalted pretzels, crackers, and bite-size pieces of cheese. For children over age 4, add trail mix, dried fruit or easy-to-eat fresh fruit, popcorn, and raw vegetable sticks. Water is the best car drink, because it doesn't stain or stick when spilled; refillable bottles with straws or squirt attachments are handy and easy to use.

▶ **Never arrive hungry.** Famished children are notoriously miserable children, and Murphy's Law dictates that the hungriest people in the restaurant will be served last. Avert disaster with bread, crackers, or the Cheerios or graham crackers you have stashed in your bag.

▶ **Order for the kids first.** There's no shame in staggering everyone's meals, regardless of the type of restaurants—the timing will benefit everyone. Before your server even finishes saying, "Hello my name is . . .," place your order for the little ones. Request grown-up drinks and fare when the server returns.

▶ **Let them eat cake.** The most brazen approach to the staggered meal works best at your hotel: feed kids their main dish via room service and later let them eat dessert while you enjoy dinner. It may raise a few eyebrows among your fellow diners, but as long as they're well behaved, who cares?

▶ **Be creative.** Don't feel shackled by the children's menu, and don't despair if there isn't one: many restaurants will be happy to adjust grown-up meals. Linguine without the clam sauce and chicken Parmesan without the Parmesan (but maybe with ketchup) are good bets.

▶ **Pack a stash of little packages of ketchup.** If your child usually slathers it on everything, come prepared. For the record: the French don't actually have a word for "ketchup."

▶ **Determine the kitchen's flexibility before you sit down**—and also ask beforehand whether the special kiddie meal has a special grown-up price.

▶ **Take a hint.** You may have the most well-behaved cherubs on the planet, but that will be irrelevant if the restaurant doesn't want them. "We don't prohibit children, but we don't recommend bringing them" is a hint. Take it and move on.

▶ **Keep your sense of humor.** The fancy macaroni and cheese made with real cheddar and Parmesan pales next to the freeze-dried cheese-food product your children love at home. The restaurant's pasta is too saucy, or your child is simply cranky. Whatever the cause of the fussiness—especially if it escalates into a meltdown—be considerate of the hapless diners around you. Pay your bill, and leave. Then enjoy your gourmet doggie bags back in your hotel room after the kids have gone to bed.

▶ **Order room service.** Kids love the ordering, the "special" delivery, and the eating in—think of it as an indoor picnic. And if they're feeling homesick, a hotel room may seem a bit more like home than a restaurant.

▶ **If all else fails, try takeout.** Grab some picnic fixings at a local food shop and head for a playground. Without the stress of a full-service meal, your kids might just become adventurous enough to sample a new flavor or two—and actually enjoy them.

▶ **Consider a finishing school.** If you'd like to try elevating your dining experiences with kids to a new level, visit one of the hotels that offers etiquette classes for children (Ritz-Carlton, for example).

▶ **Leave the kids with a sitter.** Some hotels have creative kids' programs or reputable baby-sitting services that can make it possible for the two of you to enjoy a few hours alone at a good restaurant.

10

For a Better Hotel Stay

According to travel-industry analysts, the average traveler's largest single expense is for lodging. But while many travelers spend hours seeking the best possible airfare, some spend comparatively little time researching their lodging options. To make things easier, we've broken down the process of selecting a hotel into a few simple steps and have collected our best insiders' tips to get you started. Three basic things to remember: Shop around, ask questions, and document your complaints if the lodging you choose doesn't live up to its guarantees.

CHOOSING A HOTEL

▶ **Define your needs.** Focus on hotels that will best meet your needs. Amenities, location, and price all come into play in making a determination, but do you care about a spa you won't use, a pool when it's the beach you're after, or that the clientele is all under 25? Do you want anonymity or the coziness of a small B&B? Luxury or rustic simplicity? A splurge or a super-saver? Look at photos on-line, ask around for recommendations, or call the hotel and ask them to explain what they've got to offer and who or what age their regular customers are.

▶ **Know the average rate for your destination.** Then factor in the type of hotel and add about 12% for taxes, more if you're going to a country with VAT tax. Location is everything: A room in a chichi inn going for $400 on Nantucket may go for $125 in the Florida Keys.

▶ **Look for weekend deals at business hotels.** High-end business hotels, which do most of their business during the work week, often drop their weekend rates just to fill rooms. Weekend leisure travelers might miss the best deal in town simply because they never considered staying at a business hotel.

▶ **Don't pay for amenities you won't use.** Business-oriented hotels often have higher weekday rates than vacation properties just because they have on-site business centers and amenities such as in-room fax machines and work desks. But the proliferation of portable faxes, powerful laptop computers, and other digital-communication devices has diminished the need for these perks. And since most business travelers use cell phones regardless of where they are staying, clients won't know whether they're calling you at the Plaza or the Quality Inn. (Your boss might appreciate the money-saving gesture, too.)

▶ **Be flexible when possible.** All aspects of travel are based on supply and demand, so be aware of your destination's peak season. If it's from December through April and you're coming at the end of April, you might save hundreds of dollars if you change your travel dates by a week or two. (Many properties will charge you the peak-season rate for your entire stay even if you straddle the change between peak and nonpeak seasons, so ask when the rates go down.)

▶ **Make use of frequent-flier miles.** If you have a credit card that gives you frequent-flier miles for purchases, contact the company (or visit its Web site) and ask about hotel deals or promotions during the time you'll be traveling. Also check with the airline(s) on which you have frequent-flier miles. Web sites such as www.webflyer.com track current promotions and offer tips about maximizing your miles.

▶ **Consider credit card privileges.** Travelers are often eligible for discounts they didn't know existed. If you throw out everything that comes in your credit card bill but your statement, for example, you many not notice the coupons for chain hotels. Look into perks affiliated with any professional memberships or ask the hotel to which organizations they grant discounts and deals.

▶ **Check the Web but consider the source.** To draw customers into booking on-line, major hotel chains offer Web-only deals you might not hear about over the phone. The Web is also a great place to find reviews of a single property, as well as pictures, maps, and even video clips that will help you narrow down your options. On many Web sites, you can find out what other travelers have to say about individual properties. As you browse, take what you see with a grain of salt. Photos can be framed so that you don't see the eyesores or snapped with a wide angle lens to make tiny quarters look spacious. And one past guest's "wonderful" and "charming" is another's "quirky" or worse. How someone responds to a property depends on his or her point of view—and that's where no two travelers are alike.

▶ **Create a user profile on your favorite chains' Web sites.** (Many independent properties also offer this service.) This way, your preferences—for no-smoking rooms or a king-size bed—can be automatically included in each reservation. You can store your credit card information, too, which will save time, and you'll usually be able to confirm or cancel reservations on-line even if you didn't book on-line.

▶ **Save on lodging costs by staying at hostels.** In some 4,500 locations in more than 70 countries around the world, Hostelling International (HI), the umbrella group for a number of national youth-hostel associations, offers single-sex, dorm-style beds and, at many hostels, rooms for couples and family accommodations. Membership in any HI national hostel association, open to travelers of all ages, allows you to stay in HI-affiliated hostels at member rates; one-year membership is about $25 for adults; hostels run about $10–$30 per night. Members have priority if the hostel is full; they're also eligible for discounts around the world, even on rail and bus travel in some countries.

▶ **Save your pennies for quality lodging.** It's one thing to stay in a fleabag hotel when you're a 20-year-old with a backpack. It's something else entirely when said backpack has a child in it.

RESERVING YOUR ROOM

▶ **Make hotel reservations way ahead.** In popular places, like Paris, rooms are sometimes booked a year in advance.

▶ **Compare prices and book on-line.** Many properties are listed on multiple Web sites. Depending on who is selling the room, prices can vary dramatically—by as much as 200% or more for the same room for the same date. You'll often find good prices at large on-line reservations services like Expedia, Travelocity, Orbitz, and Trip.com, but if the hotel that interests you has its own site, check there, too. And if the property is part of a chain, check the chain's site. Web discounters like Onetravel.com are another option, and some guarantee their rates: If you find a lower price within 24 hours, they'll refund the difference or let you cancel your reservation without penalty.

▶ **Bid for your rate on-line.** Depending on the destination, you can save 40% or more on hotels' regular rates on bidding sites liked Priceline or Hotwire. You choose an area and quality level of a hotel and then bid on a price—you'll hear back within minutes if your bid was accepted (and your credit card will be automatically charged).

▶ **Call the lodging, not a toll-free number.** If you've got specific needs or preferences, try this old-fashioned strategy: Use the telephone. But call your chosen hotel directly. Reservations agents at the toll-free numbers of major chains usually don't know much about individual lodgings. If you call the property itself, you're more likely to end up speaking with someone familiar with the rooms and the general lay of the land. (Don't be cheap: If the property doesn't have a toll-free number, foot the bill for a toll call.) Or call both and compare the price you're quoted by the person at each number. The reservationists manning the toll-free line may well be unaware that a large meeting group has just canceled, leaving a bunch of rooms empty the next week—and reservationists on-site are offering all kinds of deals just to fill the space.

▶ **Learn a few basic phrases in the local language.** For hotels in foreign countries, sometimes you need basic communications skills to determine whether the choice is appropriate for you—or whether rooms are even available for your travel dates.

▶ **Make your reservations via e-mail.** E-mails in place of long-distance calls which often entail figuring out time zones are a great way to go. When trying to communicate with hotel staff whose languages you don't speak, you can send an e-mail in English with the hope that they'll have a bit more time to track down a translator.

▶ **Have a bilingual friend make your reservations.** If you don't speak the language, have a friend who writes in French, say, send an e-mail, fax, or make a phone call on your behalf. Just be sure to communicate to them exactly what you're looking for.

▶ **Take the time to play investigative reporter.** You can ask the reservations agent straight out what's the best room in your price range or what rooms are most popular. But you can also play the reporter. Interview the agent about the various types of rooms available and ask what the advantages and disadvantages of each are. Ask to speak with the person's supervisor or someone at the front desk if the agent is unable to help you—surprisingly, even some on-site agents have never seen many (or any) rooms at the places they work. It's your money—make sure you get what you want.

▶ **Look for a floor plan.** Some Web sites contain floor plans of the hotel or of individual rooms. These will tell you definitively whether the photos have distorted the reality or conveyed it accurately. They will also show the relative locations of different features, and help you avoid a room by the elevator or at the remote end of a long corridor.

▶ **Make your desires clear.** If you have preferences about the room you'll be staying in, make them clear to the reservations agent. Some things to consider are: room size, smoking or nonsmoking, king or two queens (or double or two twins), high floor or low floor, patio or balcony. Need quiet? Insist on a room away from the elevator, or other high-traffic areas like bars, pools, restaurants, and service areas with ice and vending machines. Make sure you have all your questions answered before you give out your credit card number.

▶ **Check out the view.** If you hear the words "city view" or "ocean view," ask whether the view is obstructed or unobstructed. Also, in beach locations, be sure that your room is "beachfront" and not simply "waterfront." In Florida and many Caribbean destinations, for example, many visitors arrive at their "waterfront" hotels only to find themselves on the Intercoastal Waterway, a canal, or a bay, 10 or more minutes' drive from the actual beach.

▶ **Be detail-oriented.** If driving, ask if the hotel has a parking lot or covered garage and whether or not there is an extra fee for parking. In large cities like New York, some hotels have regular parking and valet parking in the same garage. If you don't ask, the attendant will assume you want your car valet parked, which has a higher daily surcharge than regular parking.

▶ **Play the newlywed game.** If you're going on your honeymoon, say so—mentioning the fact when you're making reservations might earn you a modest room upgrade. Hotels have also been known to furnish hungry honeymooners with free breakfast or champagne. One caveat: Hoteliers are becoming hip to the practice of fake honeymooning, so you might have to convince the person taking your reservation that you actually have just married.

▶ **Ask about planned renovations on-site or nearby.** It's hard for a reservations agent to predict construction too far in advance, but by all means, ask. (If you arrive at your hotel and find construction going on, request another room immediately. If the hotel cannot move you, request a rate reduction. Most hotel managers will accommodate you without argument.)

▶ **Hold your room with a credit card.** Most chain properties will hold your reservation until 6 PM; call ahead if you plan to arrive late. To hold a late reservation you may need to give your credit card number.

Some smaller properties, usually independently owned hotels and B&Bs, will charge your credit card even if you don't show up (or if you cancel from one day to two weeks before your scheduled arrival), so be sure you ask about the hotel's guaranteed reservations policy when booking.

▶ **Ask for written confirmation.** After you've made your reservation, ask for written confirmation by snail mail or e-mail and when you get it, read it. Make sure everything you've asked for is in the confirmation, and take the confirmation with you when you travel and present it upon arrival. If there are any discrepancies between what you were promised and paid for and what you got, you'll have all the evidence you'll need to have the situation righted.

▶ **Call if you're going to be late.** If your reservation is for a certain hour, alert the hotel if you will be arriving later—even if it's only 15 minutes later. Hotel managers are under pressure to keep occupancy rates high, so unless they know for sure you're arriving they may give your room to someone else.

Facilities and Services

▶ **Know what facilities are included in the price.** Bathroom facilities in B&Bs and in hotels in France determine price. In France, state your preference for shower (*douche*) or tub (*baignoire*)—the latter always costs more. If you want a double bed, you should request one (*lit matrimoniale* in France); in many places twin beds are still common. If you're counting on air-conditioning or an in-room safe, ask if there's a surcharge. Staying in a remote jungle lodge? A Japanese ryokan? It might be tough to know what to expect, and your assumptions may be way off. For exotic and unique properties, it's even more important to call the property or do a little research if you don't like surprises.

▶ **Ask if there's a restaurant or room service.** Many lodgings offer room service, but not necessarily 24 hours a day. Moderately priced business-oriented hotels often keep menus of local restaurants that will deliver to your room.

▶ **Expect to forego some basics at budget hotels.** Most hotels have in-room telephones, for example, but double-check this at inexpensive properties, especially if you are traveling outside the United States. The same goes for TVs and air-conditioning. Most hotels and motels have in-room TVs, often with cable, in the United States, but the terms change when outside North America. International chain hotels tend to be the most predictable in terms of what in-room amenities you can expect.

▶ **Stairmaster? Free weights? Know the gym.** It could be anything from a room with a treadmill to a fully stocked gym. If you care about specific brands, speak up. At the very least, you'll know what to expect. Don't forget to ask about the hours, too.

▶ **If you have a disability, ask detailed questions.** Are there any stairs, inside or out? Are there grab bars next to the toilet and in the shower/tub? How wide is the doorway to the room? To the bathroom? Make sure there's accessibility not only in your bedroom but also in the bathroom and in the hotel's public facilities, such as lounges, pools, and restaurants. If you reserve through a toll-free number, also call the hotel to confirm the information from the central reservations office. Get confirmation in writing when you can.

If You're Bringing the Kids

▶ **Ask if the property welcomes children.** If you're planning to stay at a bed-and-breakfast, be sure to ask the owners in advance whether the B&B welcomes children. Some establishments are filled with fragile antiques, and owners may not accept families with children of a certain age. Motels, hotels, condos, and cottages, which cater to children, tend to offer more practical furnishings, kitchens, and sometimes laundry facilities. Often cottage or condo communities have play yards and pools, sometimes even full children's programs.

▶ **Find out the cutoff age for children's discounts.** Many hotels allow children under a certain age to stay in their parents' room at no extra charge, but others charge for them as extra adults. Remember that it's rare to find an inn with two beds in a room—stick with hotels with varied room configurations or two double beds per room.

▶ **Don't assume that you can get a crib.** Ask whether there will be an additional charge, and make sure it is a crib that meets current child-safety standards. If you show up and it doesn't, remove a bureau drawer and pad it up with towels—instant bassinet.

ON THE WAY TO YOUR HOTEL

▶ **The night before you go, reconfirm the rate.** If you have a hotel reservation and you suspect business might be a little slow, call the front desk directly—not the 800 number—just before you arrive and ask what the best rate is for the evening. In many cases, if it's late and the hotel is not full, you will be quoted a better rate than the one you got when you made the reservation— hotel managers are fully aware that an empty room generates no revenue. If the rate is not better, simply show up with your reservation as planned. However, if you have guaranteed reservations—the kind that charge your card even if you don't show up—this trick won't fly.

▶ **Make sure you are in the hotel's computer.** If you haven't booked the room yourself or with the hotel directly, there is room for error. Double-check that your reservation has been honored before you leave home and if your hotel engages in the practice of double-booking, they'll know you intend to honor your reservation.

▶ **Find out when your room will be available.** It might make more sense to head from the airport to a restaurant for lunch if your plane gets in at 11 AM and you can't check in until 2.

▶ **Bring your confirmation information.** Show it to the staff person when checking in. This is particularly important if you've booked on-line or through a third party, or are traveling as part of a tour package.

▶ **Don't head for the wrong hotel.** This may sound obvious, but in larger cities where chains have multiple properties you need to know whether you're heading to the Heavenly Hotels Downtown, the Heavenly Hotels Seaport, or the Seaside Heavenly Hotels Resort and Conference Center. Keep both the name and address handy, and ask about nearby landmarks when booking.

▶ **Get your name onto the computer.** Don't miss your phone calls. If you've left the kids with Grandma or are traveling for business and it's important that you can be reached at your hotel while you're en route, let the staff know ahead of time. Calls may not be waiting for you when you arrive otherwise. Similarly, late arrivals are often handled by night auditors who give you your key and leave the paperwork for the morning desk clerk; make sure he or she adds your name to the hotel's guest roster—particularly if you're expecting an early morning call.

AT THE HOTEL

▶ **Give up a copy of your passport—not the original.** The policy of leaving your passport with the desk is now somewhat moot—in-room safes mean travelers can store them there and all a hotel really needs for their protection is to see your passport and copy down the passport number. It's best not to be separated from your identification—this has become even more important in our post-9/11 world. Bring a few extra copies of your passport information page along and hand over those instead.

▶ **Ask to leave your bags if your room isn't ready.** You can start your vacation right away. Go grab something to eat, tour a museum, or head to the hotel pool or beach.

▶ **Request a late checkout, if there's no extra charge.** As a courtesy, most hotels will grant you an extra hour or two to leave your room, especially if it isn't booked for the upcoming evening. But you must call the front desk in advance and request a late checkout. If not, you'll likely be billed for additional hours or an entire day. If late checkout isn't available and you don't want to deal with your bags, ask to leave your bags with the bellhop.

▶ **Leave a fair tip.** Give inn staff and porters $1 per bag carried to your room, and leave about $2–$5 per night of your stay for maid service—more if extra service, like shoe shines, warrants it.

IN YOUR ROOM

▶ **See if everything is working.** Upon arriving, make sure everything works—lights and lamps, TV and radio, sink, tub, shower, and anything else that matters. Report any problems immediately. Also, check out the fire emergency instructions. Know where to find the fire exits, and make sure your companions do, too.

▶ **Make sure you've got everything you need.** If you're going to need extra pillows or blankets or an ironing board, call housekeeping right away so the items will be there when you want to use them.

▶ **Go easy on the unpacking.** If you will be staying in a hotel room for only one night, put anything you take out of your suitcase in one place or into a single drawer. That way you won't have to go looking through closets and under beds to make sure you didn't leave anything.

▶ **Pump up the volume (a little).** When you leave your hotel room—even at a nice lodging—be sure to leave the TV on with the volume turned up just loud enough to be heard outside the door. Thieves are less likely to try anything if they think someone is in the room watching TV.

▶ **Use the in-room safe.** Don't leave anything of value out in the room. In lieu of this, the hotel should be willing to store your items in their safe. You should itemize the objects you're asking them to store and have a staff person sign it.

▶ **Sleep soundly by providing your own white noise.** Raucous Parisian partying keeping you up at night in your hotel? Pack a small transistor radio and turn the dial to one of the channels that only beams "static"— white noise that sounds like an air-conditioner. Play this at sufficient volume and the noisy world outside your window will disappear.

▶ **Let the hotel know if your neighbors are noisy.** Some amount of noise is par for the course, but if it continues into the wee hours, let the hotel know and have them correct the problem. One way of convincing a hotel to take immediate action is to imply that there might be some destruction of property going on.

IF THINGS DON'T WORK OUT

If you've done everything we've described, your hotel stay should go swimmingly. If things are somewhat more complicated and something goes wrong, the strategies listed below can be helpful in rectifying matters.

▶ **Know how to handle overbooking.** Hotel managers routinely deal with problems associated with "over-sales," the industry term for booking more reservations than there are rooms. Even the best hotels engage in the practice, because a consistent percentage of all reservations are either canceled or result in no-shows.

Often the hotel will have a nearby "sister" property or an arrangement with another chain or hotel to honor overbooked reservations. If this is the case, you can usually get an upgrade to a larger room or suite at the substitute property for no extra charge. If the room is the same or inferior to the one you have reserved, demand a rate reduction for your inconvenience and inquire as to when a room at the hotel you originally chose will become available.

▶ **If there's a problem, deal with someone in authority.** Try to settle your dispute with the front-desk personnel, but if you're still not satisfied, ask to speak to the general manager. Keep in mind that it's the job of the front-desk staff to solve problems without involving the general manager. Use this knowledge to your advantage in disputes over small matters. If your problem is a big one, though, cut to the chase and demand an audience with a person in authority.

▶ **Pretend you're already in court.** Write down the names of everyone you speak with, when you spoke with them, and what he or she said. If you have a camera, take photos relevant to your complaint. This information is handy for presenting to corporate public-relations personnel, who are very sensitive to these occurrences, and are often quick to compensate unhappy guests—sometimes quite generously—for their troubles.

▶ **Ask for an adjustment or complete refund.** If hotel personnel are unable to deliver what you were promised, ask for an adjustment—a lower rate, for example, if you've gotten a lesser room than the one you were promised. If you received a confirmation notice and brought it with you, your claims will be all the more convincing.

▶ **Be specific, focused, and fair.** Regardless of the problem, be very specific about how you would like to see the situation resolved, but be fair: If noisy neighbors kept you awake one night of your two-night stay, don't demand a refund for both nights. You have a better chance of resolving your dispute if your expectations seem reasonable. Also, hotel managers have been trained to let aggravated customers vent until they tire of arguing, so be sure to initiate a dialogue rather than droning on ad nauseam. Stay focused, and reiterate your specific demands if the conversation veers away from the problem at hand.

▶ **Get confirmation in writing.** Hotel managers have been known to say anything to put an end to a disagreeable situation. Once you and management have agreed on a solution, get confirmation of your agreement in writing.

▶ **Contest the charge.** If you believe your complaint was not handled satisfactorily, get the names of the people involved, keep your receipts, and call your credit card company when you get home. Major credit card companies have departments that deal with contested charges, and most companies will not charge your card while the matter is under investigation.

11

Destinations

Some travel rules are fairly universal, such as "Do not show up late to the airport and expect the plane to be held for you." Others are specific to the destination to which you're traveling, and these may be harder to find out about if you're more of an armchair traveler or have never been to the place before. Many travelers innocently bring their home perspectives with them to their vacation destination, only to find they just don't work.

Fodor's hundreds of writers based around the world know the score. They don't just describe their exotic home or chosen land when they're authoring guidebooks; they also share the essential details of what the inherent quirks to life are and just how to see and do it all as a visitor—without a misstep.

AFRICA

Kenya and Tanzania

▶ **Before leaving home, make sure your credit cards can be used in East Africa.** Your bank card may not work or may access only your checking account.

▶ **Reconfirm international flights.** Call about flights to and from East Africa at least 72 hours before departure. Reconfirm your internal flights at least 48 hours before departure.

▶ **Bring your child's own car seat.** You may not be able to obtain one here.

▶ **Purchase faster film to help prevent overexposure.** The sun is more intense this close to the equator. A filter and lens hood will help to reduce the glare.

▶ **Use a telephoto lens to photograph wildlife.** Even standard zoom lenses of the 35- to 88-millimeter range won't capture a satisfying amount of detail. Buy one if needed.

▶ **Fend off mosquitoes.** Bites transmit malaria. In the evenings cover your arms and legs and apply plenty of insect repellent. Burning mosquito coils at night also helps to ward off mosquitoes; coils can be purchased everywhere. Travel with mosquito netting in case this is not provided by a hotel.

▶ **Dress conservatively.** East Africans, as a rule, are a reserved and religious people. Wearing revealing clothing is considered very disrespectful.

▶ **Stay calm.** If you are unhappy with something, discuss your dissatisfaction calmly and clearly. East Africans do not respond well to displays of anger, which often make people less inclined to help resolve a problem.

Morocco

▶ **Avoid coming to Morocco during Ramadan.** The Muslim calendar is lunar and dates for Ramadan and other religious holidays shift back 11 days each year. Non-Muslim travelers will probably want to avoid a visit at this time. During this monthlong fast, all cafés and nearly all restaurants are closed during the day, and the pace of work is reduced.

▶ **Don't wear shorts.** They're simply not acceptable for either sex anywhere in Morocco, except at the beach. Although this is a moderate Islamic society, it is best to adhere to modest dress in public.

▶ **Put a hold on the PDA.** Public Displays of Affection are not common between straight or same-sex couples. Furthermore, there is no "out" gay life in Morocco. Homosexual acts are strictly illegal, and travelers have been imprisoned as a consequence.

▶ **Know market prices when shopping.** You must negotiate when purchasing Moroccan specialties. There's no rule for the percentage by which you should aim to reduce the price, because some vendors start with a decent price and others start by inflating the price ten- or twenty-fold. Any kind of intermediary, like a guide, will inflate the price.

▶ **Decide whether you'll want a guide.** Official guides have a badge to prove it and cost about 300 DH a day. The rates of unofficial guides are negotiable, and you should fix it in advance. In places like Fez you'll find you need a guide just to protect you from being approached by other guides.

▶ **Practice local politeness.** Moroccans shake hands with each other every time they meet. Nothing can happen without politeness: if you have a problem and you lose your temper, you give up hope of solving it. A combination of courtesy and persistence is the best approach. Remember that people come first; the actions to be accomplished are secondary.

▶ **Be a good guest.** Know the customs. If you're invited to someone's home, do not enter until invited to do so. In more traditional homes, you'll have to leave your shoes at the door. For all food served in a communal dish and meant to be eaten by hand, be sure to use only your right hand. Using the left for any right-hand activities is generally thought of as rude, since the left hand is considered a means for attending to personal hygiene. Don't take or refuse food. Wait until offered and partake of something from the dish offered.

Egypt

▶ **To direct a taxi driver, name a nearby landmark.** Street addresses in Egypt are generally useless when it comes to locating a museum or a hotel or a restaurant. As you get closer to the destination, give more specifics; this will avoid confusion between you and your driver.

For mailing addresses, postal codes have been recently instituted. However, like street names, they're not commonly used.

▶ **Ask directions more than once.** Some people are loath to admit that they don't know where something is, partly out of pride and partly out of a misplaced desire to help. The result is that three people on the same block will give you entirely different directions to the destination you're trying to reach.

▶ **Do not photograph government buildings.** Even when the building looks innocuous, this action is viewed as a threat to national security and can lead to an uncomfortable confrontation with security personnel or even passersby.

▶ **Honk your horn to signal your presence.** If you don't, the other vehicle may not know you're there. In both rural and urban areas, Egyptians make constant use of their horns—to warn other drivers and cars of their presence, to tell them to get out of the way, to signal their desire to pass, or to signal a turn.

▶ **Dress more conservatively for mosques and churches.** Women should bring along a light scarf to place over their heads if necessary.

▶ **Don't accept any dog-eared bills.** Many vendors will refuse to take them. Just politely give it back and ask for a newer bill.

▶ **Observe local etiquette.** In any situation it is considered rude to put one's feet on the furniture or table. The more traditional taboo against using one's left hand to eat has largely disappeared as communal meals are less common and eating utensils are the norm. Still, if you find yourself sharing a meal from the same plate with someone, use your right hand to take food from the main plate.

▶ **Drink only bottled water.** In Egypt the major health risk is "gippy tummy"—traveler's diarrhea varying in intensity from mild to disablingly severe. It's almost certainly attributable to contaminated water, and, consequently, you are strongly advised to drink only bottled water (or water that has been boiled for at least 10 minutes), avoid uncooked vegetables with a high water content (lettuce, green salads, watermelon), and be very wary of taking ice in drinks.

▶ **Avoid locally produced spirits.** There is no quality control and cases of alcohol poisoning are not unheard of. If you're invited to someone's house, don't bring alcohol unless you're sure that your hosts drink.

▶ **Watch out for come-ons.** Offers to "take you to my uncle's shop" are annoying but mostly harmless. Although most people will treat you with genuine kindness and honesty, there are exceptions. This proposition is invariably proffered by an unofficial guide who gets a percentage from the shop owner on any purchase you make.

▶ **Know a dangerous scam artist from a cop.** Rare instances of scams have been pulled by rogue "cops." These are usually police impersonators who will ask to see your passport and/or wallet, then will make off with whatever you give them. Do not turn over your passport to any unidentified person claiming to be a police officer, and certainly do not get into any unmarked "police" car.

Southern Africa

▶ **Protect yourself from malaria.** Travelers heading into malaria-endemic regions should consult a health-care professional at least one month before departure. Take great care to avoid being bitten by mosquitoes. Always sleep in a mosquito-proof room or tent, and if possible, keep a fan going in your room. If you are pregnant or trying to conceive, avoid malaria areas if at all possible.

▶ **Check your existing health plan.** Make sure you're covered while abroad and supplement it if necessary. Southern Africa has no national health system.

▶ **Pack lightweight clothes that you can layer.** Bring at least one sweater. Take along a warm jacket, too, especially if you're going to a game lodge.

▶ **Set up international roaming cell phone service before you leave home.** This is your best, cheapest, and least complicated way of making and receiving phone calls here. In Botswana and Swaziland, there are no access agreements to allow you to use U.S. long-distance services. Thus, you will not be able to make calls using your U.S. calling card from Botswana or Swaziland.

▶ **Be sure you can access your money.** Program your credit cards for ATM use in South Africa before leaving home. (Most South African ATMs take five-digit PIN numbers.) In both Namibia and Zambia MasterCard and Visa are preferred by business owners to American Express because of substantial charges levied by Amex to proprietors. Business owners in Zambia often prefer cash (or traveler's checks) to credit cards, and some smaller hotels levy a fee up to 10% to use credit.

► **On foot, look right before crossing the street.** Southern Africans drive on the left.

► **Be car savvy.** Keep your car doors locked at all times, and leave enough space between you and the vehicle in front so you can pull into another lane if necessary.

► **Avoid areas with land mines.** Never, under any circumstances, drive off the road in Mozambique unless it is a detour that has obviously been used by lots of other vehicles. There may still be land mines in the least likely places.

► **Do not walk alone at night.** Be cautious even by day. Avoid wearing flashy jewelry (even costume jewelry), and don't invite attention by wearing an expensive camera around your neck.

ASIA

China

► **Don't get rejected for your visitor's visa.** It takes about a week to get a visa in the United States. Note: the visa application will ask your occupation. The Chinese do not like journalists or anyone who works in publishing or media. Americans and Canadians in these professions routinely state "teacher" under "Occupation."

► **Register your foreign-made camera or laptop with U.S. Customs before departing.** If your equipment is U.S.-made, call the Chinese consulate to find out whether the device should be registered with local customs upon arrival.

► **Bring a surge protector and a 220-volt adapter.** Although some outlets accept American plugs, it's a good idea to carry several types of adapters in case the Asian one (with diagonal prongs slanting inward) doesn't fit. Chinese sockets come in several different configurations.

▶ **Buy train tickets from the China Travel Service.** Get them at the local CTS office or ask your hotel concierge to make the arrangements, since communicating is difficult, even at a train station's counter for foreigners. Make reservations at least a day or two in advance, if you can.

▶ **Arrive at train stations two hours before departure.** Trains are always crowded.

▶ **If you're traveling by bus, ask your hotel travel agent about the reputation of the company.** Safety and comfort vary. The more expensive bus companies, such as INTAC, are usually safer because drivers are held accountable for accidents by the government. You may be charged for insurance on more dangerous, mountainous long-distance bus routes.

▶ **Carry a small bottle of antibacterial hand sanitizer.** And do wash your hands frequently. Similarly, stay away from ice, uncooked food, and unpasteurized milk and milk products, and drink only bottled water or water that has been boiled for at least 10 minutes to guard against getting traveler's diarrhea.

▶ **Do not buy prescription drugs in China.** Quality control is unreliable. Bring more than enough of your usual medicines for your trip, and take a supply of a physician-prescribed antidiarrheal to use in emergencies.

▶ **Bring trinkets from home as gifts forr your guides.** American cigarettes, candy, T-shirts, or small cosmetic items, such as lipstick and nail polish are appreciated. Do not give American magazines and books as gifts, as this could be considered propaganda and get your Chinese friends into trouble. CTS tour guides are not allowed to accept tips.

Hong Kong

▶ **Always ask your carrier about its check-in policy.** Check in at least two hours before departing from Hong Kong International Airport at Chek Lap Kok. If you plan on taking the train to the airport, check your luggage at the Airport Express Railway station on Hong Kong Island. You must check in at least three hours in advance for this wonderfully efficient, time-saving service.

▶ **Avoid renting a car on Hong Kong Island or Kowloon.** Driving conditions, traffic jams, and limited parking are bound to make your life difficult. Public transportation is excellent here, and taxis are inexpensive.

▶ **Ask your hotel to write your destination in Chinese.** Many taxi drivers do not speak English.

▶ **Don't miss dim sum.** These light snacks, served for lunch or breakfast in local teahouses as well as fine restaurants, are usually served in steaming bamboo baskets. Dim sum includes a variety of dumplings, buns, and pastries containing meat and vegetables.

▶ **Brace yourself for the crowds.** Hong Kong is extremely crowded; pushing, shoving, and gentle nudges are commonplace. As difficult as this may be to accept, it's not considered rude, it's unavoidable. Becoming angry or taking offense to an inadvertent push is considered rude.

▶ **Brush up on your use of chopsticks.** Silverware is common in Hong Kong, but it might be seen as a respectful gesture if you try your hand at chopsticks. Dining is a communal event. Everyone orders at least one dish, which are then placed in the center of the table and shared. Your meal will usually include rice or soup. It is considered proper to hold the bowl close to your lips and push the rice or soup into your mouth. At the end of the meal, most Chinese will use a toothpick at the table while covering their mouth with the non-toothpick-holding hand. This is common at all gatherings at all types of restaurants.

▶ **Pack a folding umbrella.** At any time of year it's wise to have one with you to anticipate the frequent rainfalls.

India

▶ **Buy tickets for internal and transatlantic flights at the same time.** Although some domestic carriers don't sell their tickets outside of India, you should try to get your tickets as early as possible and from your home country.

▶ **Don't schedule back-to-back domestic flights within India.** Delays and cancellations are frequent.

▶ **Reconfirm all flights.** Do this twice—72 hours before departure and again right before leaving for the airport. Ticket or no ticket, you may lose your seat if you don't confirm well in advance.

▶ **Don't expect full-service airports in India.** Regional airports in particular may not have the services of other airports world-over. Insufficient waiting areas and lack of food services are a drag. But in some cases the lack of real infrastructure can be a time killer, too. Reclaiming your luggage can take an hour, for example, if one conveyer belt serves the entire terminal. On the other hand, security measures in India's airports are stricter than in North America. It's not uncommon to go through two security checks, both including a total pat down.

▶ **Have a prepaid taxi meet you in Bombay.** It can be overwhelming to face the crowds that meet flights of tourists just outside the airport terminal, and it's best to have a driver waiting for you with your name on a sign.

▶ **Arrange a car and driver with care.** Use a licensed, government-approved operator or, for a bit more money, through your hotel. Establish terms, rates, and surcharges in advance.

▶ **Read up on the country.** For many first-time travelers, the rich culture and daily life in India requires some interpreting. Try to get a good sense of what to expect before you go, by immersing yourself in travel guides, historical fiction, or nonfiction, and you'll be more prepared to enjoy your trip—and less inclined to feel overwhelmed.

▶ **Bring bathroom supplies with you everywhere.** Carry toilet paper and moist towelettes with you at all times. Clean bathrooms are hard to come by in cities and the countryside. Also pack all necessary medicines as well as rash creams, zinc oxide, sunscreen, diapers, and diaper wipes.

▶ **Be scrupulous about your lodging arrangements.** Secure all room reservations before arrival. Regardless of where you stay, inspect your room before checking in. Avoid leaving unlocked suitcases in your hotel room, and unless your room has a safe, never leave money, traveler's checks, passports, or jewelry in a hotel room.

▶ **Carry spare batteries and adapter for laptops.** New batteries and replacement adapters are expensive and hard to find. Never plug your computer into a socket before asking about surge protection.

▶ **Be respectful of religious places.** With all of India's faiths, you must remove your shoes before entering a shrine, even if it appears to be in ruins. Don't smoke, drink alcohol, or raise your voice on the premises. Some temples and mosques are off-limits to travelers who don't practice the faith; don't try to bribe your way inside.

▶ **Dress modestly.** Only children can get away with short shorts. Men should wear comfortable jeans or longer shorts. Women visiting sacred places should dress modestly and cover their heads before entering a Sikh temple or a mosque.

▶ **Expect some sex segregation.** Men and women are sometimes separated (by roles and social customs) in Indian society, and some distinguishing practices may be expected of you. Observe the prevailing rules applied to seating, for example, if you're invited to a traditional Indian home. Men often sit separate from women.

▶ **Watch what you eat.** Don't eat from street vendors. Stay away from uncooked or cold food and unpasteurized milk and milk products. Avoid raw vegetables and fruit, even those that have been peeled. Raw produce served at luxury hotels is mostly hygienic, but many buffets and salad bars soak produce in an iodine preparation to kill parasites; ask the waiter about this before you indulge. Drink only water that has been bottled or boiled for at least 10 minutes; avoid tap water, ice, fruit juices, or drinks to which water has been added. Buy bottled water from a reputable shop and turn down offers of "filtered" or "aquaguard" water; it may have been filtered to take out particles but not purified to kill parasites.

▶ **Always use authorized money changers.** Also, insist on receiving an encashment slip. Some banks now charge a nominal fee for this slip, which you'll need if you want to pay hotel bills or travel expenses in rupees, and again if you want to reconvert rupees into your own currency upon departure from India. Reject torn, frayed, taped, or soiled bills, as many merchants, hotels, and restaurants won't accept them.

Japan

▶ **Do not try to open the taxi door.** Japanese taxis have automatic door-opening systems.

▶ **Direct taxi drivers by naming nearby landmarks.** Do not assume the taxi driver will be able to find your destination with just a written address.

▶ **Be sure of your bus route and destination.** The bus driver, particularly on routes outside Tokyo, probably won't speak English.

▶ **Be careful crossing the street.** In Japan, driving is on the left. Look right when crossing.

▶ **Avoid alcohol entirely if you plan to drive.** There's almost zero tolerance for driving under the influence of alcohol and given the occasional evening police checkpoint, it's wisest to designate a driver who will avoid alcohol altogether.

▶ **If you plan to travel by train, get a Japan Rail Pass.** This pass offers unlimited travel on Japan Railways (JR) trains. A one-week pass is less expensive than a regular round-trip ticket from Tōkyō to Kyōto on the Shinkansen. Note that you must obtain a rail-pass voucher prior to departure for Japan, and the pass must be used within three months of purchase. The pass is available only to people with tourist visas, as opposed to business, student, and diplomatic visas.

▶ **Be prompt for both social and business occasions.** Tardiness is a major faux pas. Japanese addresses tend to be complicated, and traffic is often heavy, so allow for adequate travel time.

▶ **Bow upon meeting someone.** It's as common as saying "hello" is at home.

▶ **Stick to last names and use "san" after the name.** In business situations, most Japanese are not accustomed to using first names. Even coworkers of 20 years' standing use surnames. Unless you are sure that the Japanese person is extremely comfortable with Western customs, it is best to use last names only, followed by the honorific, "san."

▶ **Pack your best socks and stockings.** Upon entering a home, it's customary to remove your shoes in the foyer and put on the slippers that are provided; in Japan shoes are for wearing outdoors only. You don't want to be caught with holes in your socks!

▶ **Don't pour your own drink.** Similarly, if a glass at your table happens to be empty, show your attentiveness by filling it for your companion.

▶ **Take instant coffee.** All lodgings provide a thermos of hot water and bags of green tea in every room, but for coffee you'll either have to call room service (which can be expensive) or buy very sweet coffee in a can from a vending machine.

Nepal, Tibet, and Bhutan

▶ **Know the health risks.** Check with the Centers for Disease Control and your physician about current risks and recommended vaccinations before you go. Immunizations for hepatitis A, meningitis, and typhoid fever are advised.

▶ **Reconfirm all flights.** This goes for both domestic and international flights out of Kathmandu. Do it at least 24 hours in advance, particularly since weather often causes delays and cancellations of domestic flights.

▶ **Get a lock for your luggage.** Don't leave passports, cameras, laptop computers, and other valuables in your hotel room unless the room has a safe.

▶ **Check on surge protection before plugging in your computer.** IBM sells a pen-size modem tester that plugs into a telephone jack to check if the line is safe to use. This tester is an invaluable gadget in Nepal, where telephone lines are not always reliable and could destroy your modem.

▶ **Be careful what you eat and drink.** Leafy vegetables are known to carry parasites, so avoid those of dubious origin or those likely to have been washed in tap water. Also, try to eat only fruit that has a skin you can peel. Avoid drinking tap water as well as beverages with ice, which often is made of local water. Most good restaurants either make their own ice using boiled water or buy ice in bulk from huge freezer warehouses, where purified water is used.

▶ **Dress modestly.** Dress in Bhutan, Nepal, and Tibet is informal but conservative. Shorts, short skirts, and revealing tops put women at risk of encountering unflattering remarks and, increasingly, unwanted touching.

Thailand

▶ **Don't assume that Thais eat with chopsticks.** Unless they're eating Chinese dishes, Thais use a fork and a spoon.

▶ **If you're not sure what to order, start with staples.** One good bet is *tom yam kung* (prawn and lemongrass soup with mushrooms). Then move on to *pad Thai* (fried noodles with tofu, vegetables, eggs, and peanuts).

▶ **Ask for your dishes *mai phet* ("not spicy").** Thai food can get really spicy—know what you're in for. (Phet means spicy.)

▶ **On a low-sodium diet? Skip the *nam pla*.** This fish sauce is used instead of salt, and is added just as commonly.

▶ **Drive carefully.** The main rule when driving in Thailand is to remember that traffic laws are routinely disregarded. Bigger vehicles have the unspoken right of way, motorcyclists seem to think they are invincible, and bicyclists often don't look around them. Avoid driving at night in rural areas, especially north and west of Chiang Mai and in the south beyond Surat Thani, as highway robberies have been reported.

▶ **Avoid inadvertent offense.** Displays of anger, raised voices, and confrontations are considered very bad form. Thais also disapprove of public shows of affection and revealing outfits or going shirtless other than at the beach or pool.

▶ **Women should dress modestly and wear a scarf in temples.** Don't wear shorts or tank tops. If you show up improperly attired, some temples have wraps you can borrow; but you're better off having your own, as others will not let you enter.

▶ **Remove your shoes before entering the temple.** Also, don't point your toes at any image of the Buddha, as it is considered sacrilegious.

▶ **Don't step over a seated person or someone's legs.** Don't point your feet at anyone; keep them on the floor, and take care not to show the soles of your feet. For similar reasons, never touch a person's head, even a child's (the head is considered sacred), and, if you are a woman, you should avoid touching a monk.

▶ **Carry toilet paper or a small package of tissues.** It's rarely provided in older buildings or in rural areas, where you still may find squat toilets. Often a bucket is placed under a tap next to the toilet; you are expected to fill the bucket with water and flush out the toilet manually. Note that Western-style facilities are usually available in the main tourist areas and are the norm in hotels.

Singapore
▶ **Buy drinks to keep hydrated.** This is true even when you're casually walking around Singapore City midday. Or plan to head to one of the outdoor cafés which blow a fine mist of water over you as you sip on a bubble tea (an iced tea or fruit drink with tapioca pearls). The heat can really do a number on you.

▶ **Visit a food hawker center.** These government-regulated food courts are clean and safe, and are a good way to eat what the locals do at about the same prices. Prices vary depending upon the center, and some try to fleece tourists, so ask at your hotel or check your guidebook for specific recommendations.

▶ **Go to a fixed-price store, if you hate bargaining.** Otherwise, haggling is the norm; even in many shops and stores.

▶ **Bring your own chewing gum.** It's not sold here.

▶ **Be careful with counterfeits when shopping.** You could have a problem with customs—there or at home, even if selling and buying imitations, whether computers or watches, are everywhere in Singapore.

▶ **Stick to public transportation.** Taxis can't access the reserved bus lanes, which means buses whiz by those stuck in traffic. It's usually unnecessary to rent a car—and there are confusing driving restrictions to know and extra licenses to acquire if you do. Plus driving is on the left in both Malaysia and Singapore.

▶ **If you rent, make sure your car has the right tags.** You need an Electronic Road Pricing (IU) tag and an Area Licensing Scheme (ALS) pass. A prepaid "in-vehicle unit" (IU) automatically deducts your toll when passing through Electronic Road Pricing tollgates. It's essential during rush hour. You can buy a temporary one, if you're entering Singapore without one. An ALS pass (either half or full day) allows you to drive to the Central Business District between 7:30 AM and 7 PM, when traffic here is strictly regulated.

▶ **Keep your tank full.** If you don't and you're taking the Causeway out of Singapore to Malaysia you could be fined. This is a government ruling, although an understandably unpopular one: the republic incurs huge losses in revenue as a result of Singaporeans' driving to Malaysia to gas up cheaply. (Unleaded gas starts at S$1.25 per liter in Singapore, significantly less in Malaysia.)

▶ **Use your right hand.** Don't use your left hand for shaking or giving something to a Malay or an Indonesian, as in both countries the left hand is considered a means for attending to personal hygiene. Since both are predominantly Muslim, it's also improper for a male to kiss a female acquaintance on the cheek; and a man shouldn't offer his hand to most women until she has offered hers first.

▶ **Don't gape at same-sex affection.** When members of the same sex hold hands, link arms, or act affectionate with one another, the behavior is purely social, not sexual. (The rights of gays and lesbians, on the other hand, are not protected in Singapore; but there is a large gay community which abides a "don't ask, don't tell" philosophy.) In fact, affections between members of the opposite sex are generally not displayed in public and may be considered offensive.

▶ **Know who to tip—and who not to.** Tipping isn't customary in Singapore. It's prohibited at the airport and discouraged in hotels (except for bellboys, who generally receive S$1 per bag) or restaurants that levy a 10% service charge. Unlike in other countries, waitstaffs don't receive a percentage of this service charge, except in the more progressive establishments, which need to retain the best waiters and waitresses. Hence, after experiencing some Singapore service you may begin to wish that tipping was the norm. Taxi drivers don't receive tips from Singaporeans, who become upset when they see tourists tip.

Bali

▶ **When renting a car, tell the agent your itinerary.** Don't sign the contract before doing so. Some rental contracts may limit the areas to which you can drive. For example, you need to obtain a special permit to cross from Bali to Lombok—but it's really just a letter from the rental agency.

▶ **Avoid highway scams.** In northern Bali, for example, a car will pull up, its occupants waving their arms, implying that something is wrong with your car. Ignore them. This is likely to be a scam in which they will have you pull over, "fix" a problem that doesn't exist, and then charge you for it. Pay attention to similar warnings that come from car-rental operations.

▶ **Expect touching as part of conversation.** The Balinese are extremely polite. Shaking hands has become a common practice, and Indonesians are very tactile, so touching happens often. Smiling is the national pastime, so do it frequently, and you'll have a much easier time transcending language barriers.

▶ **Don't point with your index finger.** Gesture with your whole hand instead. Similarly, don't cross your arms, or place your hands on your hips; these are signs of anger.

▶ **Don't touch food or people with your left hand.** It is considered unclean.

▶ **Wear a sash in Balinese Hindu temples.** Sashes are usually rented on-site for a few thousand rupiah. It's considered improper to wear shorts and other above-the-knee clothing in temples, so avoid them or take along a sarong when visiting a holy place.

▶ **Get familiar with the Indonesian toilet.** There are several models: the long porcelain bowl in the floor, which flushes; the usual Western throne; its seatless cousin, often used in mid-price hotels, which is flushed with a dipper of water; and the hole in the ground. Instructions for floor toilets: squat and go. This can be hard on the knees, and requires balance, but most people actually find it easy with practice. Most tourist hotels and restaurants have Western-style toilets. Note that the sink is often outside the room with the toilet, and there is sometimes a nominal charge (rupiah 100) for rest room use in such public places as bus terminals. If you need to find a bathroom, ask for the WC (way-say).

▶ **Don't fall prey to a "tour guide" in Bali.** Some attach themselves to you and then proceed to drag you to all the stores of their friends and relatives (in hopes that you will buy something and make a commission for them in the process).

SOUTH PACIFIC

Australia

▶ **Unless you have tons of time, limit where you go.** Australia is enormous. Don't pack in too much if you've only got a couple of weeks—it would be like trying to see the entire United States in 14 days. Instead, start by determining what the best activities are during the time of year you plan to go—touring wineries, bushwalking, skiing, diving. Then plan your trip around them including a couple of noteworthy areas that will keep you happy and busy, rather than frazzled and run ragged.

▶ **Know how to read a menu.** Down Under, entrée means appetizer and main courses are American main courses.

▶ **Get sporty.** Catch a local sports event. Cricket in summer (October–March) or Australian–rules football (soccer) are a blast. If you've never gone diving, there's no better place to try than the Great Barrier Reef.

▶ **Look right before stepping into the street.** Driving is on the left and stepping off a curb can be dangerous if your instincts have you looking left.

▶ **Know the rules of the road.** Pick up a copy of the Highway Code from the local automobile association for any state or territory in which you plan to drive. If you drive through the Outback, carry plenty of water and always tell someone your itinerary and schedule.

▶ **Make rail reservations well in advance.** This is especially true during peak tourist seasons, roughly from November through February. Advance purchase train fares, which afford a 10%–40% discount between some major cities, are best bought before departure for Australia, as they tend to be booked up far in advance. Contact your travel agent or the appropriate Rail Australia office.

New Zealand
▶ **Mind the strong sun.** When was the last time you stood under the equator? Cover up with a long-sleeve shirt, a hat, and long pants or a beach wrap because the primary health hazard is sunburn or sunstroke. Likewise, avoid dehydration. The wisest approach

when dressing is to wear layered outfits. Frequently, particularly at the change of seasons, weather can turn suddenly.

▶ **Don't plan to tour Auckland on foot.** It isn't the easiest place to figure out. It has built out, rather than up, and the sprawl makes the greater city close to impossible to explore on foot. What might look like short walking distances on maps can turn out to be far longer.

▶ **For some local flavor, rent a Holden Commodore.** This popular New Zealand car is manufactured by General Motors but not sold in the U.S. Most major agencies will have this as a luxury option.

▶ **Keep a sense of humor.** You'll find yourself in a constant comedy of errors when you go to use directional signals and windshield wipers—in Kiwi cars it's the reverse of what you're used to. You won't be able to count how many times those wipers start flapping back and forth when you go to signal a turn (it'll happen in reverse when you get back home).

▶ **Remember this simple axiom: drive left, look right.** That means keep to the left lane, and when turning right or left from a stop sign, the closest lane of traffic will be coming from the right, so look in that direction first. By the same token, pedestrians should look right before crossing the street. Americans and Canadians can blindly step into the path of an oncoming car by looking left as they do when crossing streets at home. So repeat this several times: drive left, look right.

▶ **Beware New Zealand's one health hazard.** While the country's alpine lakes might look like backdrops for mineral-water ads, some in South Island harbor a tiny organism that can cause "duck itch," a temporary but intense skin irritation.

CANADA

▶ **Bring the right identification.** You'll need proof of citizenship (a birth certificate or valid passport) or a naturalization certificate to enter Canada, plus some form of photo identification. Children need the same identification. Children traveling with one parent or other adult should bring a letter of permission from the other parent, parents, or legal guardian. Divorced parents with shared custody rights should carry legal documents establishing their status.

▶ **Get a GST refund.** A goods and services tax (GST) of 7% applies on nearly every transaction in Canada. Nonresidents can get a refund on purchases taken out of the country and on short-term accommodations of less than one month; rebate forms, which must be submitted within 60 days of leaving Canada, may be obtained from certain retailers, duty-free shops, customs officials, or from the Canada Customs and Revenue Agency. Instant cash rebates up to a maximum of $500 are provided by some duty-free shops when you leave Canada, and most provinces do not tax goods that are shipped directly by the vendor to your home. Always save your original receipts from stores and hotels (not just credit card receipts), and be sure the name and address of the establishment is shown on the receipt. Original receipts are not returned. To be eligible for a refund, receipts must total at least $200, and each individual receipt must show a minimum purchase of $50.

▶ **For the best exchange rate, go to a bank.** U.S. dollars are accepted in much of Canada (especially in communities near the border). To get the most favorable exchange rate, however, you should use an ATM or convert currency into Canadian funds at a bank or other financial institution.

▶ **Carry insect repellent in the woods in summer.** This is particularly true in northern Canada, and in June, which is blackfly season.

▶ **Learn a few French phrases.** They'll be appreciated in the province of Québec or to French-Canadian communities elsewhere.

THE CARIBBEAN

▶ **Ask about island-hopping passes.** They're costwise if you're flying to more than one island. Air ALM, Air Jamaica, American Airlines and American Eagle, BWIA, and LIAT are among the airlines that offer them.

▶ **Reconfirm your flights on interisland carriers.** You may be requested (actually, told) to take another flight or departure time that's more convenient for the airline, or your plane may make unscheduled stops.

▶ **Travel light.** Regional carriers use small aircraft with limited baggage space, and they often impose weight restrictions. You could be subject to outrageous surcharges or delays in getting your luggage if you don't pay attention to the limits.

▶ **Save up to 50% at resorts off-season.** From April 15 through December 15, you can save a bundle.

▶ **Know which side of the island you want.** Decide whether you want a hotel on the leeward side of an island (with calm water, good for snorkeling and swimming) or the windward (with waves, good for surfing, not good for swimming). At less expensive properties, an ocean-view room may mean a difference in price of only $10–$20 per room; at luxury resorts on pricey islands, however, it could amount to as much as $100 per room. Smaller hotels and guest houses or those that are a short walk from the beach offer very pleasant accommodations that are priced considerably lower than their larger, beachfront neighbors.

▶ **Ask for a room away from the entertainment area.** This is a must if you are a light sleeper.

▶ **When renting a car, don't overlook local firms.** Their cars are mechanically sound, and prices are competitive. It's not crucial to reserve a rental car prior to your arrival.

▶ **Bring an adapter for your laptop plug.** Even if your computer can be used on either a 100v or 220v system, the prongs on your U.S. standard plug won't fit into Caribbean 220v wall outlets.

▶ **Use a good repellent to ward off tiny no-see-ums.** These sand flies often appear after a rain, near swampy ground, and around sunset; mosquitoes can also be annoying.

Bahamas

▶ **Give hurricane season a miss.** It's roughly from June through November, with greatest risk for a storm from August through October. Delays and flight cancellations are common during this time. The low airfares are alluring for a reason.

▶ **Avoid spring break.** Between the end of February and mid-April you'll find a lot of vacationing college students, beach parties, sports events, and entertainment.

▶ **Don't forget to drive on the left.** This can be confusing because most cars are American with the steering wheel on the left. Similarly, pedestrians must look right, left, right when crossing the street.

▶ **Go easy at first on new foods.** Mangoes, conch, and rum punch top the list. The major health risk is traveler's diarrhea, caused by ingesting fruits, shellfish, and drinks to which your body is unaccustomed.

Bermuda

▶ **Ask about the island's water source.** You'll get a very interesting local lesson on the island's practice of collecting rainwater. No, they've never run out, and no one has even gotten sick.

▶ **When it comes to dress, err on the formal side.** It is an offense in Bermuda to appear in public without a shirt, even for joggers. Also, leave your cutoffs, short shorts, and halter tops at home. This rule may seem arcane, but most Bermudians appreciate this decorum. This also holds true for the beach—thong bathing suits and topless sunbathing are not acceptable.

▶ **Use American money.** The Bermudian dollar is on par with the U.S. dollar, and the two currencies are used interchangeably. (Other non-Bermudian currency must be converted.) You can use American money anywhere, but change is often given in Bermudian currency. Also, avoid accumulating large amounts of local money, which is difficult to exchange for U.S. dollars in Bermuda and expensive to exchange in the United States.

▶ **Don't plan on renting a car.** In fact, you cannot rent a car in Bermuda. It has strict laws governing against overcrowded roads, so even Bermudians are only allowed one car per household. A popular (albeit somewhat dangerous) alternative is to rent mopeds or scooters, which are better for negotiating the island's narrow roads.

Cuba

▶ **Check on travel-related rules right before your trip.** U.S. citizens require special permission to visit Cuba. For details on the latest regulations and on licenses for travel, contact the U.S. Department of the Treasury's Office of Foreign Assets Control (OFAC; tel. 202/622–2520 in Washington; 305/810–5140 in Miami).

▶ **Know how to get there.** Many Americans have visited via Canada or Mexico, and have a blank piece of paper tucked in their passport to be stamped, rather than their actual passport. Although few people have been prosecuted for violating the restrictions upon return to the United States, be aware that there are stiff penalties on the books for unlicensed travel to Cuba. Do a lot of research before you go.

▶ **Bring film, videotapes, and extra batteries.** Put in more than you expect to need—supplies are limited at the government-owned Photo Service chain.

▶ **Stock your first-aid kit/medicine bag.** You need basic bandages and topical ointments as well as sunscreen; insect repellent; and your favorite brands of over-the-counter allergy, cold, headache, and stomach/diarrhea medicine. Stores and pharmacies are not well-stocked, and you, like most Cubans, will have a hard time getting even the most basic medicines, should you need them.

▶ **Make sure your car reservation is confirmed.** Before setting out, check the car carefully for defects, and make sure your car has a jack and spare tire. The two biggest agencies are Havanautos and Transautos, and because they have the most branches, they can get another vehicle to you fairly quickly if you have problems. Roadside assistance is handled primarily through car-rental companies, so ask your rental agent for the most up-to-date emergency number.

Puerto Rico

▶ **In peak seasons, reserve your car from home.** This is not only because of possible discounts but also to ensure that you get a car and that it's a reliable one. Always opt for air-conditioning. You'll be glad you did when it's high noon and you're in a San Juan traffic jam.

▶ **Drive cautiously after heavy rains or hurricanes.** Roads and bridges might be washed out or damaged. Many of the mountain roads are very narrow and steep, with unmarked curves and cliffs. Locals are familiar with such roads and often drive at high speeds, which can give you quite a scare. When traveling on a narrow, curving road, it's best to honk your horn as you take any sharp turn.

▶ **Vegetarians, plan ahead.** You may quickly grow tired of beans and rice. Most of the dishes feature some kind of meat or seafood, and meals can be heavier than some travelers are used to. You might want to bring a box of protein bars or other nutritious snacks from home.

▶ **Wear a shirt and shoes.** It's considered highly disrespectful to enter a store or a restaurant in a bathing suit or other inappropriate attire, even though you may be spending a great deal of time on the beach.

CENTRAL AMERICA

▶ **Consider domestic flights.** Flying can often be cheaper than driving, as rental cars are commonly priced for North Americans—at North American rates.

▶ **Always begin an interaction with a polite greeting.** Central Americans are more formal than North Americans, and a polite *"Buenos dias. ¿Como estas usted?"* (not the Mexican *¿Que pasa?*) will go a long way. Whether you're asking how much something costs or where the hotel entrance is located, be sure to acknowledge the person with a greeting first.

▶ **Keep poor road conditions in mind.** Given Central America's often difficult driving conditions, distances that appear short on a map can represent hours of driving on dirt roads pocked with craters. Always make sure you have a spare tire and a jack before setting off.

▶ **Respect local etiquette.** Dress modestly. Revealing clothing is frowned upon, especially in more rural areas. Be quiet when visiting a house of worship, and don't photograph people praying. When on a bus, give up your seat to an elderly person or a woman carrying a child. Strangers still rely on a handshake for first introductions—although a hearty abrazo (hug) will sometimes replace the handshake on your second meeting. Other customs are more nuanced and vary from country to country, so you should observe locals and follow their lead.

▶ **Don't count on using plastic.** Carry enough cash or traveler's checks outside cities. Major credit cards are accepted at most of the larger hotels and more expensive restaurants throughout Central America. As the phone system improves, many smaller hotels, restaurants, and other facilities are accepting credit cards. Still, it's not common. Some hotels, restaurants, tour companies, and other businesses will give you a 5%–15% discount if you pay cash.

▶ **Avoid people who offer to exchange money.** They are notorious for shortchanging tourists unfamiliar with the local currency.

▶ **Do not take photos of anyone without permission.** Always ask first—especially for children. Some children are expected to earn a little money by asking tourists if they'd like to take a picture of them. In either case, it's customary to offer a few pesos for any pictures you take.

▶ **Know each Central American country's history.** Generalizations about all countries won't go over well. Not every one of them has recently endured a civil war, for example. Belize and Costa Rica have never really seen the kind of political turmoil of the others.

▶ **Bring a flashlight.** Streetlights are not pervasive, which means when the sun goes down, it's dark. (Take a moment to look at the stars.) At jungle lodges and many resorts, power is often from generators. At a certain time of night, they are usually shut off and illumination is provided via lanterns and torches. During the rainy season, in El Salvador and possibly elsewhere, the electricity can go out for hours at time.

Belize

▶ **Know when to go.** The rainy season lasts from around June through November; the high season (mid-November through April) coincides with the dry season, which runs from December through May. The busiest time is Christmas, followed by Easter and Thanksgiving.

▶ **Don't bother brushing up on your Spanish.** The language spoken in Belize is English.

▶ **Pack for the region you're visiting.** The Cayo (cool nights) and the Cayes (hot, hot, hot) have different climates, so your wardrobe might require a warm polar-fleece jacket and some lightweight T-shirts and shorts.

▶ **Save by using the municipal Belize City airport.** Costs are as much as 45% lower on internal flights, compared to flights to or from Philip Goldson International Airport, north of the city in Ladyville.

▶ **Not traveling by bus or shuttle? Rent a four-wheel-drive vehicle.** Unpaved roads, mudslides in rainy season, and a general off-the-beaten-path landscape are status quo here. Note that most agencies do not permit you to take their vehicles over the border into Guatemala or Mexico.

▶ **Plug in your laptop cautiously.** If you bring a laptop, be aware that the power supply may be uneven, and most hotels do not have built-in current stabilizers.

Costa Rica

▶ **Once you get to the capital, leave.** San José is not representative of what Costa Rica has to offer. Don't plan to stay long; use the city just as a transportation hub and for any last-minute necessities—although there are a few good international restaurants, if you do have a night to kill.

▶ **Take the day's first flight to your next destination.** Most international flights arrive in San José, you won't likely catch internal connecting flights to the coastal beach towns, which leave early.

▶ **Reconfirm your flight by phone.** Failure to do so within 72 hours of departure may result in cancellation of your reservation.

▶ **Reserve rental cars several months in advance.** This is a must if you plan to rent any kind of vehicle between December 15 and January 3, or during Holy Week around Easter, in April.

▶ **Pack light.** A luggage weight limit of 11.3 kilograms or 25 pounds is almost always enforced on the tiny domestic planes.

▶ **Leave your jeans behind.** They take forever to dry and aren't acceptable for evening attire. Bring at least one good, wrinkle-resistant outfit for going out at night. (Costa Ricans tend to dress up a bit more than Americans.)

▶ **Hire a professional, bilingual nature guide.** To get the most out of your trip, hire one who knows well the country's diverse landscapes, birds, and animals and where to find them.

► **Bring or borrow binoculars.** Let your hardened city slicker self be impressed with the array of birds and rain-forest foliage.

► **Bring along enough film for your trip.** Most film costs at least 20% more in Costa Rica than in the United States.

Guatemala

► **Avoid crowds or book early.** The busiest time of the year is around Holy Week, from Palm Sunday to Easter Sunday. Hotels in Antigua, Panajachel, and Chichicastenango fill up months ahead of time.

► **Spend the night at Tikal.** The best way to experience the incomparable Maya ruins is to get up just before the birds do, from a hotel within the park, and head toward the deserted plaza with a guide. From the top of one of the scalable pyramids, the well-trained guards can show you an enormous array of wildlife that disappears from the park during the day. It is unbelievably breathtaking.

► **Attend a market.** Each major town has one—each seemingly better than the last. Some reach their pinnacle on Sunday, like the one in Chichicastenango, which is a favorite with locals and international visitors. Colorful handicrafts, leather goods, handwoven fabrics, and carved masks of mythological animals are just some of the gorgeous wares.

► **For comfort, travel in private shuttles.** Shuttles are private minivans that hold up to eight passengers. They are faster and more comfortable than public buses (former school buses) and maintain a fairly reliable schedule—but they cost more than the alternatives. Advance reservations are usually required. Shuttles can be arranged at the airport, at travel agencies, and at most hotels.

▶ **Drink carefully.** Avoid iced beverages and drink only bottled water while in Guatemala.

MEXICO

▶ **Bring proper identification for children.** All children must have proof of citizenship (a birth certificate) for travel to Mexico. All children up to age 18 traveling with a single parent must also have a notarized letter from the other parent stating that the child has his or her permission to leave their home country. If the other parent is deceased or the child has only one legal parent, a notarized statement saying so must be obtained as proof.

▶ **Visit a city during a festive holiday.** Although these holidays, like the Day of the Dead, may bring lots of international visitors to Oaxaca or Mexico City, it's a wonderful cultural experience to visit when the streets teem with colorful ornaments and parades—and it's a very different kind of vacation than a trip to one of the country's beach resorts.

▶ **Know the rules about driving a car.** To drive in Mexico you must carry Mexican auto insurance, which you can purchase near border crossings on either the U.S. or Mexican side. If you enter Mexico with a car, you must leave with it. Look into the other strict rules regarding bringing any car into the country.

▶ **Use common safety sense everywhere.** Exercise particular caution in Mexico City. Don't advertise you're a tourist and don't wear any valuables, including watches. Wear a money belt, put valuables in hotel safes, and carry your own baggage whenever possible, unless in a luxury hotel. Keep your passport in the hotel's safe. Take only registered hotel taxis or have a hotel concierge call for one—do not hail taxis on the street under any circumstances. Use ATMs during the day and in big, enclosed commercial areas. Avoid the glass-enclosed street variety of banks where you may be more vulnerable to thieves who force you to withdraw money for them; abduction is also possible. This cannot be stressed strongly enough.

▶ **Avoid certain remote, less-traveled areas.** In Oaxaca, Chiapas, and Guerrero, crime can be life-threatening. Do not pick up hitchhikers or hitchhike yourself. For travel by bus, buy tickets for first class or better. Women should not venture alone onto uncrowded beaches, and everyone should ignore urges to get away from it all (even as a couple) to go hiking in remote national parks.

▶ **Watch what you eat.** Stay away from ice, uncooked food, and unpasteurized milk and milk products, and drink only bottled water or water that has been boiled for at least 10 minutes, even when you're brushing your teeth.

EUROPE

▶ **Before booking, compare modes of transport.** Many city pairs are so close together that flying hardly makes sense. For instance, it may take just half an hour to fly between London and Paris, but you must factor in time spent getting to and from the airports, plus check-in time. A three-hour train ride from city center to city center might be a better alternative. It makes sense to save air travel for longer distances and do your local traveling from these hubs—unless of course you find a great airfare deal that negates the time you'll spend on airport transfers.

▶ **Buy EurailPasses before leaving for Europe.** It was once necessary for non-Europeans to purchase their passes before arriving in Europe. This remains the recommended option, but you can now buy a pass in person within six months of your arrival in Europe from Rail Europe in London.

▶ **Note that EurailPasses are not honored in Britain.** They are effective in the following 17 countries only: Austria, Belgium, Denmark, Finland, France, Germany, Greece, Holland, Hungary, Italy, Luxembourg, Norway, Portugal, Republic of Ireland, Spain, Sweden, and Switzerland.

▶ **Know which currency you'll be using.** Denmark, Great Britain, Greece, Sweden, and Switzerland, although a part of the European Union, are not part of the monetary union, and therefore each uses its local currency. A U.S. dollar is almost equal to the euro; whereas it takes a little over 1.5 of them to equal a British pound.

▶ **Reserve a car before you leave home.** This is the way to get the best car-rental rates.

▶ **Know the numeric equivalent of your ATM password.** Some ATM keypads show no letters, and you'll be unable to access your money if you can't remember the number of your PIN.

Belgium

▶ **Rent bicycles as part of a train-and-bike package.** Bike paths border Belgium's scenic canals and seaside roads, and many towns have bike lanes parallel to main streets, making it a quite a bike-friendly country (unless you count those cobbled streets!). The train-and-bike package, available at approximately 30 train stations in the country's most popular tourist destinations, includes one round-trip one-day ticket and bike rental at your destination station, with a total cost running from $10 to $20. Four stations also offer mountain bikes for $20 to $25 a day. You are required to make a deposit, which is reimbursed when you return your bicycle. A booklet called B-Excursions, available at major train stations, lists participating stations.

▶ **Be able to read signs in both French and Flemish.** Depending upon whether you are in the south or the north of the country, you need to know that Antwerp is Antwerpen in Dutch and Anvers in French; likewise, Brugge is Bruges in French, and Brussels is Bruxelles in French and Brussel in Dutch. Even more confusing is the introduction of Dutch: Mons (French) and Bergen (Dutch), or Tournai (French) and Doornik (Dutch). On the Brussels-Liège/Luik motorway, signs change language with alarming frequency as you criss-cross the Wallonia-Flanders border. *Uitrit* is Dutch for exit.

▶ **Eat french fries.** They are far superior to North American ones. Stands (*friterie* in French or *frituur* in Flemish) serve them in large cones, with a selection of condiments that go far beyond banal ketchup. Another favorite snack that beats the poor American replica is the famous Belgian waffle (*gaufres* in French, *waffels* in Flemish), which you can buy at waffle stands and in some bakeries in cities. Waffles are considered an afternoon snack, so waffle stands do not generally open until noon.

France

▶ **Make an effort to speak a little French.** A simple, friendly bonjour (hello) will do, as will asking if the person you are greeting speaks English. Be patient, and speak English slowly.

▶ **Call ahead.** When planning to visit museums, restaurants, and hotels, phone in advance to make sure they will be open. With 11 national *jours feriés* (holidays) and five weeks of paid vacation, the French have their share of repose. In May there is a holiday nearly every week, so be prepared for stores, banks, and museums to shut their doors for days at a time.

▶ **Traveling in a group? Rent a car.** Though renting a car in France is expensive—about twice as much as in the United States—as is gas (€0.90–€1.25 per liter), it can pay off if you're traveling with two or more people.

▶ **For good seats, board trains early.** A half hour before departure is optimal. Before boarding, you must punch your ticket (but not EurailPass) in one of the orange machines at the entrance to the platforms, or else the ticket collector will fine you €15.

▶ **Complain if taxes and service charges show up as extra on your bill.** By law, restaurant and hotel prices must include these surcharges amounting to 19.6%.

▶ **Know the distinction between private and public beaches.** All along the coast, the waterfront is carved up into private frontage, roped off and advertised by coordinated color awnings, parasols, and mattresses. These private beaches usually offer full restaurant and bar service, and rent mattresses, umbrellas, and lounge chairs by the day and half day. But interspersed between these commercial beaches is plenty of public space, with open access and (usually) the necessary comforts of toilets and cold-rinse "showers" for washing off the salt.

▶ **Get used to secondhand smoke.** Whereas smoking laws are fairly strict in North America, the right to puff is permitted in all manner of public places in France. A few hotel properties or restaurants may be willing to accommodate your preferences if you need a little breathing room by giving you a table in an empty area, but it's considered quite rude to expect locals to stop. Moreover, you should refrain from getting self-righteous about the pervasiveness of smoking. Remember, you're a guest in someone else's house, so to speak.

▶ **Forget your dieting plans.** When was the last time you were in a country with over 500 types of cheese? It would be a shame to come all this way only to deny yourself participation in the French culinary traditions and eating practices. Help yourself to big slabs of cheese and bread, and wash it all down with a good red wine. And don't worry about getting hooked: You'd be hard-pressed to eat this well at home.

Paris

▶ **Learn how to read Parisian addresses.** A site's location in one of the city's 20 arrondissements is noted by its mailing code or, simply, the last one or two digits of that code (for example, Paris 75010 or 10^e, both of which indicate that the address is in the 10th arrondissement; Paris 75005 or 5^e indicates the address is in the 5th arrondissement).

▶ **Head to cheap neighborhoods.** Paris is expensive. Places where you can generally be certain to shop, eat, and stay without overpaying include the streets surrounding Montmartre (not the Butte, or hilltop, itself); the St-Michel/Sorbonne area on the Left Bank; the mazelike streets around Les Halles and the Marais in central Paris; in Montparnasse, south of the boulevard; and the Bastille, République, and Belleville areas of eastern Paris.

▶ **Consider a Museums and Monuments Pass.** Get the Carte Musées et Monuments (www.intermusees.com) if you want to skip long museum lines. Unless you're a rabid museum goer, it may not otherwise be worth the cost—you'd have to do three museums in one day, or six in three days, to make any real savings. It may seem like even less of an attractive proposition now that the museums owned by the City of Paris are free. However, a pass is a good way to avoid the long lines when you have limited time.

▶ **Eat at the counter.** Note that in cafés, bars, and some restaurants in Paris, it's less expensive to eat or drink standing at the counter than it is to sit at a table. Most restaurants have two basic types of menu: à la carte and fixed price (prix fixe). The prix-fixe menu is usually the best value.

▶ **Ask for the lunch menu.** Even Paris's best restaurants have prix-fixe lunch menus that are dramatically more affordable (but much more limited) than ordering from their regular à la carte menus. If it's not offered, feel free to ask for one.

Germany

▶ **If you want an automatic car, ask in advance.** The typical rental cars come with manual transmission.

▶ **Always address acquaintances formally.** Use Herr (Mr.) or Frau (Mrs.) plus their last name, and do not call them by their first name unless invited to do so.

▶ **Take the waters.** In Germany, this tradition of spa going, whether for curing the body or merely beautifying it, has been popular since Roman times. More than 300 health resorts, most equipped for hot mineral, mud, or brine treatments, are set within pleasant country areas or historic communities. The word Bad before the name of a town usually means it's a spa destination.

Berlin

▶ **Be willing to take buses.** Berlin is a spread-out city and distances between subway stations can be greater than they appear on a map. If your destination isn't near a subway, try to decipher the bus routes posted at stops—buses move fairly quickly through the city.

▶ **Validate your transportation card.** It must be done the first time you use public transportation whatever type of transportation card you purchase.

▶ **Consider a Berlin State Museums ticket package.**

▶ **Buy a phone card.** It's time-consuming trying to find a public phone; if you do find one, have a phone card handy, since many no longer accept coins.

▶ **Be prepared for a few cloudy and wet days.** Summers are usually sunny and warm, though.

Great Britain

▶ **Reserve hotel rooms weeks ahead (months for London).** Most hotels have rooms with "en suite" bathrooms—as private bathrooms are called in Great Britain. When you book a room in the mid-to-lower price categories, it's best to confirm your request for a room with en suite facilities.

▶ **Save with passes or memberships.** These can shave the high price of visiting castles, gardens, and historic houses. Some passes, including the British Tourist Authority's Great British Heritage pass and English Heritage's Overseas Visitor pass, are for specific amounts of time from a week to a month. The British Tourist Authority Web site (www.visitbritain.com) has information about these and other discounts. Be sure to match what the pass or membership offers against your itinerary; you may or may not be visiting enough places to make it worthwhile.

▶ **Buy your BritRail Pass before you leave home.** Train travelers should consider purchasing a BritRail Pass, which gives unlimited travel on the British rail network and will save you money. EurailPasses are not honored in Britain. Make train reservations whenever possible; there are often discounts for early booking.

▶ **Drive on the left in Britain.** This takes a bit of getting used to, and it's much easier if you're driving a British car where the steering and mirrors are designed for U.K. conditions. Note that off main streets, roads can be very narrow and winding. For driving rules and illustrations of signs and road markings, pick up a copy of the official Highway Code (£1.50) at a service station, newsagent, or bookstore. Pedestrians should also look right, left, right when crossing the street.

London

▶ **Plan your airport transfer—it's not cheap.** Tube, taxi, or the Heathrow Express are the most common ways to go, each with its perks and downfalls. Taking the tube (London's Underground subway system) is the cheapest means for reaching most points in central London (£3.50), but you'll have to lug your bags. Taxi trips from Heathrow can take more than an hour and cost £30–£40, depending upon traffic. From Gatwick, the taxi fare is at least £50 plus tip. Another option is the Heathrow Express train, which makes the trip to London Paddington in 15 minutes. Standard one-way tickets cost £12 (£22 round-trip). But then you'll likely need a taxi to your city hotel.

▶ **Buy a Travelcard for the Underground.** It's useful if you are planning several trips on the Underground subway system (or "tube") or bus system in one day. It's good for unrestricted travel on both tube and bus. Buses are a good way of seeing the town, particularly if you plan to hop on and off to cover many sights, but don't take a bus if you are in a hurry.

▶ **Don't try to do everything.** You might get more out of a visit to this sprawling city if you pick one or two attractions per day that are in proximity of each other, like taking in a show at Shakespeare's Globe Theatre and touring the Tate Modern.

▶ **Always check if tipping is necessary.** At many restaurants and nearly all cafés and pubs, a tip is not customary. Unlike in North America where food servers and bartenders make most of their income through gratuities, workers in England get an hourly wage. Many upscale or international restaurants and large hotels (particularly those belonging to chains) will automatically add a 10%–15% service charge to your bill. So check before you hand out extra money.

Scotland

▶ **Research bringing your own clubs.** Call the golf course and your airline for details. Airlines may not necessarily treat golf clubs as typical luggage and you may have to pay an extra fee or follow packing instructions in order to bring them over on your flight. When you book your tee time, which you should do in advance, ask about clubs. It might be best to rent them.

▶ **Expect to get your own drinks at pubs.** Most pubs do not have any waitstaff, and you're expected to go to the bar and order a beverage and your meal—this can be particularly disconcerting when you are seated in a "restaurant" upstairs but are still expected to go downstairs and get your own drinks and food.

▶ **Beware the midge.** Pack some insect repellent to deter this tiny biting fly if you are traveling in the Highlands and islands in summer: the Highland midge is a force to be reckoned with. You might want to set out on hike after a windy spell, when the creatures have been temporarily beaten back. Antihistamine cream is helpful in reducing swelling of bites you do get.

▶ **Go shopping.** Tartans, tweeds, and woolens may be a Scottish cliché, but nevertheless the selection, generally of high quality, and the reasonable prices of these goods make them a must-have for many visitors.

▶ **Ask for clarification if you don't understand.** Scots English can be a tough accent to understand and the abbreviation of many colloquial words can make it even more challenging. Virtually everyone will "modulate" either unconsciously or out of politeness into understandable English when conversing with a non-Scots speaker.

Holland

▶ **Book well in advance.** Accommodation in the incredibly popular Randstad region (the provinces of North and South Holland, and Utrecht) is at a premium.

▶ **Go to museums early.** You might have come all this way to see a Vermeer or van Gogh and not be able to get close enough because of all the tourists and school-children.

▶ **Avoid Amsterdam's Red Light District at night.** The streets are jammed with noisy groups of young men, who don't seem to pose much of a threat, but can behave obnoxiously (hence the outdoor lavatories and signs forbidding urination in the nearby canal).

▶ **Know a coffee shop from a Starbucks.** Coffee shops might sell coffee and snacks, but the licensed ones also sell marijuana, hash, and drug paraphernalia, which can be used on the spot.

▶ **Don't worry about speaking Dutch.** Most Dutch in major cities are bilingual in Dutch and English—at least.

▶ **Know your station.** Be sure of the exact name of the train station from which your train will depart, and at which you wish to get out. In some Dutch cities (including Amsterdam, Rotterdam, The Hague, and Delft) there are two or more stations, although one is the principle station.

▶ **Try local Dutch brews.** The Dutch are especially fond of their pils, a light golden lager usually served with a large head. Locals claim that it tastes better if sipped through the foam, so asking for a top-up may offend. There are stronger beers, usually referred to as bokbier—typically seasonal, they are made with warming spices in the winter. In summer, witte bier (white beer) is a refreshing drink, a zesty brew served cool with a twist of lemon. There's almost nothing better than a beer and sandwich taken at a canal-side café.

▶ **Go out for Indonesian rijstafel.** This multi-ingredient dish with rice, vegetables or meat, and sweet and spicy condiments is a tasty legacy of Dutch colonialism.

▶ **Stamp the date on your ticket.** Do this before you board the train on your day of travel, if you buy a non-dated train ticket. If you forget to stamp your ticket in the machine, or you didn't make it in time to buy a ticket, you could should actively seek out an inspector and pay the onboard fare, a stinging 70% more expensive than at the railway station counter.

▶ **Rent a bike.** It's a magnificent way to see the city—the locals will agree. Never leave your bike unlocked: there is a rapid turnover of stolen bikes no matter what quality or condition. Use a "D" lock, which can't be cut with the average thieves' tools, and lock your bike's frame to something that can't be shifted, like a railing.

Italy

▶ **If you can, avoid Italy in August.** Much of the population is on the move, especially around Ferragosto (August 15). Deluxe and four-star hotel rates in cities can be downright extravagant. In those categories, ask for one of the better rooms, since less desirable rooms—and there usually are some—don't give you what you're paying for. Light sleepers should request a quiet room when making reservations.

▶ **Avoid Naples in summer.** The area can become a sweltering inferno in summer, the archaeological sites swarm, and the islands and Amalfi Coast resorts are similarly overrun with tour buses and bad tempers. Any other time of year would be preferable.

▶ **Take your own soap to budget hotels.** It's not often provided.

▶ **For sightseeing, pack binoculars.** They will help you get a good look at wondrous painted ceilings and domes.

▶ **Buy a travel guide and books on art and wine.** You'll know where to find the paintings you came all the way to see and which wine regions have the varietal you seek.

▶ **Have coins handy for the luce (light) machines.** These illuminate the works of art in the perpetual dusk of ecclesiastical interiors.

▶ **Expect that no-smoking areas may be smoky.** If you try to enforce a no-smoking policy, especially with a local, don't expect him or her to respond or respect your request. Your best bet for finding as smoke-free an environment as possible is to stick to large establishments and, weather permitting, to eat outside.

▶ **Don't be too bashful to make requests of waiters.** As you wish, ask for salt, extra Parmesan cheese, or olive oil on the side or to have a dish prepared without ingredients you do not care for.

▶ **Plan train travel way ahead.** Buy train tickets and make seat reservations up to two months in advance at travel agencies displaying the FS emblem, which stands for Ferrovie dello Stato, the Italian railway system. Trains can be very crowded and lines are usually long at station windows. Seat reservations can be made at agencies (or the train station) up until about five hours before the train departs from its city of origin. Campania's bus network is extensive and in some areas buses can be more direct (and therefore, faster) than local trains, so it's a good idea to compare bus and train schedules.

Rome

▶ **Always check times locally for museum hours.** They vary and may change with the seasons. Sightseeing in churches during religious rites is usually discouraged.

▶ **Mind the dress codes.** They are especially strict for visits to the Basilica di San Pietro and the Musei Vaticani: shorts, tank tops, and halter tops are taboo. Shoulders must be covered. Women should carry a scarf or shawl to cover bare arms if the custodians insist. Those who do not comply with the dress code are refused admittance.

▶ **Ask for the bill in restaurants.** In Rome, the bill will not be brought until you ask for it. Unless otherwise written on the menu, service is included. However, it's customary to leave an additional 5%–10% tip for the waiter, depending on the quality of service.

▶ **Beware of pickpockets on buses.** Especially dicey are Line 64 (Termini–St. Peter's train station); the line

40 Express, which takes a slightly different route and takes you closer to the basilica; and subways—and when making your way through the corridors of crowded trains. Pickpockets may be active wherever tourists gather, including the Roman Forum, the Colosseum, the Piazza Navona, and Piazza di San Pietro.

▶ **Beware purse snatchers.** They often work in teams on a single motor scooter or motorcycle: one drives and the other grabs.

Venice and Veneto

▶ **Buy a map at a newsstand.** It's essential to have a good map showing all street names and vaporetto routes. Signs are posted on many corners pointing you in the right direction for the nearest major landmark—San Marco, Rialto, Accademia, etc.—but don't count on finding such signs once you're deep into residential neighborhoods.

▶ **Take a late gondola ride.** Go in the late afternoon or early evening hours, when the Grand Canal isn't so heavily trafficked. Avoid low tide, when the odors of the canals are at their worst. It's best to start from a station on the Grand Canal, because the lagoon is usually choppy. Make it clear that you want to see the smaller canals, and agree to a price and length of ride before you start. Few tourists know about the two-man gondolas that ferry people across the Grand Canal at various fixed points. They are the cheapest and shortest gondola ride in Venice and can save a lot of walking. The fare is €0.40, which you hand to the gondolier when you get on. Look for TRAGHETTO signs.

Portugal

▶ **Fly to London and pick up a charter.** You might save money and have a wider choice of destinations in Portugal. There are often good deals to Faro, in particular, as the Algarve is popular with British vacationers. In summer, last-minute, round-trip flights have cost as little as $150. From Australia or New Zealand, look for a cheap charter to London or Amsterdam and then a second direct charter to Portugal.

▶ **Don't eat food served that you haven't ordered.** While you ponder the menu in a restaurant, you may be served an impressive array of appetizers. If you eat any of these, you'll probably be charged a fee called a couberto or couvert. If you don't want these appetizers, you're perfectly within your rights to send them back or push them to the end of the table.

▶ **Look for money-saving set menus.** As in many European countries, Portuguese restaurants serve an ementa (or prato) do dia, or set menu. This can be a real bargain—usually 80% of the cost of three courses ordered separately.

▶ **Prepare for hills in Lisbon.** Turn-of-the-20th-century funicular railways and outdoor elevators make getting around a little easier, but you shouldn't assume the distance between two places is flat and easily or quickly walkable. It's like San Francisco.

▶ **Learn a few basic phrases in Portuguese.** Not everyone speaks English, even in cities.

▶ **Tour a port bottler.** In Vila Nova de Gaia, a town across the River Douro from Porto, are the country's port manufacturers—the view of the lodges bearing their huge brand-name signs from the Porto side of the river is beautiful. Each lodge is open to the public (call for hours), some have free tours, others charge a fee, and a few also have a restaurant.

▶ **Avoid driving.** Portugal has one of the highest rates of auto accidents and fatalities in Europe and local driving habits (nary a brake is used) quickly explains why. Taxis are cheap and the long-distance trains are really comfortable. If you take a train in the peak season, however, get tickets in advance since seats are assigned.

Greece

▶ **Learn to recognize letters in the Greek alphabet.** This helps to make finding your way around as easy as possible. Most areas, even Athens, have few signs in English.

▶ **Expect variable place-name transliterations.** Examples: Agios or Ayios, Georgios or Yiorgos. Also, the English version may be quite different from the Greek, or even what locals use informally: Corfu is known as Kerkyra; island capitals are often just called Chora (town) no matter what their formal title; Vasilissis Sofias (Queen Sofia), a main Athens boulevard, now reads Eleftheriou Venizelou on maps since royalty was banned, but if you ask for that name, no one will know what you're talking about.

▶ **Name nearby landmarks to direct taxi drivers.** And know the district you're headed for. A street may change names several times, and a city may have more than one street by the same name. Note that there are odd- and even-numbered sides of the streets, but don't assume No. 124 is across from No. 125, which could be several blocks down the street.

▶ **When choosing a ferry, read the schedule carefully.** Determine how many stops you'll make and the estimated arrival time. Sometimes a ferry that leaves an hour later for your destination gets you there faster. Timetables change frequently, and boats may be delayed by weather conditions, especially when the northwestern winds called meltemia hit in August, so stay flexible, one advantage to not buying a ticket in advance. Don't travel by boat around August 15, when most ferries are so crowded the situation becomes comically desperate.

▶ **Price 24-hour transportation tickets.** A ticket costs (1,000 dr./2.94) and may save you money if you take the bus, trolley, and metro several times in one day during your Athens stay. When assessing whether it's worth the money, remember that you must use a new ticket (120 dr./0.35–250 dr./0.73) for each leg of the journey for each method of transportation. A pass also saves you the hassle of validating your tickets numerous times.

▶ **Be careful with your gestures.** Some communicate their opposite message. A gesture you should remember is the "no" that looks like "yes": a slight or exaggerated (depending on the sentiment) tipping back of the head, sometimes with the eyes closed and eyebrows raised. When you wave with your palm towards people, they may interpret it as "come here" instead of "goodbye"; and, Greeks often wave goodbye with the palm facing them, which looks like "come here" to English speakers.

▶ **Don't be tricked into buying overpriced drinks.** Men in Athens around Syntagma Square should be careful of any stranger who tries to talk them into going to a local bar. Here, the unsuspecting foreigner will order drinks under the encouragement of hostesses hired by the establishment without realizing these cocktails are astronomically expensive. Hesitation in paying your whopping bill may result in uncomfortable encounters. Grab a policeman or call the tourist police (171).

▶ **Ask advice from the tourist police.** Often stationed near the most popular tourist sites, tourist police can answer questions in English about transportation, steer you to an open pharmacy or doctor, and locate phone numbers of hotels, rooms, and restaurants.

▶ **Register laptop computers with customs on entry.** This is essential for non-EU citizens. Also you must then show the stamped passport page with the computer's serial number upon exit to prove they did not buy it in Greece. Although officials may never check you coming or going, it's good to follow procedure to avoid last-minute trouble on departure.

Moscow and St. Petersburg

▶ **Get to the airport early to avoid being bumped in Russia.** Check-in officially ends 40 minutes before departure, and if you arrive late you may have to beg to be allowed onto the plane.

▶ **Pack as much as you can in your carry-on.** That goes for all of your valuables, since checked luggage is frequently lost or pilfered.

▶ **Bring a sweater.** No matter what time of year you visit, you're bound to use it.

▶ **Carry small packages of tissues.** Toilet paper is plentiful in hotels but less so in public buildings.

▶ **Speed your transit through passport control.** Bring a photocopy of your visa and hand it along with the original, to the official. Write down on the customs form the exact amount of currency you are carrying (in cash as well as traveler's checks); you may enter the country with any amount of money, but you cannot leave the country with more money than you had when you entered. Include on your customs form any jewelry (particularly silver, gold, and amber) as well as any electronic goods you have. It is important to include any valuable items on the form to ensure that you will be allowed to export them, but be aware that you are expected to take them with you, so you cannot leave them behind as gifts.

▶ **Drink only boiled or bottled water.** The water supply in St. Petersburg is thought to contain an intestinal parasite called Giardia lamblia, which causes diarrhea, stomach cramps, and nausea. The gestation period is two to three weeks, so symptoms usually arise after you return home. Imported, bottled water is widely available.

▶ **Pay in rubles even if prices are stated in dollars.** Prices are often listed in dollars in order to retain stability (and to avoid printing new menus every week), but payment must actually be made in rubles.

▶ **Carry your passport and a copy of your visa at all times.** Regardless of whether or not carrying your visa is a legal requirement (the law is hazy on the subject), a crooked cop will use it as an excuse to demand a "fine."

▶ **Ride solo in taxis.** As well as avoiding taxis that already have occupants, never allow your driver to stop to take an extra passenger after you have gotten in.

▶ **Travel by train.** In general, the best, safest, and most efficient way to get around Russia is by train. You can travel in relative comfort and there are plenty of overnight trains between Moscow and St. Petersburg.

Spain

▶ **Come between September and June to avoid crowds.** Spain is the number-one destination for European travelers.

▶ **Make reservations well in advance.** Paradors, usually government-operated hostelries, are extremely popular with foreigners and Spaniards alike

▶ **Specify if you want an automatic rental car.** Virtually all cars in Spain have a manual transmission—if you don't want a stick shift, reserve weeks in advance and specify automatic transmission, then call to reconfirm your automatic car before you leave for Spain.

▶ **Pay attention at the gas pump.** Most pumps offer a choice of gas, including leaded, unleaded, and diesel, so be careful to pick the right one for your car.

▶ **Never, ever leave anything valuable in a parked car.** That goes no matter how friendly the area feels, no matter how quickly you'll return, or how invisible the item seems once you lock it in the trunk. Thieves can spot rental cars a mile away, and they work very efficiently. In airports, laptop computers are choice prey.

▶ **Do not tip more than 10% of the bill.** Leave less if you eat tapas or sandwiches at a bar—just enough to round out the bill. Restaurant checks almost always include a service charge, which is not the same as a voluntary tip.

▶ **Don't assume holidays last just a day.** If a public holiday falls on a Tuesday or Thursday, many businesses also close on the nearest Monday or Friday. If a major holiday falls on a Sunday, businesses close on Monday.

▶ **Remember the siesta.** Almost all shops in Spain close at midday for at least three hours. You might find yourself about to faint of hunger or restless without a museum or shop to frequent, so plan your day around the break, taking it easy by the pool, say, or going for a bike ride.

Switzerland

▶ **Don't plan to use your euros.** Switzerland still uses its own currency, the Swiss franc (SF).

▶ **Look for the vignette.** To use the main highways, you must have this sticker on the top-center or lower corner of the windshield. There are no other tolls in Switzerland. You can buy it at the border (cash only; euros are accepted). It costs 40 SF and can also be purchased from any post office and from most gas stations; it's valid to the end of the year. Cars rented within Switzerland already have these stickers; if you rent a car elsewhere in Europe, ask if the company will provide the vignette for you.

▶ **Take it easy up high.** Limit strenuous excursions on the first day at extra-high-altitude resorts, those at 5,248 ft and above. Adults with heart problems may want to avoid all excursions above 6,560 ft.

▶ **Pack smart.** Bring a warm sweater. Even in July and August the evening air grows chilly in the mountains. And bring a hat or sunscreen, as the atmosphere is thinner at high altitudes. Glaciers can be blinding in the sun, so be sure to bring sunglasses, especially for high-altitude excursions. Good walking shoes or hiking boots are a must, whether you're tackling medieval cobblestones or mountain trails.

Scandinavia

▶ **Research Scandinavian air passes.** The SAS Visit Scandinavia/Europe Air Pass offers up to eight flight coupons for one-way travel within and between Scandinavian cities (and participating European cities). These money-saving passes can only be bought in conjunction with a round-trip ticket between North America and Europe on SAS airline.

▶ **Plan road trips carefully.** In a few remote areas, especially in northern Norway, Sweden, and Finland, road conditions can be unpredictable. Several mountain and highland roads in these areas close during winter. When driving in remote areas like these, especially in winter, it is best to let someone know your travel plans. It is also wise to use a four-wheel-drive vehicle and to travel with at least one other car in these areas.

▶ **Make reservations whenever possible.** Even countryside inns, which usually have space, are sometimes packed with vacationing Europeans.

▶ **Bring an eye mask and dark sunglasses.** Otherwise you may have trouble sleeping when it is light or be irritated by the strong sun. The sun rises as early as 4 AM in some areas, and the far-northern latitude causes it to slant at angles unseen elsewhere on the globe.

▶ **Take advantage of tax-free shopping.** One way to beat high prices throughout Scandinavia is to show your passport. Major purchases are free of tax if you have a foreign passport. Ask about getting your items tax-free when you're considering a purchase of 50 SF or more.

▶ **Consider a Scanrail Pass or Scanrail'n Drive Pass.** These are available for travel in Denmark, Sweden, Norway, and Finland. Depending on your travel plans, these can save you money.

Eastern Europe

▶ **Never photograph Gypsies, however colorful.** Ask for permission and agree on payment. Photographing anything military, assuming you'd want to, is usually prohibited. Otherwise, although people are pleased to be photographed, it's respectful to ask first.

▶ **Buy fresh fruits and vegetables at street markets.** Regular grocery stores often don't sell them.

▶ **Vegetarians should pack vitamins and protein bars.** Vegetarians and those on special diets may have a problem with the heavy local cuisine, which is based largely on pork and beef.

▶ **Beware unpasteurized milk products.** In Romania, unrefrigerated milk sold in outdoor markets or in villages may not be pasteurized and can make Westerners sick. In Bulgaria, mayonnaise-based fillings are very common in *sandvitchee*—the ubiquitous toasted sandwiches sold at many street kiosks; avoid them.

▶ **Bring necessities.** Some items that you take for granted at home are occasionally unavailable or of questionable quality in Eastern and Central Europe, though the situation has been steadily improving.

Toiletries and personal-hygiene products have become relatively easy to find, but it's always a good idea to bring necessities when traveling in rural areas.

▶ **In Bulgaria, have a flashlight with you at all times.** Streetlights are rare, even in city centers, and often interior hallways are unlit.

▶ **Beware of pickpockets in crowded areas.** That's especially true on public transportation, at railway stations, and in big hotels. Crime rates are still relatively low in Eastern and Central Europe, but you should always keep your valuables with you—in open bars and restaurants, purses hung on or placed next to chairs are easy targets. Men: make sure your wallet is safe in a buttoned pocket. Women: watch your handbag.

▶ **Avoid getting ripped off as a tourist.** In the Czech Republic and Slovakia, ask taxi drivers what the approximate fare will be before getting in, and asking for a receipt (paragon in the Czech Republic and potvrdenka in Slovakia) might also discourage a driver from charging you an enormous fare—or it could be used when complaining about a fare to a taxi dispatcher. Carefully look over restaurant bills; be extremely wary of handing your passport to anyone who accosts you with a demand for ID; and never exchange money on the street.

▶ **Know local scams.** A notorious scam in some Romanian cities involves men flashing fake police badges and accusing you of exchanging currency illegally. Do not hand over your passport or money; instead, offer to accompany them (on foot) to your hotel or a police station. If you spot a uniformed policeman, summon him. On trains and buses, groups sometimes cause distractions, then make off with your valuables.

SOUTH AMERICA

▶ **Keep on top of the latest travel warnings.** The U.S. State Department has a 24-hour hot line (202/647–5225) and a Web site (travel.state.gov), with details on each country.

▶ **Andes bound? Check with your doctor.** The area can be hard on you if you have high blood pressure and a history of heart trouble.

▶ **Price both buses and planes for long trips.** They're often similar. When traveling by bus, expect to pay with cash, as credit cards aren't accepted everywhere.

▶ **Expect to pay a hefty airplane-departure tax.** Most countries charge at least the equivalent of US$25 for nonresidents. You can use your remaining local currency or pay in U.S. dollars.

▶ **Consider hiring a car and driver.** Go through your hotel concierge, or make a deal with a taxi driver for some extended sightseeing at a longer-term rate. Drivers often charge an hourly rate, regardless of the distance traveled. You'll have to pay cash, but you'll often spend less than you would for a rental car.

▶ **Watch what you eat and drink.** Stay away from food that is uncooked or has been sitting around. Drink only bottled water or water that has been boiled for at least 10 minutes, even when you're brushing your teeth. If you plan to visit remote regions or stay for more than six weeks, check with the Centers for Disease Control (CDC) Travelers Hot Line: 877/394–8747.

▶ **Be sure to clarify if you want a double mattress.** A double room doesn't guarantee a mattress for two. If you'd like to avoid twin beds, ask for a *cama de casal* ("couple's bed") in Spanish or *cama de casal* in Portuguese.

▶ **Visit any room before accepting it.** Price is no guarantee of charm or cleanliness, and accommodations can vary dramatically within one hotel. Be especially careful in the countryside.

▶ **Check the hotel shower.** Some hotels have electric-powered showerheads rather than central water heaters. If you want hot water you have to turn the water pressure down; if you want pressure, expect a brisk rinse. Don't adjust the power when you're under the water—you can get a little shock.

▶ **Pack appropriately for each country.** Sure climates change, but so do local preferences. If there's a rule for dressing in South America, it's to dress more conservatively on the west coast than on the east.

Argentina

▶ **Register your computer upon leaving home.** Also, declare your computer at customs upon entering Argentina—you'll need to produce either a document from U.S customs or its receipt, and be sure to declare it on the way out (keep your receipts for this purpose).

▶ **Buy your train tickets a few days ahead.** Do so two months ahead in summer—and arrive at the station well before departure time. Reservations must be made in person at the local train station.

▶ **Don't expect a deal on a rental car.** A midsize car costs around $85 per day plus tax. Extras such as car seats and air-conditioning drive the fee even higher. Ask about special rates; generally a better price can be negotiated. Reserve ahead if you plan to rent during a holiday period, when vehicles may be in short supply. However, you can probably get the best rate by renting upon arrival, particularly from a smaller, local company. Keep in mind that almost all cars have manual transmission rather than automatic.

▶ **Change your money in cities.** You may not be able to change currency in rural areas at all, so don't leave cities without adequate amounts of pesos in small denominations.

Brazil

▶ **Buy an air pass before you leave home.** These are useful if you plan to travel a lot within Brazil (these can only be purchased outside Brazil). Passes from TAM, Transbrasil, or Varig can save you hundreds of dollars.

▶ **Be prepared to pay a hefty departure tax.** Expect to shell out about R$78 ($36) for international flights. A departure tax also applies to flights within Brazil. Although the amount varies, figure on R$11–R$22 ($5–$10). Although some airports accept credit cards as payment for departure taxes, it's wise to have the appropriate amount in reais.

▶ **Get peak-season bus tickets and reservations early.** It's a must when traveling to resort areas during high season—particularly on weekends—or during major holidays and school-break periods. In general, arrive at bus stations early, particularly for peak-season travel.

▶ **Watch your belongings closely.** Be extra vigilant especially in bus stations.

▶ **Bring water and toilet paper along for day trips.** You may not find it provided.

▶ **Bring your own film.** It's expensive in Brazil and is frequently stored in hot conditions.

▶ **Be careful of the water.** Drink only bottled water or water that has been boiled for at least 10 minutes. Stay away from ice, uncooked food, and unpasteurized milk and milk products. Peel or thoroughly wash fresh fruits and vegetables.

Chile

▶ **Always check with your doctor about shots.** All travelers to Chile should get up-to-date tetanus, diphtheria, and measles boosters, and a hepatitis A inoculation is recommended. Children traveling to Chile should have current inoculations against mumps, rubella, and polio.

▶ **Pack for all seasons.** No matter what time of year you're traveling, you'll need clothing to suit a wide range of temperatures.

▶ **Avoid altitude sickness by ascending slowly.** Spend a few nights at 6,000–9,000 feet before you head higher. If you must fly straight in, plan on doing next to nothing for your first few days. If you begin to experience symptoms—shortness of breath, nausea, and splitting headaches—the traditional remedy is herbal tea made from coca leaves.

▶ **Arrive at bus stations extra early in peak seasons.** Companies are notoriously difficult to reach by phone, so it's often better to stop by the terminal to check on prices and schedules.

▶ **Ask permission before taking pictures of people.**
Chileans seem amenable to having picture-taking
tourists in their midst, but you should ask first.

▶ **Don't drive after mulithour rains.** Between May
and August, roads, underpasses, and parks can flood
when it rains. It's very dangerous, especially for drivers
who don't know their way around.

Contacts and Resources

AIRLINE ASSOCIATIONS

Air Transport Association of America

www.air-transport.org
1301 Pennsylvania Ave.
NW, Suite 1100
Washington, DC 20004-1707
202/626–4000

The trade organization of the principal U.S. airlines.

Association of Flight Attendants

www.afanet.org
1275 K St. NW, Suite 500
Washington, DC 20005
202/712–9799

The world's largest labor union organized by flight attendants for flight attendants. Ellen Church, the first "skygirl," founded the profession in 1930; the union was founded in 1945 to combat current industry practices—women were forced to retire at 32, remain unmarried, and observe weight, height, and appearance standards—and now represents over 49,000 flight attendants at 27 airlines.

Baggage Claim

Unclaimed Baggage Center

www.unclaimedbaggage.com
509 W. Willow St.
Scottsboro, AL 35768
256/259–1525

The packing tips come from a unique perspective on the Web site of this Alabama store (which sells merchandise and clothing from baggage that has been officially declared unclaimed).

Consolidators

Air by Pleasant

www.airbypleasant.com
4015 Camino del Rio S,
Suite 210
San Diego, CA 92108
800/877–8111

D-FW Tours

www.dwftours.com
7616 LBJ Fwy., Suite 524
Dallas, TX 75251
800/527–2589

Jax Fax Travel Marketing Magazine

www.jaxfax.com
48 Wellington Rd.
Milford, CT 06460
203/301–0255

Pacific Gateway

www.pacificgateway.com
320 S.W. Stark St., Suite 315
Portland, OR 97204
800/777–8369

United States Air Consolidators Association

www.usaca.com
926 L St.
Sacramento, CA 95814
916/441–4166

United States Tour Operators Association

www.ustoa.com
275 Madison Ave.,
Suite 2014
New York, NY 10016
212/599–6599

Consumer Advocacy

Aviation Consumer Action Project

www.acap1971.org/acap.html
529 14th St. NW, Suite 923
Washington, DC 20045

Ralph Nader founded this nonprofit in 1971 to represent air travelers, pilots, and other flight crew, air-disaster victims, air traffic controllers, and the like. Publishes "Facts and Advice for Airline Passengers" ($5), outlining passengers' rights under federal law. Nader also has written the 378-page Collision Course: The Truth about Airline Safety ($12), detailing the effect of economics and politics on air safety. The Web site has many useful links.

International Air Passengers Association

www.iapa.com
Box 700188
Dallas, TX 75370-0188
972/404–9980 or 800/821–4272

Advocacy and discounted travel services, including discounted admission to 300 airport lounges worldwide.

PassengerRights.com

www.passengerrights.com

Horror stories you'll want to avoid, summaries of passenger rights; on-line forum for complaints.

Couriers

Air Courier Association

www.aircourier.org
350 Indiana St., Suite 300
Golden, CO 80401
800/282–1202 or 800/822–0888

True courier operation that also provides access to low fares from consolidators and discounters, last-minute sales, and other deals.

International Association of Air Travel Couriers

www.iaatc.com
Box 980
Keystone Heights, FL 32656
352/475–1584

Delays

Bureau of Transportation Statistics

www.bts.gov/ntda/oai
U.S. Department of Transportation
400 7th St. SW
Washington, DC 20590

Source of airline on-time performance ratings and airport-delay stats.

Frequent-Flier Programs

FrequentFlier.com

A lively site full of tips and updates plus airport links, forums, a history of airline loyalty programs, and a detailed up-to-date discussion of the pros and cons of various programs.

Inside Flyer

www.webflyer.com
800/209–2870

Definitive source of everything to know about frequent travel programs.

Points.com

www.points.com
134 Peter St.
Toronto, Ont. M5V 2H2
Canada
866/340–3717

Here you can buy miles and exchange miles from one program for miles in another. Many links.

General

Airline Alliances
OneWorld
www.oneworld.com

Airline Policies
www.onetravel.com

You can find most airlines' contracts of carriage on their Web sites. But these are hefty documents. "Rules of the Air" is helpful if you want to look up something specific.

Airports Council International (ACI)
www.airports.org
Box 16
1215 Geneva 15—Airport
Switzerland
(41)22/717–8585

Airports trade group, with publications and statistics.

Airports International
www.airportsintl.com

Links to airports worldwide.

Johnny Jet Travel Portal
www.johnnyjet.com

A former fearful flier–turned–frequent flier maintains this very rich site where you can link to anything and everything from the Passport Service to pilots' bulletin boards to newspaper travel sections; look for flight schedules, in-flight movie lineups, TV schedules everywhere, the latest weather, and much more.

Qualiflyer
www.qualiflyer.com

RudyMaxa.com
www.rudymaxa.com

The PBS travel columnist's site. You can browse or sign up for an e-mail newsletter ($60).

SkyTeam
www.SkyTeam.com

Smarter Living
www.smarterliving.com

This site is jammed with current consumer travel information from deals and the latest developments in frequent-flier programs to airport delays. The money-saving tips are good (as in the interesting discussion of back-to-back ticketing and hidden-cities tickets at www.smarterliving.com/columns/tightwad/Questionable20010925.1.html). No ticket sales.

Star Alliance
www.star-alliance.com

Government Help

Air Travelers Association
www.1800airsafe.com
202/686–2870 or 800/247–7273

Publishes an Air Safety Report Card for 250 airlines

worldwide as well as a newsletter; represents consumers with complaints.

Aviation Consumer Protection Division
www.dot.gov/airconsumer
U.S. Department of
Transportation
400 7th St. SW
Washington, DC 20590
202/366–2220

U.S. Carriers' customer-service commitments are at www.dot.gov/airconsumer/customerservice.htm. The site also publishes statistics on bumping and oversells; a series of fact sheets called "Plane Talk" on topics ranging from frequent-flier plans to baggage to passengers with disabilities; and "Consumers Tell It to the Judge," about how to negotiate in small-claims court. All of these are available on the Web at www.dot.gov/airconsumer/pubs.htm and www.dot.gov/airconsumer/telljudge.htm.

Federal Aviation Administration (FAA)
www.faa.gov
800 Independence Ave. SW
Washington, DC 20591
202/366–4000 or 800/255–1111; 800/322–7873 Consumer Hotline; 866/289–9673 Transportation Security Hotline; 800/255–1111

Aviation Safety Hotline for time-critical events.

Current information on airport procedures, airline regulations, forbidden carry-ons, and much more. For countries whose safety standards are below accepted international levels, see www.faa.gov/avr/iasa and click on "assessment results."

In-Flight Health

Aerospace Medical Association
www.asma.org
320 S. Henry St.
Alexandria, VA 22314-3579
703/739–2240

Centers for Disease Control
www.cdc.gov/travel/sprayair.htm

Overview and links explaining disinfection, spraying aircraft for insects.

Healthy Flying
www.flyana.com

Author and former flight attendant Diana Fairechild holds forth on cabin air quality, pesticide spraying in flight, and other topics.

Jet Lag Diet
www.newton.dep.anl.gov/askasci/gen99/gen99875.htm
Argonne National
Laboratory

c/o Public Affairs
9700 S. Cass Ave.
Argonne, IL 60439
630/252–2000

The often-quoted jet lag diet was developed by a scientist here; copies can be mailed or faxed.

Pesticides Onboard
www.afanet.org/pesticides_what_you_need_to_know.htm

The flight attendants' union's view of required pesticide applications abroad.

U.S. Department of Transportation
www.ostpxweb.dot.gov/policy/safety/disin.htm

Has telephone numbers of various airline disinsection specialists.

Pets in the Air

Air Travel for Your Dog or Cat
www.airlines.org/public/publications

Detailed information from the Air Transport Association and U.S. Department of Agriculture.

Transporting Live Animals
www.dot.gov/airconsumer/animals.htm

Published by the DOT's Aviation Consumer Protection Division.

Traveler Information: Pets/Animals
www.customs.ustreas.gov/travel/travel.htm

Information from U.S. Customs, with specifics for various species.

Traveling with Your Pet
www.aphis.usda.gov/oa/pubs/petravel.htm

The U.S. Department of Agriculture weighs in on the subject.

Plane Manufacturers

Airbus
www.airbus.com

Boeing
www.boeing.com/commercial

Details on various models.

Fokker
www.fokker.com

Plane Models in Airline Fleets
av-info.faa.gov/detail.asp

Click on Air Operator Certificate Information, then search by Operator Type; choose Domestic and Flag (Pax/Cargo).

Safety

AirSafe.com
www.AirSafe.com

The project of airline-safety analyst Todd Curtis, AirSafe.com includes safety tips and answers to such common questions as "Where's the safest place to sit?" as well as perversely fascinating coverage of airline fatalities by model, aircraft type, region, and the like. Many links.

Anna's Inflight Safety Page
www.plsys.co.uk/~Eanna/inflight.html

Anna, a former flight attendant who now trains other attendants for British Airways, gives examples of and suggestions for dealing with fire, smoke, decompression, and other inflight emergencies.

Aviation Safety Network
aviation-safety.net

Full-text accident reports involving aircraft damaged beyond repair, links to accident cockpit voice recordings; sign up for e-mail notifications.

Flight Safety Foundation
www.flightsafety.org
601 Madison St., Suite 300
Alexandria, VA 22314-1756
703/739–6700

An independent, international nonprofit forum for safety concerns.

National Air Disaster Alliance/Foundation
www.planesafe.org

2020 Pennsylvania Ave. NW
Washington, DC 20006-1846

An advocacy group that aims to raise the standard of safety, security, and survivability for aviation passengers.

National Transportation Safety Board
www.ntsb.gov/aviation/aviation.htm
490 L'Enfant Plaza SW
Washington, DC 20594
202/314–6000

An independent federal agency that investigates U.S. civil aviation accidents. You can review accident synopses and read reports on major investigations, forums, and public hearings.

Schedules and Seating Plans

Official Airline Guide
www.oag.com
800/342–5624

Flight schedules are published in book form and in an on-line version (downloadable onto PDAs). Seating charts.

Tickets and Reservations

Air Brokers
www.airbrokers.com
415/397–1383 or 800/883–3273

California-based travel agent specializing in complicated itineraries; established 1987.

AirTreks
www.AirTreks.com
c/o High Adventure Travel
442 Post St.
San Francisco, CA 94102
415/912–5600 or 800/350–0612

Travel agent specializing in writing multistop international tickets.

Bestfares.com
Collects little-known offers; members have access to the best.

Bidding Sites
Bid4Vacations.com
www.thedailyauction.com

Cheapfares.com
Tickets from major U.S. cities to popular destinations outside the country.

Cheaptickets.com
888/922–8849

Research fares and availability here, but call to confirm your fare is the lowest available.

Expedia Travel
www.expedia.com

Hotwire.com
A hybrid booking site where you are given the price before you purchase your ticket.

LastMinuteTravel.com
Displays offers from various providers, with many late-breaking specials. Book through the provider.

Lowestfare.com
Uses American Airlines' Sabre system.

Orbitz
www.orbitz.com

Agency started and owned by American, Continental, Delta, Northwest, and United.

Priceline.com
Air travelers agree to one stop if necessary. Bids are accepted within an hour.

Qixo.com
Searches 20 top travel Web sites. You can buy on the site or from the vendors.

Skyauction.com
All auctions have a starting bid of $1.

Travelocity
www.travelocity.com
Largest on-line agency.

YouPriceIt.com
Lets you know within two hours (24 hours for international flights). If rejected, you're told the lowest list-price fares available.

AIRLINES

Domestic Carriers

AirTran (FL)
www.airtran.com
770/994–8258, 800/825–8538,
or 800/247–8726

Alaska Airlines (AS)
www.alaska-air.com
800/252–7522; 206/870–6062
customer service

Aloha Airlines (AQ)
www.alohaair.com
800/367–5250

America West (HP)
www.americawest.com
800/235–9292; 480/693–6019
customer service

American Airlines (AA)
www.aa.com; amrcorp.com
800/433–7300; 817/967–2000
customer service

American TransAir/ATA (TZ)
www.ata.com
800/225–2995 or 800/435–9282; 877/617–1139 or 317/243–4140 customer service

Continental Airlines (CO)
www.continental.com
800/525–0280 domestic; 800/231–0856 international; 800/525–0280 in Canada; 800/932–2732 customer service

Delta Air Lines (DL)
www.delta-air.com
800/221–1212 domestic; 800/231–0856 international; 800/525–0280 in Canada; 404/715–1450 customer service

Frontier Airlines (F9)
www.frontierairlines.com
800/432–1359; 800/265–5505
customer relations

Hawaii Airlines (HA)
www.hawaiianair.com
800/367–5320; 888/246–8526
customer advocate department

Horizonair (QX)
www.horizonair.com
800/547–9308; 206/431–3647
consumer comments

JetBlue Airways (B6)
www.jetblue.com
800/538–2583; 800/944–4840
customer relations fax

Mesa Airlines (YV)
www.mesa-air.com
800/637–2247; 602/685–4000
customer service

Midway Airlines (JI)
www.midwayair.com
800/446–4392

Midwest Express (YX)
www.midwestexpress.com
800/452–2022; 414/570–4080
consumer affairs

National Airlines (N7)
www.nationalairlines.com
888/757–5387; 877/625–7378
customer service

Northwest Airlines (NW)
www.nwa.com
800/225–2525 domestic; 800/447–4747 international; 612/726–2046 customer service

Southwest Airlines (WN)
www.iflyswa.com
800/435–9792; 214/792–4223
customer service

Spirit Airlines (NK)
www.spiritair.com
800/772–7117; 954/447–7965
corporate office

United Airlines (UA)
www.ual.com
800/824–6200 automated
flight info; 800/241–6522
domestic; 800/538–2929 international; 877/228–1327
customer service

US Airways (US)
www.usairways.com
800/428–4322 domestic; 800/
622–1015 international; 336/
661–0061 customer service

Vanguard Airlines (NJ)
www.flyvanguard.com
800/826–4827; 913/789–1746
customer service fax

International Carriers

Aer Lingus (EI)
www.aerlingus.com
800/223–6537

Aerolineas Argentinas (AR)
www.aerlineas.com
305/648–4100 or 800/333–
0276; 800/688–0008 in
Canada

Aeromexico (AM)
www.aeromexico.com
800/237–6639 in the U.S.
and Canada

Air Canada (AC)
www.aircanada.ca
888/247–2262 in the U.S.
and Canada

Air France (AF)
www.airfrance.com
800/237–2747; 800/667–2747
in Canada

Air-India (AI)
www.airindia.com
800/223–7776; 800/223–2250
first and executive class; 416/
865–1033 in Canada

Air Jamaica (JM)
www.airjamaica.com
800/523–5585

Air New Zealand (NZ)
www.airnz.com
800/262–1234; 800/663–5494
in Canada

Alitalia Airlines (AZ)
www.alitalia.it
800/223–5730; 800/361–8336
in Canada

ANA All-Nippon Airlines (NH)
www.fly-ana.com
800/235–9262 in the U.S.
and Canada

Austrian Airlines (OS)
Also Tyrolean Airways
www.aua.com
800/843–0002; 888/817–4444
in Canada

Avianca (AV)
www.avianca.com
800/284–2622; 800/387–8667
in Canada

British Airways (BA)
www.british-airways.com
800/247–9297; 416/250–0880
in Canada

British Midland Airways (BD)
www.flybmi.com
800/788–0555 in the U.S.
and Canada

Buzz
www.buzzaway.com
870/240–7070 in the U.K.

BWIA (BW)
www.bwee.com
800/538–2942; 800/538–2942
in Canada

Cathay Pacific Airways (CX)
www.cathay-usa.com
800/233–2742; 800/268–6868
in Toronto; 604/606–8888 in
Vancouver

Cayman Airways (KX)
www.caymanairways.com
800/422–9626; 345/949–2311
outside the U.S.

Czech Airlines (OK)
www.csa.cz
212/ 765–6022, 800/223–
2365, or 800/628–6107

EasyJet (EZ)
www.easyjet.com/en
870/600–0000 in the U.K.

El Al Israel Airlines (LY)
www.elal.co.il
800/223–6700; 800/361–6174
or 416/967–4222 in Canada

Finnair (AY)
www.finnair.com

800/950–5000; 800/361–6174
or 416/967–4222 in Canada

Go (GO)
www.go-fly.com
127/966–6388 in the U.K.

Iberia Airlines (IB)
www.iberia.com
800/772–4642

Icelandair (FI)
www.icelandair.com
800/223–5500 in the U.S.
and Canada

Japan Airlines (JL)
www.jal.com
800/525–3663 in the U.S.
and Canada

KLM (KL)
www.klm.com
800/447–4747 in the U.S.
and Canada

Lacsa Costa Rica (LR)
www.centralamerica.com/
cr/lacsa/lacsa.htm, www.
taca.com
800/225–2272; 416/968–2222
in Canada

LanChile (LA)
www.lanchile.com
800/735–5526; 905/673–1297
in Canada

Lauda Air (NG)
www.laudaair.com
800/843–0002; 888/817–4444
in Canada

Lufthansa (LH)
www.lufthansa.com
800/645–3880; 800/563–5954
in Canada

Malaysia Airlines (MH)
www.malaysiaairlines.com
800/552–9264; 888/627–8477
first and business class; 310/
535–9288 N.A. headquarters

Mexicana (MX)
www.mexicana.com.mx
800/531–7921 in the U.S.
and Canada

Olympic Airways (OA)
www.olympic-airways.gr
800/223–1226; 416/964–2720
in Canada

Qantas Airways (QF)
www.qantas.com.au
800/897–0106; 800/227–4500
in the U.S. and Canada

Royal Air Maroc (AT)
www.royalairmaroc.com
800/344–6726; 514/285–1937
in Canada

Ryanair (FR)
www.ryanair.com
870/156–9569 in the U.K.

SAS (SK)
www.scandinavian.net
800/221–2350 in the U.S.
and Canada

Singapore Airlines (SQ)
www.singaporeair.com
800/742–3333; 800/663–3046
in Canada

**South African Airways
(SA)**
www.flysaa.com
800/722–9675; 800/387–4629
in Canada

Swiss (LX)
www.swiss.com

877/359–7947; 800/221–4750
in Canada

TAP Air Portugal (TP)
www.tap.pt/eportal/v10/EN/
jsp/index.jsp
800/221–7370

Thai Airways (TG)
www.thaiair.com
800/426–5204; 800/668–8103
in Canada

Varig (RG)
www.varig.com.br/english
800/468–2744; 800/898–2744
in Canada

**Virgin Atlantic Airways
(VS)**
www.virgin-atlantic.com
800/862–8621; 1293/450–150
in the U.K.

AIRPORTS

Acapulco (ACA)

Albany, NY (ALB)
www.albanyairport.com

Albuquerque (ABQ)
www.cabg.gov/airport

Amarillo (AMA)
www.amarillo-cvb.org/
airport.html

**Amsterdam Schiphol
(AMS)**
www.schiphol.nl

Anchorage (ANC)

Athens (ATH)
www.athensairport-2001.gr

Atlanta (ATL)
www.atlanta-airport.com

Auckland (AKL)
www.auckland-airport.co.nz

Austin (AUS)
www.ci.austin.tx.us/
newairport

Baltimore (BWI)
www.bwiairport.com

Bangkok (BKK)
www.airportthai.or.th/
airportnew/bia/html

Barcelona (BCN)
www.barcelona-airport.com

Baton Rouge (BTR)
www.ci.baton-rouge.la.us/
dept/airport

Beijing (PEK)

Belfast (BFS)
www.bial.co.uk

Belize City (BZE)

**Berlin-Brandenburg-
International (BER)**
www.berlin-airport.de

Billings (BIL)

Birmingham, AL (BHM)
www.bhamintlairport.com

Boise (BOI)
www.ci.boise.id.us/
transportation/airport

Bombay (BOM)
www.mumbaiairport.com

Boston Logan (BOS)
www.massport.com/logan

Brisbane, Australia (BNE)
www.brisbaneairport.net

Brussels (BRU)
www.brusselsairport.be

Budapest (BUD)
www.budapest-airport.lri.
hu/english

Buenos Aires (EZE)

Buffalo (BUF)
www.buffaloairport.com

Burbank, CA (BUR)
www.burbankairport.com

Burlington, VT (BTV)
www.burlingtonintlairport.
com

Cancun (CUN)

Capetown (CPT)
www.airports.co.za/acsa/cia/
cia_home.html

Caracas (CCS)

Charleston, SC (CHS)
chs-airport.com/index.htm

Charlotte, NC (CLT)
www.charlotteairport.com

Chattanooga (CHA)
www.chattairport.com

Chicago Midway (MDW)
www.ohare.com/midway/
home.asp

Chicago O'Hare (ORD)
www.ohare.com/ohare/
home.asp

Cincinnati (CVG)
www.cvgairport.com

Cleveland (CLE)
www.clevelandairport.com

Columbus, OH (CMH)
www.port-columbus.com

Copenhagen (CPH)
www.cph.dk

Cozumel (CZM)

Dallas-Ft. Worth (DFW)
www.dfwairport.com

Dallas Love Field (DAL)
www.guidelive.com/topic/
visitors_topic/features/love/
home.htm

Dayton (DAY)
www.daytonairport.com

Delhi (DEL)
www.delhiairport.com

Denver International
(DEN)
www.flydenver.com

Des Moines (DSM)
www.dsmairport.com

Detroit Metro (DTW)
www.metroairport.com

Dubai (DXB)
www.dubaiairport.com

Dublin, Ireland (DUB)
www.dublin-airport.com

Durango (DRO)
co.laplata.co.us/airport.html

Edinburgh, Scotland (EDI)
www.baa.co.uk/main/
airports/edinburgh

Eugene (EUG)
www.eugeneairport.com

Fairbanks (FAI)

Fort Lauderdale (FLL)
www.co.broward.fl.us/fll.
htm

Fort Myers, FL (RSW)
www.swfia.com

Frankfurt (FRA)
www.frankfurt-airport.de

Geneva, Switzerland
(GVA)
www.gva.ch/en/default.htm

Glasgow (GLA)

Grand Rapids (GRR)
www.grr.org

Green Bay (GRB)

Guatemala City (GUA)

Hamburg (HAM)
www.hamburg-ham.com

Hartford (BDL)
www.bradleyairport.com

Helsinki (HEL)

Hong Kong (HKG)
www.hkairport.com

Honolulu (HNL)
www.honoluluairport.com

Houston Hobby (HOU)
www.houstonairportsystem.
org

Houston Intercontinental
(IAH)
www.houstonairportsystem.
org

Indianapolis (IND)
www.indianapolisairport.
com

Islip, NY (ISP)
www.stewartintlairport.com

Istanbul (IST)
www.ataturkairport.com
(in Turkish only)

Jacksonville, FL (JAX)
www.jaxairports.org

Johannesburg (JNB)
www.airports.co.za

Kalamazoo/Battle Creek, Michigan (AZO)
www.kalcounty.com/airport.htm

Kansas City, MO (MCI)
www.kcairports.com/kci

Key West (EYW)
www.keywestinternationalairport.com

Knoxville (TYS)
www.tys.org

Lansing (LAN)
www.capitalcityairport.com

Las Vegas (LAS)
www.mccarran.com

Lima, Peru (LIM)
www.lap.com.pe

Lincoln, NE (LNK)
www.lincolnairport.com

Lisbon, Portugal (LIS)
www.ana-aeroportos.pt/eng/aeroportos/lisboa/lisboa.htm

Little Rock (LIT)
lrairport.dina.org

London Gatwick (LGW)
www.baa.co.uk/main/airports/gatwick

London Heathrow (LHR)
www.baa.co.uk/main/airports/heathrow

London Luton (LTN)
www.london-luton.com

London Stansted (STN)
www.baa.co.uk/main/airports/stansted

Long Beach, CA (LGB)
www.lgb.org

Los Angeles (LAX)
www.airports.ci.la.ca.us/

Louisville (SDF)
www.louintlairport.com

Madison, WI (MSN)
www.co.dane.wi.us/airport/index.html

Madrid Barjas (MAD)
www.aena.es/ae/mad/homepage.htm

Manchester, England (MAN)
www.manairport.co.uk

McAllen, TX (MFE)
www.mcallenairport.com

Melbourne, Australia (MEL)
www.melbourne-airport.com.au

Memphis (MEM)
www.mscaa.com

Mexico City (MEX)
www.mexico-city-mex.com

Miami (MIA)
www.miami-airport.com

Milan Malpensa (MXP)
www.sea-aeroportimilano.it/malpensa

Milwaukee (MKE)
www.mitchellairport.com

Minneapolis-St. Paul (MSP)
www.mspairport.com

Mobile, AL (MOB)
www.mobairport.com

Montgomery, AL (MGM)
www.montgomeryairport.org

Montréal-Dorval (YUL)
www.admtl.com/dorval/en/
1_bienvenue/bienvenue-e.
shtml

Montréal-Mirabel
www.admtl.com/mirabel/en/
1_bienvenue/bienvenue-e.
shtml

Munich (MUC)
www.munich-airport.de

Nairobi (NBO)
www.meteo.go.ke/obsv/
stations/jomo.html

Nashville, TN (BNA)
www.nashintl.com

Nassau, Bahamas (NAS)

New Haven (HVN)
www.
tweednewhavenairport.com

New Orleans (MSY)
www.flymsy.com

**New York John F. Kennedy
(JFK)**
www.panynj.gov/aviation/
jfkframe.htm

**New York La Guardia
(LGA)**
www.panynj.gov/aviation/
lgaframe.htm

Newark (EWR)
www.panynj.gov/aviation/
ewrframe.htm

Oakland, CA (OAK)
www.flyoakland.com/
index2.cfm

Ontario, CA (ONT)
www.airports.ci.la.ca.us/ont/
ontframe.html

Orange County, CA (SNA)
www.ocair.com

Orlando (MCO)
www.state.fl.us/goaa

Osaka (KIX)
www.kansai-airport.or.jp/
english/index.htm

Oslo (OSL)
www.osl.no

Ottawa (YOW)
www.ottawa-airport.ca

Palm Springs, CA (PSP)
www.ci.palm-springs.ca.
us/Departments/airport/
airport.html

Palma de Mallorca (PMI)
www.aena.es/ae/pmi/
homepage.htm
(in Spanish)

Paris Orly (ORY)
www.adp.fr

**Paris Roissy Charles de
Gaulle (CDG)**
www.adp.fr

Philadelphia (PHL)
www.phl.org

Phoenix (PHX)
www.phxskyharbor.com

Pittsburgh (PIT)
www.pitairport.com

Portland, ME (PWM)
www.portlandjetport.org

Portland, OR (PDX)
www.portlandairportpdx.
com

Prague (PRG)
www.csa.cz/en/let/letiste.
htm

Providence, RI (PVD)
www.pvd-ri.com

Raleigh-Durham (RDU)
www.rdu.com

Richmond, VA (RIC)
www.flyrichmond.com/
Index_Splash.html

Rio de Janeiro (GIG)
Rome Fiumicino (FCO)
www.adr.it/en/fiumic/
fiumic-00.html

Sacramento (SMF)
airports.co.sacramento.ca.us

Salt Lake City (SLC)
www.slcairport.com

San Antonio (SAT)
www.ci.sat.tx.us/aviation

San Diego (SAN)
www.portofsandiego.org/
sandiego_airportindex.html

San Francisco (SFO)
www.flysfo.com

San Jose, CA (SJC)
www.sjc.org

San Juan, PR (SJU)

Sanford, FL (SFB)
www.orlandosanfordairport.
com

Santiago (SCL)
www.aeropuertosantiago.cl

Santo Domingo (SDQ)

Sao Paulo (GRU)
www.infraero.gov.br

Sarasota, FL (SRQ)
www.srq-airport.com

Seattle-Tacoma (SEA)
www.portseattle.org/seatac

Seoul Kimpo (SEL)
www.kimpo-airport.co.kr
(in Korean)

Singapore (SIN)
www.changi.airport.com.sg

Spokane (GEG)
www.spokaneairports.net

St. Louis (STL)
www.lambert-stlouis.com

St. Maarten (SXM)

St. Thomas (STT)

Stockholm (ARN)
www.lfv.se/site/airports/
arlanda/eng/index.asp

Sydney (SYD)
www.sydneyairport.com.au

Taipei (TPE)
www.cksairport.gov.tw

Tampa (TPA)
www.tampaairport.com

Tel Aviv (TLV)
www.ben-gurion-airport.
com/english.htm

Tokyo Haneda (HND)
www2f.biglobe.ne.jp/
~Emasaho/us/indexus.htm
(in Japanese)

Tokyo Narita (NRT)
www.narita-airport.or.jp/
airport_e

Toronto (YYZ)
www.gtaa.com

Tucson (TUS)
www.tucsonairport.org

Vancouver (YVR)
www.yvr.ca

Vienna (VIE)
www.viennaairport.com

Warsaw (WAW)

Washington, D.C., Dulles (IAD)
www.metwashairports.com/
Dulles

Washington, D.C., National (DCA)
www.metwashairports.com/
National

West Palm Beach (PBI)
www.pbia.org

Westchester County, New York (HPN)
www.westchestergov.com/
airport

Zurich (ZRH)
www.zurich-airport.ch

BUSINESS TRAVEL

Biz Trip
www.business-trip.com
Airlines, car rentals, weather forecast, city links, tips.

Joe Sent Me
www.joesentme.com
Business travel tips and news.

CAR TRAVEL

AAA
AAA.com
888/859–5161
Roadside assistance, maps, and trip-planning in the United States.

Cracker Barrel
www.crackerbarrel.com
800/333–9566
Trip-planning assistance and shop locations with books-on-tape exchange.

Rand McNally
www.randmcnally.com
Driving directions, weather reports, road maps and atlases, and a Road Explorers program, with roadside and travel planning assistance.

CAR-RENTAL AGENCIES

Avis Rental Car
avis.com
800/230–4898

Budget Rental Car
drivebudget.com
800/527–0700

Dollar Rental Car
dollar.com
800/800–3665

Hertz Rental Car
hertz.com
800/654–9998

Thrifty Car Rental
thrifty.com
800/847–4309

Car-Rental Wholesalers in Europe

Auto Europe
autoeurope.com
800/223–5555

Also has information on hotels and discounted airfares.

Destination Europe Resources (DER)
der.com
800/782–2424

Also has an American office.

Europe by Car
www.europebycar.com
800/223–1516

Kemwel
kemwel.com
800/678–0678 or 800/576–1590

CRUISE LINES

American Hawaii Cruises
cruisehawaii.com
800/543–7637

Carnival Cruise Lines
carnival.com
800/327–9501

Celebrity Cruises
celebrity-cruises.com
800/437–3111 ext. 7823

Commodore Cruise Line
commodorecruise.com
800/237–5361

Costa Cruise Line
costacruises.com
800/445–8020

Crystal Cruises
crystalcruises.com
800/265–3838

Cunard Line
cunardline.com
800/528–6273

Disney Cruise Line
disneycruise.com
800/939–2784

EuroCruises
eurocruises.com
800/688–3876

First European Cruises
first-european.com
800/688–3876

Holland America Line
hollandamerica.com
800/426–0327

Mediterranean Shipping Cruises
msccruiseusa.com
800/666–9333

Norwegian Cruise Line
ncl.com
800/327–7030

Orient Lines
orientlines.com
800/333–7300

Princess Cruises
princesscruises.com
800/774–6237

Radisson Seven Seas Cruises
rssc.com
800/333–3333

Regal Cruises
regalcruises.com
800/270–7245

Renaissance Cruises
renaissancecruises.com
800/525–5350

Royal Caribbean International
rccl.com
800/327–6700

Royal Olympic Cruises
royalolympiccruises.com
800/827–6400

Seabourn Cruise Line
seabourn.com
800/929–9595

Silversea Cruises
silversea.com
800/722–9955

United States Line
unitedstateslines.com
877/330–6871

Uniworld
uniworldcruises.com
800/298–0318

Windstar Cruises
windstarcruises.com
877/827–7245

World Explorer Cruise (Universe Explorer)
wecruise.com
800/854–3835

Ferries and Freighters

Alaska Marine Highway System (ferry)
dot.state.ak.us/external/
amhs/index.html
800/642–0066

Cruise and Freighter Travel Association
travltips.com
800/872–8584

Ivaran's Americana (freighter)
800/451–1639

Norwegian Coastal Voyage (ferry)
coastalvoyage.com
800/323–7436

River Cruises

Abercrombie & Kent
abercrombiekent.com
800/323–7308

American Canadian Caribbean Line
accl-smallships.com
800/556–7450

American West Steamboat Company
columbiarivercruise.com
800/434–1232

B&V Waterways
bvwaterways.com
800/546–4777

Clipper Cruise Line
clippercruise.com
800/325–0010

Compagnie des Îles du Ponant
ponant.com
33–2/40–58–14–95

Continental Waterways
abercrombiekent.com
800/323–7308

Cruise West
cruisewest.com
800/888–9378

Delphin Cruises
eurocruises.com
800/686–3876

Delta Queen Steamboat Company
deltaqueen.com
800/543–1949

Étoile de Champagne
etoiledechampagne.com
800/280–1492

Eurocruises
eurocruises.com
800/686–3876

European Waterways
europeanwaterways.com
800/217–4447

Global Quest
globalquesttravel.com
800/221–3254

Grand Circle Travel
grandcircle.org
800/248–3737

Intrav
intrav.com
800/456–8100

Julia Hoyt Canal Cruises
800/852–2625

KD River Cruises of Europe
rivercruises.com
800/346–6525

Lindblad Special Expeditions
specialexpeditions.com
800/762–0003

MTS
meltours.com
675/852–2276

Nabila Tours and Cruises
nabilatours.com
800/443–6453

Peter Deilmann EuropAmerica Cruises
deilmann-cruises.com
800/348–8287

Premier Selections
premierselections.com
800/234–4000

Regal China Cruises
regalchinacruises.com
800/808–3388

Riverbarge Excursions
riverbarge.com
888/456–2206

St. Lawrence Cruise Lines
stlawrencecruiselines.com
800/267–7868

Travcotels Ltd.
ebitravel.com
800/426–5492

Victoria Cruises
victoriacruises.com
800/348–8084

Viking River Cruises
vikingrivercruises.com
800/707–1287

Specialty Cruises

Abercrombie & Kent
abercrombiekent.com
800/323–7308

Alaska Sightseeing/Cruise West
cruisewest.com
800/888–9378

Alaska's Glacier Bay Tours and Cruises
glacierbaytours.com
800/451–5952

American Canadian Caribbean Line
accl-smallships.com
800/556–7450

Butterfield and Robinson
butterfieldandrobinson.com
800/678–1147

Classic Cruises of Newport
cruisenewport.com
800/395–1343

Classical Cruises
classicalcruises.com
800/252–7745

Clipper Cruise Line
clippercruise.com
800/325–0010

Club Med 2
clubmed.com
800/453–7447

Cruise West
cruisewest.com
800/888–9378

Delta Queen Steamboat Company
deltaqueen.com
800/543–1949

French Country Waterways Ltd.
fcwl.com
800/222–1236

Global Quest
globalquesttravel.com
800/221–3254

Intrav
intrav.com
800/456–8100

KD River Cruises of Europe
rivercruises.com
800/346–6525

Lindblad Special Expeditions
specialexpeditions.com
800/762–0003

Marine Expeditions
marineex.com
800/263–9147

Metropolitan Touring
ecuadorable.com
593–2/464–780

Mountain Travel Sobek
mtsobek.com
888/687–6235

Norwegian Coastal Voyage
bergenline.com
800/323–7436

Peter Deilmann EuropAmerica Cruises
deilmann-cruises.com
800/348–8287

Quark Expeditions
quarkexpeditions.com
800/356–5699

Riverbarge Excursions
riverbarge.com
888/456–2206

Sea Cloud Cruises, Inc.
seacloud.com
201/227–9404 or 888/732–2568

Society Expeditions
societyexpeditions.com
800/548–8669

Star Clippers
starclippers.com
800/442–0553

Swan Hellenic
swan-hellenic.co.uk
877/219–4239

Temptress Cruises
temptresscruises.com
800/336–8423

Victoria Cruises
victoriacruises.com
800/348–8084

Windjammer Barefoot Cruises
windjammer.com
800/327–2601

Windstar Cruises
windstarcruises.com
800/258–7245

CRUISE RESOURCES

Cruise Publications

Agent's Cruise Monthly
World Ocean & Cruise
Liner Society
Box 92
Stamford, CT 06904
203/329–2787

Annual subscription $30.

Cruise & Vacation Views
www.e-travelnews.com
25 Washington St.
Morristown, NJ 07960
973/605–2442

Bimonthly publication for cruise agents and interested vacationers. Yearly subscription including annual Cruise Preview is $48 in the United States and $54 in Canada.

Cruise Industry News Quarterly Magazine
Cruise Industry News
www.cruiseindustrynews.com
441 Lexington Ave., Suite 1209
New York, NY 10017
212/986–1025

Annual subscription $30.

"Cruise News"
seavacations.com
800/749–4950

Newsletter. No advertising. Annual subscription $28.

Cruise Travel
travel.org/cruisetravel
990 Grover St.
Evanston, IL 60201
847/491–6440

Subscription six issues for $19.97.

Ocean and Cruise News
World Ocean & Cruise
Liner Society
oceancruisenews.com
Box 92
Stamford, CT 06904
203/329–2787

$2.50 per issue or $30 annual subscription.

Porthole Cruise Magazine
PPI Group
porthole.com
7100 W. Commercial Blvd.,
Suite 106
Fort Lauderdale, FL 33319
954/746–5554 or 800/776–
7678

Serious reviews. One-year
subscription $19.95 for 6 is-
sues; two-year subscription
for 12 issues for $29.95.

Cruise Trade Organizations

Cruise Lines International Association (CLIA)
cruising.org
500 5th Ave., Suite 1407
New York, NY 10110
212/921–0066

The official trade organization of the cruise industry.

International Council of Cruise Lines
iccl.org
2111 Wilson Blvd., 8th floor
Arlington, VA 22201
703/522–8463

A non-profit trade organization with information on 16
cruise lines.

Cruise Web Sites

Cruise @ddicts
cruise-addicts.com

Photo galleries, chat rooms,
reviews, downloads, and
news.

Cruise Critic
cruisecritic.com

Reviews, destinations.

Cruise Mates
cruisemates.com

Ratings, reviews, itineraries,
news, classifieds, chat rooms,
and links.

Cruise Reports
cruise-report.com

Reports, ratings, feedback,
evaluation, cruise lines, and
links.

Cruise Reviews
cruisereviews.com

Reviews, newsletters.

Deja
deja.com

Cruise ratings by cabins,
food quality, entertainment,
cost.

Epinions
epinions.com/trvl-Cruises

Cruise recommendations.

DISABILITIES

New Horizons
www.dot.gov/airconsumer/
horizons.htm

Information for travelers
with disabilities from the
Aviation Consumer Protec-
tion Division.

Society for Accessible Travel and Hospitality (SATH)

Formerly Society for Advancement of Travelers with Handicaps
www.sath.org
347 5th Ave., Suite 610
New York, NY 10016
212/447–7284

EMERGENCIES ABROAD

Centers for Disease Control and Prevention
cdc.gov
1600 Clifton Rd.
Atlanta, GA 30333
800/311–3435 general information; 877/394–8747 travelers' information

Foreign and Commonwealth Office
fco.gov.uk
Travel tips for all over the world.

International Association for Medical Assistance to Travelers
iamat.org
U.S. Headquarters
417 Center St.
Lewiston, NY 14092
716/754–4883

International SOS Assistance
intsos.com
8 Neshaminy Interplex, Suite 207
Trevose, PA 19053-6956

215/244–1500 or 800/523–8930

Global emergency assistance and travel health policies such as trip-cancellation and trip-interruption coverage.

MASTA (Medical Advisory Services for Travelers Abroad)
masta.org

Medicine Plus
Nim.nih.gov/medlineplus

Overseas Citizens Services
travel.state.gov
U.S. Department of State
202/647–5225 travel warnings
888/407–4747 emergency;
317/472–2328 emergency from overseas

Traveler's Health
cdc.gov
877/394–8747

Tripprep.com
International advice and doctors.

WebMD.com
Medical information site.

World Health Organization
who.int
525 23rd St. NW
Washington, DC 20037
202/861–3200

Worldwide Assistance
www.worldwideassistance.com
1133 15th St. NW, Suite 400
Washington, DC 20005

800/777–8710 ext. 417; 703/
204–1897 or 800/821–2828
for enrollment

Cruise Lines

American Hawaii Cruises
cruisehawaii.com
800/543–7637

Carnival
carnival.com
800/327–9501

Disney
disneycruise.com
800/939–2784

Holland America
hollandamerica.com
800/426–0327

Norwegian Cruise Line
ncl.com
800/327–7030

Princess Cruises
princesscruises.com
800/774–6237

**Royal Caribbean
International**
800/827–6400

Hotels

Best Western
bestwestern.com
800/780–7234

Days Inn
daysinn.com
800/544–8313

DoubleTree Hotel
doubletree.com
800/222–TREE

**Four Seasons Hotels
and Resorts**
fourseasons.com
800/819–5053

Holiday Inn
holiday-inn.com
800/465–4329

Howard Johnson
hojo.com
800/406–1411

Hyatt Hotels
hyatt.com
800/633–7313

Marriott Hotels
marriott.com
800/932–2198

Ramada Hotels
ramada.com
888/298–2054

**Sheraton Hotels and
Resorts**
sheraton.com
888/625–5144

Travel Agencies

Backroads
backroads.com
801 Cedar St.
Berkeley, CA 94710
800/462–2848

Family biking trips in the
United States; walking tours
in Canada, Hawaii, and
Washington.

Family Travel Connection
familytravelconnection.com
Family Cruise Specialists
Safety Harbor, FL 34695
888/799–2336

Represents all of the major cruise lines.

Familyworld Tours
16000 Ventura Blvd., Suite 200
Encino, CA 91436
818/990–6777

International tours for parents traveling with children ages four months and up.

Grand Travel
grandtrvl.com
6900 Wisconsin Ave., Suite 706
Chevy Chase, MD 20815
800/247–7651 or 301/986–0790

Specializing in trips for grandparents and grandchildren.

Kids Go Too
kidsgotootravel.com
Box 3478
Winter Park, CO 80482
800/638–3215

Family packages for vacations in the Rocky Mountains.

Personal Touch Travel
gio-ctc.com
65 Rombout Rd.
Poughkeepsie, NY 12603
877/485–7221

Excursions all over the world.

Rascals in Paradise
rascalsinparadise.com
Family Travel Specialists
650 5th St., Suite 505
San Francisco, CA 94107
800/U–RASCAL or 415/978–9800; 415/442–0289 fax

Packages include baby-sitters, special kids' menus, separate mealtimes for children, and organized activities.

Sealed with a Kiss
eswak.com
Box 2063
Rockville, MD 20847
800/888–7925

Custom-made travel packages

Web Sites

Air Travel with Multiples
owc.net/twins/flying.htm

Arranges flights, seating, car seats, and strollers; information on packing and in-flight issues.

American Academy of Pediatrics
aap.org

Excellent tips for keeping your kids safe from the sun.

BabyCenter.com
babycenter.com

Sells travel supplies; helps plan a safe trip.

Baby Travel Solutions
BabyTravelSolutions.com

Sells diapers, food, wipes, and infant toiletries for delivery directly to your hotel room.

Evenflo
evenflo.com

Sells car seats, strollers, and other baby-care products; provides safety information, consumer services, and helpful links.

Family Go
family.go.com

Search engine with articles about kid-friendly trips.

Family Travel Forum
familytravelforum.com

Travel specialists with airfare, restaurant reviews, information about specific destinations, and helpful links.

Family Web
familyweb.com

Childproofing and other travel tips.

Home Hardware Dealers
homehardwaredealers.com

Games for the road and plane packing lists.

Tiny Travelers
tinytravelers.net

Articles about traveling with infants; infant products.

Travel with Kids
travelwithkids.com

State-by-state guide for family attractions around the country, many articles.

HEALTH AND FITNESS

Encyclozine
encyclozine.com

Links to sites on cycling and hiking. The site also helps you make reservations.

Fitscape
fitscape.com

Information about exercise (workout programs, animated exercise instructions), nutrition (a food and nutrition calculator), and a feature that lets you search for health clubs in destinations all over the world.

Great Outdoor Recreation Pages
gorp.com

Includes all kinds of tools to help you plan active vacations.

Just Move
justmove.org

Run by the American Heart Association, this free site gives you a digital diary, weekly motivational updates, and support from other exercise aficionados across the country.

Running.com
running.com

Lists places to run, races around the world, and general running information.

Swimmers Guide Online
Lornet.com/sgol

Directory of publicly accessible, full-size, year-round pools available in 91 countries.

VegDining
vegdining.com

Guide to vegetarian restaurants around the world.

Weight Watchers International
weightwatchers.com
800/651–6000

Includes tips on healthy eating and staying fit. Also features tips from readers on sticking to their diet plans.

Yoga Movement
yogamovement.com

Features yoga basics for beginners, resources for pros, and links to other yoga sites.

Fitness Gear
Athleta
athleta.com
888/322–5515

Fitness and sports gear for women.

Living
gaiam.com
800/254–8464

Yoga videos and other relaxation products for travel.

Power Systems
power-systems.com
800/321–6975

Portable exercise equipment that can easily fit in your suitcase.

Road Runner Sports
roadrunnersports.com
800/551–5558

Clothes, shoes, and accessories for men and women.

Yoga Enterprises
stretch.com
888/YES–YOGA

"In-Flight Yoga," "Bed Top Yoga," and other audiotapes are available.

Fitness Info
Metro Sports
metrosports.com
27 W. 24th St., Suite 10B
New York, NY 10010
212/627–7040

Monthly magazines in New York, Boston, Philadelphia, and Washington, D.C., list events and retailers, covering running, in-line skating, hockey, basketball, and hiking.

Runners World
runnersworld.com
800/666–2828

Monthly features on runs around the world.

Fitness-Oriented Travel

Adventure Health Travel
adventurehealthtravel.com
800/443–9216

This on-line division of a 50-year-old agency specializes in spas, fitness, and adventure vacations.

Diving Trips and Certification
Padi.com
800/729–7234

Fitness Travel Club
hotelfitnessclub.com

Members can search on-line for hotels with health clubs and spas.

One World Journeys
oneworldjourneys.com/expeditions

Specializes in adventurous, travel-writing, and do-good vacations.

Spa Finder
spafinder.com
800/255–7727

On its Web site, the world's largest spa travel and reservation company lets you search for spas and resorts.

Spaquest
spa-quest.com
800/772–7837

Provides all the specifics you need to complete a spa reservation.

HONEYMOON TRAVEL

About Honeymoons
honeymoons.about.com

Specific places to stay, things to see while you're there, airfares, what to pack, adventure vacations, and links.

All Inclusive Honeymoons
all-inclusivetravel.com/honeymoon.htm

All-inclusive resorts throughout the Caribbean.

Anything Romantic
anythingromantic.com

Destinations and links.

Augusta Weddings
augustaweddings.com/trips.htm

Hints on packing, tips on budgets, and ways to avoid typical honeymoon mistakes.

Honeymoons
honeymoons.com

Destinations and hotels.

Island Honeymoons
islandhoneymoons.com

Tropical island and cruise vacations.

Just Honeymoons
justhoneymoons.net

Itineraries, registering.

Modern Bride Budget Calculator

modernbride.com/honeymoonplanning/budget.cfm

Computerized budgeting.

The Knot

theknot.com

Planning weddings and honeymoons.

Tipping

tipping.org

General advice on gratuities.

Wedding 411

wedding411.com

On-line to-do lists, budget calculators, and advice. Registries enable your family and friends to contribute to the cost of your honeymoon.

INTERNATIONAL TRAVEL

See also passports and visas.

American Automobile Association (AAA)

aaa.com

Authorized by U.S. State Department to issue on-line International Driving Permit applications.

American Automobile Touring Alliance (AATA)

nationalautoclub.com
1151 E. Hillsdale Blvd.
Foster City, CA 94404
800/622–7070; 650/294–7105 fax

Alternate contact for International Driving Permits authorized by U.S. State Department.

Federal Consumer Information Center

pueblo.gsa.gov

Information on entry requirements to various countries, including passport requirements.

Overseas Citizens Services

U.S. Department of State
travel.state.gov
202/647–5225

U.S. Customs Service

customs.ustreas.gov
Box 7407
Washington, DC 20044

Links to useful publications, such as the fact-packed "Know Before You Go," a classic that's mandatory reading if you're headed overseas. The URL is www.customs.ustreas.gov/travel/travel.htm.

U.S. Department of State

travel.state.gov
900/225–5674 or 888/362–8668

For passports and information regarding road security abroad. The 900 number is a toll call. The 888 number is toll-free but you will need a credit card. Download DSP-11 passport application from Web site. A live operator can tell you the status of your application (for a fee).

VAT Refunds
Global Refund
www.globalrefund.com
99 Main St., Suite 307
Nyack, NY 10960
845/348–7673 or 800/566–9828

Home Rentals and Exchanges

CyberRentals
CyberRentals.com

Exclusively devoted to rental listings.

Dejanews
DejaNews.com

Locate rentals and exchanges by posting notices to on-line newsgroups, forums, or boards.

Holi-Swaps
holi-swaps.com

Rent, trade, or exchange your home and take your family anywhere in the world.

Home Base Holidays
homebase-hols.com

Cheap travel and comfortable accommodations all around the world.

Home Exchange
homeexchange.com

Budget home rentals within the United States.

International Home Exchange Network
homexchange.com

For home exchanges and some rental listings.

Mountain Lodging
mountain-lodging.com

Mountain lodgings from inns to bungalows, all across the United States and parts of Canada.

Vacation Home Rentals
vacationhomerentals.com

An assortment of family homes from beach houses to mountain cottages across North America.

Web Home Exchange
webhomeexchange.com

Worldwide affordable homes.

Andiamo Luggage
www.andiamoinc.com
3011 S. Crobdy Way
Santa Ana, CA 92704-6304
714/751–8711 or 800/759–9738

Luggage manufacturer. Product and on-line catalog available.

Atlantic Luggage Company
www.atlanticluggage.com

10th St. and Factory Ave.
Ellwood City, PA 16117-0672
724/752–0012 or 888/828–5268

Luggage manufacturer with on-line catalog.

Backpack Traveler
www.europebytrain.com
Box 3538
Dana Point, CA 92629
949/661–9577 or 800/688–9577

Catalog retailer with on-line catalog. Sells packs and other luggage, plus travel gadgets.

Boyt
www.boyt.com
15 Sarah Ave.
Iowa Falls, IA 50126-0279
641/648–6601 or 888/289–2698

Luggage manufacturer. Product and on-line catalog available.

Briggs & Riley
www.briggs-riley.com
Box 3169
Half Moon Bay, CA 94019
650/728–2000 or 888/462–2247

Manufacturer of stylish soft-side luggage. Product catalog available on request and on-line.

Brookstone
www.brookstone.com

This retailer includes luggage and travel gadgets in its intriguing stock.

Bugatti, Inc.
www.bugatti.com
100 Condor St.
Boston, MA 02128
617/567–7600 or 800/284–2887

Manufacturer of leather casual bags and accessories with on-line catalog sales.

Campmor
www.campmor.com
201/445–5000 or 800/226–7667; 201/689–9678 fax

Catalog retailer with one store (Route 17 North, Paramus, New Jersey) and on-line catalog sales. Luggage and gear for outdoor activities and more.

Cascade Designs
www.cascadedesigns.com
4000 1st Ave. S
Seattle, WA 98134
800/531–9531

One-of-a-kind products for serious outdoor activities.

The Container Store
www.thecontainerstore.com
2000 Valwood Pkwy.
Dallas, TX 75234
888/266–8246

This nationwide chain with an on-line presence is a ready source of tiny bottles and jars that are perfect for your toiletries kit. You'll also find many travel gadgets.

CrewGear

www.crewgear.com
10855 U.S. 19N
Clearwater, FL 33764
800/848–2739

Sells luggage and travel products to airline crews and general public. Product catalog available on request and on-line (phone ordering only).

Croakies

www.croakies.com
1240 Huff La.
Box 2913
Jackson Hole, WY 83001
800/443–8620

Sells eyewear retainers so your glasses stay put.

Delsey Luggage

www.delsey.com
6735 Business Pkwy, Suite A
Elkridge, MD 21075
410/796–5655 or 800/558–3344

Manufacturer of innovative, hard- and soft-side luggage. Catalog available.

Due North Outdoor Supplies

Duenorth.net/outdoor
11345 Hwy. 17 W, Box 6264
Sturgeon Falls, Ont. P2B 3K7
705/753–2387; 705/753–6113 fax

Canada-based on-line catalog retailer of packs and other camping gear.

Eagle Creek Travel Gear

www.eaglecreek.com
3055 Enterprise Ct.
Vista, CA 92083
760/599–6500 or 800/874–9925

Travel luggage and gear manufacturer. Product catalog and list of retailers available on request or on-line.

Eastern Mountain Sports

www.emsonline.com
1 Vose Farm Rd.
Peterborough, NH 03458-2122
888/463–6367; 603/924–4320 fax

Outdoor gear retailer with on-line catalog (order by phone) and stores nationwide.

eBags

www.eBags.com
800/820–6126

Luggage.

Eddie Bauer

www.eddiebauer.com
Box 97000
Redmond, WA 98073
800/625–7935

General travel clothes and supplies.

800–LUGGAGE

www.1800luggage.com
S. Pickett St.
Alexandria, VA 22304
703/751–1109 or 800/584–4243

Washington, D.C.–area luggage discount retailer with on-line catalog (order by phone).

Ex Officio

exofficio.com
800/644–7303

On-line clothing company offering wear for adventure travel and excursions with harsh weather conditions.

Goods of the World

www.travelbags.com
3101 E. Eisenhower Pkwy.
Ann Arbor, MI 48108
734/677–0700 or 800/950–2247

Manufacturer of leather bags for travel and sports. Catalog available on request.

Hartmann Luggage Company

www.hartmann.com
1301 Hartmann Dr.
Lebanon, TN 37087
615/444–5000 or 800/331–0613

Luggage manufacturer. Mail-order and on-line catalog available.

High Sierra Sport Company

www.highsierrasport.com
880 Corporate Woods Pkwy.
Vernon Hills, IL 60061
800/323–9590

Innovation Luggage

20 Enterprise Ave. S
Secaucus, NJ 07094
800/722–1800

Luggage retailer carrying major brands. List of stores available by phone; no catalog.

JanSport

www.jansport.com
Box 1817
Appleton, WI 54912
920/734–5708 or 800/552–6776

Manufacturer of travel packs and travel and outdoor accessories. Product information and dealer names on-line and on request.

Land's End

www.landsend.com
Land's End La.
Dodgeville, WI 53595
800/332–0103

General travel clothes and supplies.

L.L. Bean Traveler

www.llbean.com
Freeport, ME 04033
800/441–5713

General travel clothes and supplies.

Lodis

www.lodis.com
2261 S. Carmelina Ave.
Los Angeles, CA 90064-1001
310/207–6841 or 800/421–8674

Laptop cases, hands-free bags, small leather accessories, and travel items.

Magellan's

magellans.com
800/962–4943

Offers a range of necessary items from jet-lag prevention medicine to outdoor wear.

McKlein USA

www.mckleinusa.com
964 Northpoint Blvd.
Waukegan, IL 60085
847/785–1715 or 877/625–5346

Manufactures luggage for traveling professionals.

Orvis Travel

www.orvis.com
1711 Blue Hills Dr.
Box 12000
Roanoke, VA 24012
800/541–3541; 800/635–7635 customer service

Retailer with catalog and stores nationwide. Sells luggage, clothing, and accessories.

Patagonia

www.patagonia.com
Box 32050
Reno, NV 89523-2050
800/638–64646; 800/336–9090 catalog requests

Manufacturer of outdoor gear, including luggage, backpacks, and accessories, with retail stores and complete on-line and mail-order catalogs.

REI

www.rei.com
1700 45th St. E
Sumner, WA 98352-0001
253/891–2500 or 800/426–4840; 253/891–2523 fax

Manufacturer of outdoor gear and clothing with retail stores, catalog, and on-line sales.

Samsonite

www.samsonite.com
11200 E. 45th Ave.
Denver, CO 80239
303/373–2000 or 800/262–8282

Longstanding luggage manufacturer with many innovative products. Product listing on request.

Sharper Image

sharperimage.com
800/344–5555

Offers a range of top-quality products from luggage to alarm clocks.

Skymall

www.skymall.com
Box 52824
Phoenix, AZ 85072
602/254–9777 or 800/424–6255

On-line and product catalog retailer; catalog is available in airplane seat backs or phone. Travel gear.

Tilley Endurables

www.tilley.com
900 Don Mills Rd.
Toronto, ON M3C 1V6
416/441–6141 or 800/363–8737

High-performance travel clothing is the specialty of this company built around a sailing hat; most dry overnight even under humid conditions.

Title 9 Sports

www.title9sports.com
6201 Doyle St.
Emeryville, CA 94608
800/342–4448

Casual performance wear for women—lots of Supplex and Cool Max.

Travel Goods Association

www.travel-goods.org
5 Vaughn Dr., Suite 105
Princeton, NJ 08540
609/720–1200

Can help you find a retailer near you or get in touch with manufacturers or luggage-repair services and suppliers. Provides general information on innovative products, airline carry-on regulations, and preventing luggage theft.

Travel 2000

www.travel2000.com
3120 Spanish Oak Dr.
Lansing, MI 48911
517/882–2988 or 800/903–8728

Catalog retailer with luggage and travel gear.

Travelers Club

www.travelersclub.com
13003 S. Figueroa St.
Los Angeles, CA 90061
310/323–5660 or 800/368–2582

Luggage manufacturer and wholesaler with on-line catalog.

Travelpro

www.travelpro.com
700 Banyan Tr.
Boca Raton, FL 33431
561/998–2824 or 800/741–7471

Luggage manufacturer with catalog. Web page lists international resources.

TravelSmith

travelsmith.com
800/950–1600

Quality travel gear.

Walkabout Travel Gear

www.walkabouttravelgear.com

Box 1115
Moab, UT 84532
435/259–4974 or 800/852–7085

Catalog and on-line retailer of luggage and travel gadgets and gear.

Zero Halliburton
www.zerohalliburton.com
500 W. 200 N.
Salt Lake, UT 84054
801/298–5900 or 888/909–9376

Manufacturer of classic aluminum suitcases and briefcases.

PASSPORTS AND VISAS

American Passport Service
www.americanpassport.com
603/431–8482 or 800/841–6778

Express Visa Services
www.expressvisa.com
18 E. 41st St., Suite 1206
New York, NY 10017
212/679–5650

7 locations around the United States process visas for travel anywhere.

National Passport Center
www.travel.state.gov/passport_services.html
888/362–8668 or 603/334–0500

Passport Express
www.passportexpress.com

179 Wayland Ave.
Providence, RI 02906
401/272–4612 or 800/362–8196

Travisa
www.travisa.com
800/222–2589 or 800/421–5468

Issues passports and visas in 24 hours.

U.S. Department of State
www.travel.state.gov
202/647–5225

Publishes a number of useful information sheets, including consular information on many countries. Also good: "Your Trip Abroad," "A Safe Trip Abroad," and various sheets containing regional travel tips.

TECHNOLOGY-RELATED PRODUCTS AND INFORMATION

iGo
www.igoproducts.com
9393 Gateway Dr.
Reno, NV 89511
775/850–2545 or 800/422–9872

On-line mobile technology tools and products for traveling with a laptop, phone, and other devices.

Laptop Travel
www.laptoptravel.com
Box 46106

Plymouth, MN 55446
763/404–9497 or 888/527–
8728

Products, tips and tech support to help you take your computer on the road.

Rent-a-cellphone.com
One of many rental mobile phone businesses.

RoadNews.com
www.roadnews.com
Box 14524
Scottsdale, AZ 85267
480/225–8430

Articles, products, tips, and links to other sites related to traveling with technology.

Teleadapt
www.teleadapt.com
1762 Technology Dr.
San Jose, CA 95110
408/350–1440 or 877/835–
3232

Connectivity tips and products.

TOURISM OFFICES FOR U.S. DESTINATIONS

Alaska
AlaskaGuidebook.com
www.alaskaguidebook.com
Alaska Internet Travel Guide
www.alaskaone.com

Alaska Marine Highway System
www.dot.state.ak.us/ferry
800/642–0066

Alaska Public Lands Information Center
www.nps.gov/aplic

Alaska Travel Industry Association
www.travelalaska.com
Box 143361
Anchorage 99514-3361
907/929–2200 or 800/862–
5275

State of Alaska
www.state.ak.us
Box 110809
Juneau 99811-0809
907/465–2012 or 907/465–
3767

CITY INFORMATION

Alaska Anchorage
www.anchorage.net
Fairbanks
www.explorefairbanks.com
Juneau Web
www.juneau.com

Arizona
Arizona Office of Tourism
www.arizonaguide.com
2702 N. 3rd St., Suite 4015
Phoenix 85004
602/230–7733 or 888/520–
3434; 602/240–5475 fax

Native American Attractions
www.hopi.nsn.us

Hopi Tribe Office of the
Chairman
Box 123
Kykotsmovi 86039
928/734–2441 or 928/734–
2435

**Navajo Nation Tourism
Office**
www.navajoland.com
Box 663
Window Rock 86515
928/871–6436 or 928/871–
7371; 928/871–7942 fax

California

**California Office
of Tourism**
gocalif.ca.gov
801 K St., Suite 1600
Sacramento 95814
916/322–2882 or 800/862–
2543

LOS ANGELES

**Beverly Hills Conference
and Visitors Bureau**
beverlyhillscvb.com

**Hollywood Chamber of
Commerce Info Center**
www.hollywoodcoc.org

**Long Beach Area
Convention and Visitors
Bureau**
www.visitlongbeach.com

**Los Angeles Visitors
Information Center**
www.visitlanow.com
685 S. Figueroa St.
90017
213/689–8822

**Pasadena Convention
& Visitors Bureau**
www.pasadenacal.com

**Redondo Beach Visitors
Bureau**
www.visitredondo.com

**Santa Monica Convention
& Visitors Bureau**
www.santamonica.com

**West Hollywood
Convention and Visitors
Bureau**
www.visitwesthollywood.
com

SAN DIEGO

**International Visitor
Information Center**
www.sandiego.org
11 Horton Plaza,
at 1st Ave. and F St.
92101
619/236–1212

**San Diego Convention
& Visitors Bureau**
www.sandiego.org
401 B St., Suite 1400
92101
619/236–1212

SAN FRANCISCO

Berkeley
www.berkeleycvb.com
510/549–7040 or 800/847–
4823; 510/549–8710 for
recorded information

San Francisco Convention and Visitors Bureau's Visitor Information Center
www.sfvisitor.org
Box 429097
94142-9097
415/391–2000 or 415/974–6900

NORTHERN CALIFORNIA

Redwood Empire Association
www.redwoodempire.com
1925 13th Ave., Suite 103
Oakland 94606
510/536–8808 or 800/200–8334; 510/536–8824 fax

WINE COUNTRY

Visit www.winecountry.com for the information on the region's towns. You can narrow your search to include specific information on wineries, tours, hotels, and restaurants.

The Napa Valley Conference & Visitors Bureau
napavalley.org
1310 Napa Town Center
Napa, CA 94559
707/226–7459; 707/255–2066 fax

Colorado

Colorado Tourism Office
www.colorado.com
1625 Broadway, #1700
Denver 80202
800/265–6723

Connecticut

Connecticut Office of Tourism
www.ctbound.org
505 Hudson St.
Hartford 06106
860/270–8081 or 800/282–6863

Florida

Florida Tourism Industry Marketing Corporation
www.flausa.com
Box 1100, 661 E. Jefferson St., Suite 300
Tallahassee 32302

MIAMI

Greater Miami Convention & Visitors Bureau
tropicoolmiami.com
701 Brickell Ave., Suite 2700
Miami 33131
305/539–3000 or 800/240–4282; 305/539–3113 fax

About Greater Orlando
www.orlandoinfo.com
Orlando/Orange County
Convention & Visitors Bureau
8723 International Dr.
Orlando, FL 32819
407/363–5871

Busch Gardens
www.buschgardens.com
Box 9158
Tampa, FL 33674
813/987–5283

Orlando/Orange County Convention & Visitors Bureau
8723 International Dr.
32819
407/363–5871

SeaWorld Orlando
www.seaworld.com
7007 SeaWorld Dr.
Orlando, FL 32821
407/351–3600

Universal Studios Escape
www.uescape.com
1000 Universal Studios
Plaza
Orlando, FL 32819-8000
407/363–8000; 407/363–8265
TDD

Walt Disney World Information
www.disney.com
Box 10000
Lake Buena Vista, FL 32830
407/824–4321; 407/827–5141
TDD

Disney Reservation Center
407/934–7639; 407/939–3463
for dining; 407/560–4651 for
production information

Georgia

Georgia Department of Industry, Trade and Tourism
www.georgia.org
285 Peachtree Center Ave.
Marquis Tower Two,
Suite 1000
Atlanta 30303
404/656–3590 or 800/847–
4842; 404/651–9063 fax

Hawai'i

Hawai'i Visitors & Convention Bureau
www.gohawaii.com
2270 Kalakaua Ave.,
Suite 801
Honolulu 96817
808/923–1811; 800/464–2924
for brochures

Idaho

Idaho Travel Council
www.visitid.org
Department of Commerce
700 W. State St., Box 83720
Boise 83720
208/334–2470 or 800/635–
7820; 208/334–2175 fax

Nevada

Nevada Commission on Tourism
Capitol Complex
5151 S. Carson St.
Carson City 89710
702/687–4322 or 800/237–0774; 800/638–2328 for brochures; 702/687–6779 fax

LAS VEGAS

"Las Vegas Advisor"
3687 S. Procyon Ave.
89103
702/252–0655 or 800/244–2224

Las Vegas Chamber of Commerce
www.lvchamber.com
3720 Howard Hughes Pkwy.
89109
702/735–1616 or 702/735–2011

Las Vegas Convention and Visitors Authority
www.lasvegas24hours.com
3150 Paradise Rd.
89109
702/892–0711 or 702/892–2824

Maine

Maine Tourism Association
www.visitmaine.com
325-B Water St.
Hallowell 04347
207/623–0363 or 888/624–6345

Massachusetts

Massachusetts Office of Travel and Tourism
www.massvacation.com
10 Park Plaza, Suite 4510
Boston 02116
617/973–8500 or 800/227–6277; 617/973–8525 fax

BOSTON

Boston Common Information Kiosk
www.bostonusa.com
Tremont St. where the Freedom Trail begins
02116
617/426–3115 or 800/733–2678

Cambridge Tourism Office
www.cambridge-usa.org
4 Brattle St., Suite 208
Cambridge 02138
617/441–2884 or 800/862–5678

Greater Boston Convention and Visitors Bureau
www.bostonusa.com
2 Copley Pl., Suite 105
02116
888/SEE BOSTON; 617/424–7664 fax

CAPE COD

Cape Cod Chamber of Commerce
www.capecodchamber.org
Junction of Rtes. 6 and 132
Hyannis 02601
508/862–0700 or 888/332–2732; 508/862–0727 fax

Cape Cod National Seashore
www.nps.gov/caco
South Wellfleet 02663
508/349–3785

Destination Plymouth
www.visit-plymouth.com

MARTHA'S VINEYARD

Martha's Vineyard Chamber of Commerce
www.mvy.com
Beach Rd., Box 1698
Vineyard Haven 02568
508/693–0085

NANTUCKET

Chamber of Commerce
www.nantucketchamber.org
48 Main St.
02554
508/228–1700

Nantucket Visitor Services and Information Bureau
www.nantucket.net
25 Federal St.
02554
508/228–0925

Montana

Travel Montana
www.visitmt.com or www.wintermt.com
Department of Commerce
1424 9th Ave.
Helena 59620
406/444–2654 or 800/847–4868; 406/444–1800 fax

New Hampshire

New Hampshire Office of Travel and Tourism Development
www.visitnh.gov
Box 1856
Concord 03302
603/271–2343; 800/258–3608 seasonal events; 800/386–4664 for brochures

New Orleans

Greater New Orleans Black Tourism Network
www.soulofneworleans.com
1520 Sugar Bowl Dr.
70112
504/523–5652 or 800/725–5652; 504/522–0785 fax

New Orleans and River Region Chamber of Commerce
chamber.gnofn.org
601 Poydras St.
70190

New Orleans Metropolitan Convention & Visitors Bureau
www.neworleanscvb.com
1520 Sugar Bowl Dr.
70112
504/566–5011 or 800/672–6124; 504/566–5021 fax

New York

New York State Division of Tourism
www.iloveny.state.ny.us
Box 2603
Albany 12220
518/474–4116 or 800/225–5697

NEW YORK CITY

Brooklyn Information & Culture Inc.
www.brooklynX.org
647 Fulton St., 2nd floor
Brooklyn 11217
718/855–7882

Downtown Alliance
www.downtownny.com
120 Broadway, Suite 3340
10271
212/566–6700 or 212/566–6707

NYC & Company–Convention & Visitors Bureau
www.nycvisit.com
810 7th Ave., 3rd floor, between W. 52nd and W. 53rd Sts., Midtown West
10019
212/484–1222 or 212/397–8200; 212/245–5943 fax

Times Square Visitors Center
www.timessquarebid.org
1560 Broadway, between 46th and 47th Sts., Midtown West
10036
212/768–1560

North Carolina

North Carolina Travel and Tourism Division
www.visitnc.com
301 N. Wilmington St.
Raleigh 27601
919/733–2616 or 800/847–4862

Oregon

Portland/Oregon Visitors Association
www.pova.com
28 World Trade Center, 26 S.W. Salmon St.
97204
503/222–2223 or 800/962–3700

Pennsylvania

Pennsylvania Office of Travel and Tourism
www.experiencepa.com
717/787–5453; 800/847–4872
for brochures

PHILADELPHIA

Greater Philadelphia Tourism Marketing Corporation
www.gophila.com
215/599–0776 or 888/467–4452

Independence Visitor Center
www.independence
visitorcenter.com
6th St. between Market and Arch Sts.
19102

215/965–7676 or 800/537–7676

Philadelphia Convention and Visitors Bureau
www.pcvb.org
1515 Market St., Suite 2020 19102
215/636–3300 or 800/537–7676; 215/636–3327 fax

Rhode Island

Rhode Island Department of Economic Development, Tourism Division
www.visitrhodeisland.com
1 W. Exchange St.
Providence 02903
401/222–2601; 800/556–2484 for brochures

South Carolina

South Carolina Department of Parks, Recreation, and Tourism
www.travelsc.com
1205 Pendleton St., Suite 106
Columbia 29201
803/734–1700 or 800/872–3505; 803/734–0133 fax

Utah

Ski Utah
www.skiutah.com
150 W. 500 South St.
Salt Lake City 84101
801/534–1779

Utah County Convention and Visitors Bureau
www.utahvalley.org/cvb
51 S. University Ave.
Suite 111
Provo 84601
801/370–8393 or 800/222–8824

Utah Travel Council
utah.com
Council Hall, Capitol Hill
300 N. State St.
Salt Lake City 84114
801/538–1030; 800/200–1160 for brochures; 801/521–8102 for ski reports

Park City Chamber of Commerce/Convention and Visitors Bureau
www.parkcityinfo.com
Box 1630
Park City 84060
435/649–6100 or 800/453–1360

Salt Lake Convention and Visitors Bureau
www.saltlake.org
90 S.W. Temple St.
Salt Lake City 84101
801/521–2822

Vermont

Vermont Chamber of Commerce, Department of Travel and Tourism
www.VTchamber.com
Box 37
Montpelier 05601
802/223–3443

Vermont Department of Tourism and Marketing
www.1800VT.com
134 State St.
Montpelier 05602
802/828–3237; 800/837–6668
for brochures

Washington

Visitors Information Center
www.seattleinsider.com
520 Pike St., Suite 1300
Seattle 98101
206/461–5840

Washington State Convention & Trade Center
www.wsctc.com
800 Convention Place
Seattle, WA 98101
206/447–5000

Washington State Tourism
www.tourism.wa.gov
101 General Administration Bldg.
Olympia 98504
800/544–1800

SEATTLE

Seattle/King County Convention and Visitors Bureau
www.seeseattle.org
520 Pike St., Suite 1300
98101
206/461–5800

Seattle Visitor Center
www.wsctc.com
Washington State Convention Center
800 Convention Pl.
98104
206/461–5840

Washington D.C.

DC Chamber of Commerce
dcchamber.org
1213 K St. NW
20005
202/347–7201

Washington, DC, Convention and Tourism Corporation
www.washington.org
1212 New York Ave., NW
Suite 600
20005
202/789–7000; 202/789–7037 fax

D.C. Chamber of Commerce Visitors Center
dcvisit.com
Ronald Reagan Building and International Visitors Center
1300 Pennsylvania Ave. NW
20004
202/328–4748

Wyoming

Wyoming Tourist Office
wyomingtourism.org
I–25 at College Dr.
Cheyenne 82002
307/777–7777 or 800/225–5996; 307/777–6904 fax

TOURISM INFORMATION FOR NON-U.S. DESTINATIONS

Africa

EGYPT

Egyptian Tourist Authority
touregypt.net
630 5th Ave., Suite 1706
New York, NY 10111
212/332–2570; 212/956–6439 fax

MOROCCO

Moroccan National Tourist Office
www.tourism-in-morocco.com
20 E. 46th St., Suite 1201
New York, NY 10017
212/557–2520 or 212/949–8148

BOTSWANA

Department of Tourism, Ministry of Commerce and Industry
Private Bag 0047
Gaborone
267/35–3024 or 267/31–3314; 267/30–8675 fax
3400 International Dr. NW, Suite 7M
Washington, DC 20008
202/244–4990

KENYA

Kenya Tourist Offices
424 Madison Ave.
New York, NY 10017
212/486–1300
9150 Wilshire Blvd., Suite 160
Beverly Hills, CA 90212
213/274–6635

NAMIBIA

Ministry of Environment and Tourism
Private Bag 13346
Windhoek
061/284–2366 or 061/22–1930

Namibian Embassy
1605 New Hampshire Ave. NW
Washington, DC 20009
202/986–0540 or 202/986–0443

SOUTH AFRICA

South African Government Tourist Offices
500 5th Ave., Suite 2040
New York, NY 10110
212/764–1980 or 800/822–5368

4117 Lawrence Ave. E, Suite 2
Scarborough, Ontario M1E 2S2
416/283–0563 or 416/283–5465

Private Bag X164
Pretoria 0001

012/347–0600 or 012/347–6199

SOUTHERN AFRICA

All the countries in Southern Africa are members of RETOSA (Regional Tourism Organization of Southern Africa), based in Johannesburg. You can access them on the Web at www.retosa.co.za.

RETOSA
Box 7381, Halfway House
Johannesburg 1685, South Africa
011/315–2420 or 011/315–2422

SWAZILAND
Swaziland High Commission
3400 International Dr. NW, Suite 3M
Washington, DC 20008
202/362–6683

TANZANIA
Tanzania High Commission
2139 R St. NW
Washington, DC 20008
202/939–6125

205 E. 42nd St.
New York, NY 10017
212/972–9160

ZAMBIA
Zambian National Tourist Board
237 E. 52nd St.
New York, NY 10022
212/308–2155 or 212/758–1319

ZIMBABWE
Zimbabwe High Commission
332 Somerset St.
West Ottawa, Ontario K2P 0J9
613/237–4388

Zimbabwe Tourist Office
1270 Ave. of the Americas, Suite 2315
New York, NY 10020
212/332–1090

Box CY286
Harare
04/75–8730 through 04/75–8734, 04/75–8712 through 04/75–8714

South America

ARGENTINA
Argentina Government Tourist Offices
2655 Le Jeune Rd.
Miami, FL 33134
305/442–1366

12 W. 56th St.
New York, NY 10019
212/603–0443

BRAZIL
Consulate General of Brazil and Trade Bureau
1185 Ave. of the Americas, 21st floor
New York, NY 10036
212/827–0976

For general travel and business information on Brazil.

Riotur
3601 Aviation Blvd.,
Suite 2100
Manhattan Beach, CA 90266
310/643–2638

201 E. 12th St., Suite 509
New York, NY 10003
212/375–0801

For information on the city
of Rio.

LanChile Tourism Office
visitchile.org
6500 NW 22nd St.
Miami, FL 33122
800/244–5366; 305/670–8890

Caribbean

**Caribbean Tourism
Organization**
www.doitbahamas.com
80 Broad St., 32nd floor
New York, NY 10017
212/635–9530 or 212/697–
4258

512 Duplex Ave.
Toronto, Ontario M4R 2E3
416/485–8724 or 416/485–
8256

Aruba Tourism Authority
www.arubatourism.com
800/862–7822
L. G. Smith Blvd.
172, Eagle Beach
Aruba
297/8–23777

**Bahama Out Islands
Promotion Board**
19495 Biscayne Blvd.,
Suite 809
Aventura, FL 33180
305/359–8098 or 800/688–
4752

121 Bloor St. E, Suite 1101
Toronto M4W 3M5
416/968–2999 or 416/968–
6711

Bahamas Tourism Center
150 E. 52nd St., 28th floor N
New York, NY 10022
212/758–2777 or 800/823–
3136; 212/753–6531 fax

Bahamas Tourist Office
www.gobahamas.com
800/422–4262
8600 W. Bryn Mawr Ave.,
Suite 820
Chicago, IL 60631
773/693–1500 or 773/693–
1114

**Nassau/Paradise Island
Promotion Board**
19495 Biscayne Blvd.,
Suite 804
Aventura, FL 33180
305/931–1555 or 305/931–
3005

Center for Cuban Studies
www.cubaupdate.org
124 W. 23rd St.
New York, NY 10011
212/242–0559

Because the Cuban government has no tourist offices in the United States, the Center for Cuban Studies, which publishes the bimonthly Cuba Update, is one of the best sources of information.

Cuban Tourist Board
gocuba.ca
55 Queen St. E, Suite 705
Toronto, Ontario M5C 1R6, Canada
416/362–0700

Blvd. René Lévesque W, Suite 1105
Montréal, Québec H37 1V7, Canada
514/875–8004

Goethe 16, 3er piso, Colonia Anzures
Mexico City 06100, DF, Mexico
5/250–7974

167 High Holborn
London WC1V6PA, U.K.
44/207–240–2488

Cubanacán
416/601–0346 in Toronto;
207/537–7909 in London;
119/525–574–1523 in Mexico City

Infotur
cubaweb.cu
Calle del Obispo, e/Habana y Compostela
Havana
7/33–3333

PUERTO RICO

Puerto Rico Tourism Company
gotopuertorico.com
Box 902-3960
Old San Juan Station
San Juan, PR 00902-3960
787/721–2400

3575 W. Cahuenga Blvd., Suite 560
Los Angeles, CA 90068
213/874–5991

901 Ponce de León Blvd., Suite 101
Coral Gables, FL 33134
305/445–9112

TURKS AND CAICOS

Turks and Caicos Islands Tourist Board
turksandcaicostourism.com
649/946–2321 or 800/241–0824; 649/946–2733 fax

Central America

BELIZE

Belize High Commission
10 Harcourt House, 19A
Cavendish Sq.
London W1M 9AD
0207/499–9725

Belize Tourist Board
www.travelbelize.org
New Central Bank Bldg.
Level 2, Gabourel La.
Belize City, Belize
223/1913 or 800/624–0686 in the U.S

Belizean Embassy
2535 Massachusetts Ave.
NW
Washington, DC 20008
202/332–9636 or 202/332–
6888

COSTA RICA

Costa Rica Tourist Board
tourism-costarica.com
800/343–6332

Instituto Costarricense de Turismo
C. 5 between Advas. Central
and 2 Barrio del Catedral
San José
506/222-1090

GUATEMALA

Guatemalan Embassy
2220 R St. NW
Washington, DC 20008
561/241–7687 or 800/464–
8281

Inguat
guatemala.travel.com.gt
7a Av. 1-17, Zona 4
Guatemala City, Guatemala
331–1333 or 331–4416

South Pacific

AUSTRALIA

Australian Tourist Commission
www.australia.com
2049 Century Park E
Los Angeles, CA 90067
310/229–4870 or 310/552–
1215

Australian Capital Territory
www.act.gov.au

New South Wales
www.visitnsw.com.au

Queensland
www.queenslandtravel.
com.au

Western Australia Government
www.westernaustralia.net

NEW ZEALAND

New Zealand Tourism Board
purenz.com or tourism.
net.nz
501 Santa Monica Blvd., Los
Angeles, CA 90401
310/395–7480 or 800/388–
5494; 310/395–5454 fax

Canada

Canada Tourism Commission
www.canadatourism.com
55 Metcalfe St., Suite 600
Ottawa, Ontario
K1P 6L5
613/946–1000

BRITISH COLUMBIA

Tourism British Columbia
www.hellobc.com
Box 9830
Victoria, British Columbia
V8W 9W5
800/435–5622

Tourism Victoria
1175 Douglas St., Suite 710
V8W 2E1
250/953–2033 or 250/361–9733

Vancouver Tourist InfoCentre
tourismvancouver.com
200 Burrard St. V6C 3L6
604/683–2000

Tourism Ontario
www.ontariotravel.net

Tourism Toronto
www.torontotourism.com
207 Queen's Quay W, Suite 509, Box 106
M5J 1A7
416/203–2600 or 800/363–1990

Tourisme Québec
www.bonjourquebec.com
C.P. 979
Montréal, H3C 2W3
800/363–7777

Quebec City Tourist Information
www.quebec-region.com

Tourism Montreal
www.tourisme-montreal.org

Asia

China International Travel Service (CITS)
2 Mott St.
New York, NY 10002
212/608–1212 or 800/899–8618
www.cnto.org

350 5th Ave., Suite 6413
New York, NY 10118
212/760–8218 or 212/760–8809
www.citscanada.com

556 W. Broadway
Vancouver, BC V5Z 1E9
604/872–8787 or 604/873–2823

Hong Kong Tourist Board
discoverhongkong.com
590 5th Ave., Suite 590
New York, NY 10036
212/869–5008 or 212/730–2605

9 Temperance St., 3rd floor
Toronto, Ontario M5H 1Y6
416/366–2389 or 416/366–1098

Indonesia Tourist Board
www.indonesiatourism.com
3457 Wilshire Blvd.
Los Angeles, CA 90010
213/387–2078; 213/380–4876 fax

Embassy of Indonesia
287 MacLaren St.
Ottawa, Ontario
Canada K2P 0L9
613/236–7403; 613/563–2858 fax

JAPAN

Japan National Tourist Organization (JNTO)
www.jnto.go.jp/eng/
1 Rockefeller Plaza,
Suite 1250
New York, NY 10020
212/757–5640

165 University Ave.
Toronto, Ontario M5H 3B8
416/366–7140

2–10–1 Yūrakuchō 1-chōme,
Chiyoda-ku
Tōkyō
03/3502–1461

Kyōto Tower Bldg.
Higashi-Shiokoji-chō,
Shimogyo-ku
Kyōto
075/371–5649

Japan Travel Phone
0088/22–4800 throughout
Japan outside of Tōkyō and
Kyōto
03/3201–3331 in Tōkyō; 075/
371–5649 in Kyōto

Teletourist Service
03/3201–2911 in Tōkyō
Recorded information
24 hours a day

Tourist Information Centers
Tōkyō International
Forum B1
3–5–1 Marunouchi,
Chiyoda-ku
Tōkyō
03/3201—3331

INDIA

The following independent
Web sites also have helpful
information on travel to and
within India: www.rediff.
com/travel/travhom1.htm;
www.indiaserver.com/travel;
www.indiamart.com/travel;
and www.123india.com/
travel_and_tourism.

Government of India Tourist Offices Abroad
60 Bloor St. W, Suite 1003
Toronto, Ontario M4W 3B8
416/962–3787

30 Rockefeller Plaza, Room
15, North Mezzanine
New York, NY 10112
800/953–9399
3550 Wilshire Blvd.,
Suite 204
Los Angeles, CA 90010
213/380–8855

NEPAL

Department of Tourism
TAB@druknet.net.bt
Ministry of Trade & Industry, Royal Government
of Bhutan
Doebom Lam, Thimphu
02/3–23251 or 02/3–23252;
02/3–23695 fax

Nepal Tourism Board
ntb@mos.com.np
Bhrikuti Mandap
01/256909 or 01/256910

Singapore Tourism Board
www.stb.com.sg
Tourism Court
1 Orchard Spring La.
Singapore 247729
736-6622 or 800/736-2000
www.singapore-usa.com

590 5th Ave., 12th floor
New York, NY 10036
212/302–4861
www.singapore-ca.com

2 Bloor St. W., Suite 404
Toronto, Ontario M4W 3E2
416/363–8898

Tourism Authority of Thailand
tourismthailand.org
1600 New Phetburi Rd.
Makkasan, Ratjatevee
Bangkok 10310
66(0)/2250–5500; 66(0)/2250–5511 fax

611 North Larchmont Blvd., 1st Floor
Los Angeles, CA 90004
323/461–9814; 323/461–9834 fax

Tibet Tourism Bureau
18 Yuanlin Lam, Lhasa
0891/683–4315 information;
0891/683–4193 complaints

Mexico

Mexico Tourism Board
www.visitmexico.com
21 E. 63rd St., 3rd floor
New York, NY 10021
212/821–0314, 212/821–0367
or 800/446–3942 nationwide

2 Bloor St. W, Suite 1502
Toronto, Ontario M4W 3E2
416/925–0704 or 416/925–6061

Presidente Masaryk 172
Mexico, D.F. 11550
55/5250–0123 or 1-800/903–9200

Europe

Austrian National Tourist Office
www.austria-tourism.at
Box 1142,
Times Square Station
New York, NY 10108-1142
212/944–6880 or 212/730–4568

2 Bloor St. E, Suite 3330
Toronto, Ontario M4W 1A8
416/967–3381 or 416/967–4101

Belgian National Tourist Office
780 3rd Ave.
New York, NY 10017
212/758–8130 or 212/355–7675

Box 760 NDG
Montréal, Québec H4A 3S2

514/484–3594 or 514/489–8965

Belgian Office of Tourism
61-63, rue Marché aux
Herbes 1000
Brussels
02/513–6950 or 02/513–8803

BRITAIN

British Tourist Authority
visitbritain.com
Thames Tower
Blacks Rd., London
W6 9EL
(44)(0)20/8846–9000;
(44)(0)20/8563–0302 fax

551 5th Ave., 7th floor
New York, NY 10176
212/986–2200 or 800/462–2748
www.visitbritain.com/ca
5915 Airport Rd., Suite 120
Mississauga, Ontario L4V 1T1
905/405–1840 or 800/847–4885

London Tourist Information Centre
www.londontouristboard.com
Victoria Station Forecourt
Buckingham Palace Rd.
no phone

Londonline
09068/663–344

The London Tourist Board's Londonline phone guide to London gives information about events, theater, museums, transport, shopping, and restaurants. It's accessible only in Britain and is a toll call.

Scottish Tourist Board
www.visitscotland.com
23 Ravelston Terr.
Edinburgh EH4 3EU
0131/332–2433 or 0131/343–1513

CZECH REPUBLIC

Czech and Slovak Tourist Centre
16 Frognal Parade,
Finchley Rd.
London NW3 5HG
020/7794–3263 or 020/7794–3265

Czech Center
www.czechcenter.com
1109 Madison Ave.
New York, NY 10028
212/288–0830 or 212/288–0971

Czech Tourist Authority
c/o Czech Airlines
401 Bay St., Suite 1510
Toronto, Ontario M5H 2Y4
416/363–9928 or 416/363–0239

95 Great Portland St.
London W1N 5RA
020/7291–9920 or 020/7436–1300

DENMARK

Danish Tourist Board
55 Sloan St.
London SW1X 9SY
44/20–7259–5959 or, 44/20–7259–5955

Estonian Tourist Office

www.tourism.ee
600 3rd Ave., 26th floor
New York, NY 10016
212/883–0636 or 212/883–0648

958 Broadview Ave.,
Suite 202
Toronto, Ontario M4K 2R6
416/461–0764 or 416/461–0353

Finnish Tourist Board

www.mek.fi
655 3rd Ave.
New York, NY 10017
212/885–9700 or 212/885–9739

French Government Tourist Office

www.francetourism.com
900/990–0040 nationwide,
50¢ per minute
444 Madison Ave., 16th floor
New York, NY 10022
212/838–7855

1981 Ave. McGill College,
Suite 490
Montréal, Québec H3A 2W9
514/288–4264 or 514/845–4868

Paris

Espace du Tourisme d'Ile-de-France

Carrousel du Louvre
99 rue de Rivoli
75001 Paris
08–03–81–80–00 or 01–44–50–19–98

French Embassy

www.france.diplomatie.fr

French Ministry of Culture

www.culture.fr

Louvre Museum

mistral.culture.fr/louvre/louvrea.htm

Office du Tourisme de la Ville de Paris

www.paris.org
127 av. des Champs-Élysées
01–49–52–53–54; 01–49–52–53–56 recorded information in English

RATP

www.ratp.fr

SNCF

www.sncf.fr

German-American Chamber of Commerce

messe–frankfurt.de
212/974–8830

Information about trade fairs.

German National Tourist Office

deutschland-tourismus.de
122 E. 42nd St.
New York, NY 10168

212/661–7200 or 212/661–7174

175 Bloor St. E, Suite 604
Toronto, Ontario M4W 3R8
416/968–1570 or 416/968–1986

Beethovenstr. 68
D-60325 Frankfurt
069/974–640 or 069/751–903

Berlin Tourist Offices
berlin-tourism.de
Berlin Tourismus Marketing
Europa-Center,
Budapester Str. 45
Pariser Pl., south wing of
Brandenburg Gate
0190/016–316 [€1.21 per
min]; 030/250–250 for hotel
reservations only; 180/575–
4040 from outside Germany
for information and hotel
reservations

**Frankfurt/Main
tourist office**
Römerberg 27
069/2123–8708
Tourismus und Congress
GmbH Frankfurt/Main
www.frankfurt.de

Kaiserstr. 56
D–60329 Frankfurt am
Main
069/2123–8800

GREECE

**Greek National Tourist
Organization**
www.gnto.gr
645 5th Ave.
New York, NY 10022

212/421–5777 or 212/826–6940

1300 Bay St.
Toronto, Ontario M5R 3K8
416/968–2220 or 416/968–6533

HOLLAND

**Netherlands Board
of Tourism**
www.visitholland.com
070/370–5705
355 Lexington Ave.,
21st floor
New York, NY 10017
212/370–7360 or 888/464–
6552; 212/370–9507 fax

31 Adelaide St. E.
Toronto, Ontario M5C 2KS
416/363–1577 or 416/363–
1470

NORWAY

Norwegian Tourist Board
www.goscandinavia.com
655 3rd Ave., Suite 1810
New York, NY 10017
212/885–9700 or 212/885–
9710

HUNGARY

**Hungarian National
Tourist Office**
www.hungarytourism.hu
150 E. 58th St., 33rd floor
New York, NY 10155
212/355–0240 or 212/207–
4103

ICELAND

Iceland Tourist Board
www.goscandinavia.com

655 3rd Ave.
New York, NY 10017
212/885–9700 or 212/885–9710

IRELAND

Irish Tourist Board

ireland.travel.ie.
Baggot St. Bridge, Dublin 2
01/602–4000, 669/792083, or
1850/230330 within Ireland

345 Park Ave.
New York, NY 10154
212/418–0800 or 800/223–6470; 212/371–9052 fax

Northern Ireland Tourist Board

discovernorthernireland.com.
59 North St.
Belfast BT1 1NB
028/9023–1221 or 028/9024–0960

2 Bloor St. W, Suite 1501
Toronto, Ontario M4W 3E2
416/925–6368 or 416/925–6033

551 5th Ave., Suite 701
New York, NY 10176
212/922–0101 or 800/326–0036; 212/922–0099 fax

ITALY

Italian Government Tourist Board

www.italiantourism.com
630 5th Ave., Suite 1565
New York, NY 10111
212/245–4822 or 212/586–9249

175 Bloor St. E, Suite 907,
South Tower
Toronto, Ontario M4W 3R8
416/925–4882 or 416/925–4799

Florence

www.firenze.turismo.toscana.it
Via Cavour 1/r, next to
Palazzo Medici-Riccardi
50129
055/290832

Milan

www.mimu.it or www.provincia.milano.it
Via Marconi 1
20121
02/72524301

Naples

www.ept.napoli.it
Piazza dei Martiri 58
80121
081/405311

Palermo

www.palermoturismo.it
Piazza Castelnuovo 35
90141
091/583847

Rome

www.romaturismo.it or
www.inRoma.it
Via Parigi 5
00185
06/36004399

Venice

www.turismovenezia.it
Castello Quattromille 4421
30124
041/5298711

PORTUGAL

Portuguese National Tourist Office
www.portugal.org
590 5th Ave., 4th floor
New York, NY 10036
212/354–4403 or 212/764–6137

60 Bloor St. W, Suite 1005
Toronto, Ontario M4W 3B8
416/921–7376 or 416/921–1353

ROMANIA

Romanian National Tourist Office
14 E. 38th St., 12th floor
New York, NY 10016
212/545–8484 or 212/251–0429

SLOVAKIA

Slovak Tourist Office
www.sacr.sk
2201 Wisconsin Ave. NW, Suite 250
Washington, DC 20007
202/965–5160 or 202/965–5166

SLOVENIA

Slovenian Tourist Office
www.slovenia-tourism.si
345 E. 12th St.
New York, NY 10003
212/358–9686 or 212/358–9025

SPAIN

Tourist Offices
666 5th Ave., 35th floor
New York, NY 10103
212/265–8822

2 Bloor St. W, Suite 3402
Toronto, Ontario M4W 3E2
416/961–3131

The site okspain.org provides a basic introduction; the Spain-based tourspain.es is more sophisticated.

SWEDEN

Swedish Travel and Tourism Council
www.visit-sweden.com
Box 4649,
Grand Central Station
New York, NY 10163-4649
212/885–9700 or 212/885–9764

SWITZERLAND

Swiss Travel Centre
www.sydneytravel.com.au/swiss
Reid House Level 8,
75 King St.
Sydney, NSW 2000
02/9475–1255 or 800/251–911
www.myswitzerland.com

608 5th Ave.
New York, NY 10002
212/757–5944 or 212/262–6116

Switzerland Tourism
switzerlandtourism.ch
608 5th Ave.
New York, NY 10020

212/757–5944 or 212/262–6116

926 The East Mall, Etobicoke
Toronto, Ontario M9B 6KI
416/695–2090 or 416/695–2774

TURKEY

Turkish Tourist Office
www.turkey.org
821 UN Plaza
New York, NY 10017
212/687–2194 or 212/599–7568

360 Albert St., Suite 801
Ottawa, Ontario K1R 7X7
613/230–8654 or 613/230–3683

RUSSIA

Moscow City Tourist Office
300 Lanidex Plaza, 3rd floor
Parsippany, NJ 07054
973/428–4709 or 973/884–1711

Russian Consulate General
11 E. 91st St.
New York, NY 10128
212/348–0926

3655 Ave. du Musée
Montréal, Québec H3G 2E1
514/843–5901

Russian National Tourist Office
800 3rd Ave., Suite 3101
New York, NY 10022
212/758–1162 or 212/758–0933

1801 McGill Ave., Suite 930
Montréal, Québec H3A 2N4
514/849–6394 or 514/849–6743

TRAIN TRAVEL

Amtrak
www.amtrak.com
800/USA–RAIL

Brit Rail
britrail.com
888/BRITRAIL

The Orient Express
orientexpress.com

Rail Europe
raileurope.com
800/4EURAIL

Rovos Rail
rovosrail.com
Box 2837
Pretoria 0001
South Africa

Society of International Railway Travelers
www.irtsociety.com
800/IRT–4881

VIA Rail Canada
www.viarail.ca
Rail Travel Bureau
Central Station
Montréal, Québec H3C 3N3
514/989–2626

TRAVEL AGENTS

AAA
AAA.com
2040 Market St.
Philadelphia, PA 19103
888/859–5161

The largest leisure travel agency in the United States.

American Society of Travel Agents

astanet.com
1101 King St., Suite 200
Alexandria, VA 22314
703/739–2782 or 800/965–ASTA

Professional association of travel agents with Web site list of specialists.

API Travel Consultants

royalinsider.com/API.htm
800/401–4API

Alliance of agents and premier hotels.

Institute of Certified Travel Agents

icta.com
148 Linden St.
Wellesley, MA 02482-0012
800/542–4282

Provides names of certified travel agents.

National Association of Cruise Only Agencies

nocoa.com
305/663–5626

A nonprofit organization of cruise travel agents.

Senior Citizens

Grand Circle Travel

gct.com
347 Congress St.
Boston, MA 02210
800/597–3644

Regency Travel

regencytravel.com/seniors
10330 Friars Rd.
San Diego, CA 92120
800/362–6221

Singles

Aim Higher

aim-higher.com/sin-glestravel
Winfield, IL
877/752–1858

Singles Travel International

singlestravelintl.com

Special Needs

Access First

Randolph, MA
800/557–2047

Cobb Travel Agency

Birmingham, AL
205/822–5137

The Society for Accessible Travel & Hospitality

sath.org
212/447–7284

Tri Venture Travel

530/243–3101

The Very Special Traveler

410/635–2881

TRAVEL INSURANCE

Access America

www.accessamerica.com
800/284–8300

ASA Inc.

888/ASA–8288

The Berkely Group
www.berkely.com
100 Garden City Plaza
Box 9366
Garden City, NY 11530
800/645–2424

Sells through tour operators and travel agents.

Customized Services Administrators (CSA)
Box 939057
San Diego, CA 92193-9057
800/873–9855

International Medical Group (IMG)
www.imglobal.com
Indianapolis, IN
317/655–4500 or 800/628–4664

Travel Guard International
www.travel-guard.com
800/826–4919

Travel Insured
www.travelinsured.com
800/243–3174

Travelers Insurance Company is the underwriter.

Travelex
www.travelex-insurance.com
800/797–4515

The former Mutual of Omaha.

WEATHER

CNN Weather
www.cgi-cnn.com/weather

Lowe's Storm 2000
gopbi.com/weather/storm

National Hurricane Center
nationalhurricanecenter.com

National Oceanic and Atmospheric Administration (NOAA)
noaa.com
14th St. & Constitution Ave. NW, Room 6013
Washington, DC 20230
202/482–6090

National Weather Service, NOAA
nationalweatherservice.com
1325 East-West Hwy.
Silver Spring, MD 20910

Tropical Prediction Center
nhc.noaa.gov
11691 S.W Prediction Center
Miami, FL 33165-2149
305/229–4470

USA Today Weather
www.usatoday.com/weather/wfront.htm

Weather Channel
www.weather.com

BASIC WARDROBE OPTIONS

BUSINESS WEAR

- ❏ Dresses
- ❏ Suits

JACKETS

- ❏ All purpose jacket
- ❏ Cold weather jacket

TROUSERS

- ❏ Casual slacks
- ❏ Dress pants
- ❏ Jeans
- ❏ Shorts

SKIRTS

- ❏ Casual skirts
- ❏ Dress skirts

SHIRTS

- ❏ Dress shirts
- ❏ Casual shirts
- ❏ T-shirts
- ❏ Tanks

DRESSES

- ❏ Casual dresses
- ❏ Sundresses

SWEATERS

- ❏ Cardigans
- ❏ Pullovers
- ❏ Turtlenecks

ACCESSORIES

- ❏ Belts
- ❏ Earrings, necklaces
- ❏ Hair ties, barrettes
- ❏ Handbag
- ❏ Pareo, sarong
- ❏ Scarves
- ❏ Sunglasses

SHOES

- ❏ Boots
- ❏ Dress shoes
- ❏ Walking shoes
- ❏ Sandals

- ❑ Sneakers, athletic shoes
- ❑ Water shoes, thongs

SOCKS

- ❑ Athletic socks
- ❑ Knee socks
- ❑ Panty hose
- ❑ Trouser socks

UNDERWEAR

- ❑ Bras
- ❑ Underwear
- ❑ Long johns
- ❑ Sports bras
- ❑ Pajamas

FOR SPORTS

- ❑ Bathing suits
- ❑ Bathing suit cover-up
- ❑ Sports equipment
- ❑ Swim goggles
- ❑ Workout gear

FOR EVENING

- ❑ Dress, gown, or suit
- ❑ Evening bag
- ❑ Evening wrap, shawl
- ❑ Jewelry
- ❑ Stockings

OUTERWEAR

- ❑ Day pack
- ❑ Gloves
- ❑ Overcoat
- ❑ Parka
- ❑ Raincoat, zip-out lining
- ❑ Sun hat
- ❑ Tote bag
- ❑ Umbrella
- ❑ Windbreaker
- ❑ Winter hat

KID STUFF TO BRING

FOR KIDS IN DIAPERS

- ❑ Diapers
- ❑ Baby wipes
- ❑ Diaper-rash cream
- ❑ Baby powder
- ❑ Changing pad
- ❑ Toilet seat adapter or potty seat
- ❑ Two outfits and pajamas per day, outerwear, socks and undershirts
- ❑ Swimsuit, swim diapers, diaper cover

FOR BOTTLE-FED KIDS

- ❑ Baby formula
- ❑ Can opener, if needed
- ❑ Bottles or holders and liners
- ❑ Bottle nipples
- ❑ Rings
- ❑ Bottle caps
- ❑ Bottle brush
- ❑ Breast pump

FOR MOBILITY

- ❑ Car seat
- ❑ Baby carrier
- ❑ Collapsible stroller

BEDTIME

- ❑ Blankets
- ❑ Sleepwear
- ❑ Pacifiers and spares
- ❑ Your child's lovey
- ❑ Nightlight
- ❑ Portable crib

DIVERSIONS

- ❑ Road atlas
- ❑ Sand toys
- ❑ Toy tote

FEEDING TIME

- ❑ Snacks
- ❑ Familiar foods
- ❑ Baby cereal
- ❑ Bibs

- ❏ Drinks
- ❏ Paper towels
- ❏ Baby wipes
- ❏ Terrycloth towel
- ❏ Collapsible hook-on high chair

FOR OLDER KIDS

- ❏ One outfit per day
- ❏ Two extra tops
- ❏ An extra pair of pants
- ❏ Hair accessories
- ❏ Two swimsuits per child
- ❏ Swim goggles
- ❏ One nice outfit for dress
- ❏ An out-of-season outfit
- ❏ Sweatshirt, sweater
- ❏ Windbreaker, outerwear

- ❏ Shoes, extra laces
- ❏ Socks
- ❏ Undies

JUST IN CASE

- ❏ Medications your child may need
- ❏ Acetaminophen
- ❏ Thermometer
- ❏ Your pediatrician's phone and fax number and e-mail address

OTHER STUFF

- ❏ Babyproofing supplies
- ❏ Laundry kit
- ❏ Moist towelettes
- ❏ Paper towels
- ❏ Resealable plastic bags
- ❏ Toiletries

Index